# Conversations

Conversations

# Conversations

Contemporary Critical Theory
and the Teaching of Literature

Edited by
Charles Moran
University of Massachusetts–Amherst

Elizabeth F. Penfield
University of New Orleans

National Council of Teachers of English
1111 Kenyon Road, Urbana, Illinois 61801

NCTE Editorial Board: Richard Abrahamson, Celia Genishi, Richard Lloyd-Jones, Raymond J. Rodrigues, Brooke Workman; Charles Suhor, *chair,* ex officio; Michael Spooner, ex officio

Book Design: Tom Kovacs for TGK Design

Staff Editor: Tim Bryant

NCTE Stock Number 08601-3020

**Library of Congress Cataloging-in-Publication Data**
Conversations : contemporary critical theory and the teaching of
    literature / edited by Charles Moran, Elizabeth F. Penfield.
        p.    cm.
    Includes bibliographical references.
    ISBN 0-8141-0860-1
    1. Literature—Study and teaching—Theory, etc.  2. Literature,
Modern—History and criticism—Theory, etc.  I. Moran, Charles,
1936-    .  II. Penfield, Elizabeth, 1939-    .
PN61.C58   1990
807—dc20                                                    90-32671
                                                               CIP

# Contents

# Introduction

We think of this book as a conversation, one that began several years ago in a meeting of NCTE's College Section Steering Committee. We had been talking about the nature of the discipline: how teachers at meetings of NCTE, CCCC, and the like discussed what they were doing in their writing classes but rarely talked about what they were doing in their literature classes. This thought led us to reflect upon the past twenty years or so—a time in which the field of composition theory has been tremendously active. This activity, expressed in the quality and quantity of journal publication as well as in conference programs, has had a powerful effect on the way writing is taught in our classes.

In the past two decades literary theory has also emerged as a vigorous and exciting field. Yet the vigor and excitement have not inspired widespread conversation about the teaching of literature. Unlike composition theory, contemporary literary theory has remained somehow remote from our talk about classroom practice.

Given this remoteness, this apparent lack of connection between literary theory and our pedagogical practice, why not, we thought, initiate a conversation about the teaching of literature? Why not propose that NCTE sponsor a series of annual Summer Institutes, and to these Institutes bring the country's finest literary critics as seminar leaders? They could give morning discussion/lectures that would serve as the focus of formal conversations taking place in afternoon discussion groups. And why not do all this in a setting that would inspire informal conversations during dinner or while walking about in some pleasant place—perhaps, ideally, an ocean beach? The result of this discussion was the annual Summer Institute for Teachers of Literature to Undergraduates, held in June at Myrtle Beach, South Carolina.

This book is an extension of the conversations that took place at the first two Summer Institutes, held in June of 1987 and 1988. These Institutes focused on current topics in the teaching of literature: poststructuralism, cultural criticism, reader-response theory, and issues of gender and the canon. As we read the essays again we remember the setting and hear the voices of the seminar leaders and the participants—often disagreeing with one another, often worlds apart in background

1

or professional situation. As in the Institutes, so in this book: there is energy and there is goodwill, but there is not consensus.

The first section of the book, "Aspects of Contemporary Critical Theory," draws chiefly on the presentations of the seminar and discussion leaders. Myra Jehlen, as she did at the first Institute, begins our project by discovering an assumption shared by Institute planners and the editors of this book: the belief that multiple, or new, critical perspectives will somehow liberate, empower, change. She warns us of the limits of this belief. We need to understand, she tells us, that even in a classroom informed by the latest, and by multiple, critical perspectives, the voices of the disenfranchised are not present. The voice of authority is the voice of Mark Twain—not Jim, not Huck.

Jane Tompkins follows with an essay, an edited transcript of her June 1987 talk, that gives us a remarkably lucid explanation of a subject which by its very nature resists explanation: post-structuralist criticism. She concludes, surprisingly, that we "can't apply post-structuralism to literary texts." Though Walker Gibson and Joseph Dupras make the attempt in their essays in the latter part of the book, the silence of the other authors on this subject suggests that she may be right.

Next, Steven Mailloux, in an essay that evolved from his talk at Myrtle Beach, gives us a history of reader-response theory, suggests its likely future trajectory, and sets both past and future in the context of institutional culture. Henry Louis Gates, Jr., editor of the forthcoming *Norton Anthology of Afro-American Literature,* follows with an argument for a rethinking of the canon and an inside look at the process of creating such a new canon. James Raymond's essay begins to develop a radical critique of the impulse to create a canon, seeing such an impulse as a potentially damaging exercise of authority; and Janet Emig's essay asks what now seems the inevitable question: why is it that our new interest in theory seems to exclude *learning theory?* As we listen to the voices in this section, we feel ourselves at the beginning of a movement whose shape we cannot yet clearly discern. The text is dethroned; New Criticism is not "true" or "false," but is a culturally situated set of assumptions about the nature of texts, readers, and the transactions between the two. Now our reading of texts is infused by readings of our situation—as we operate within or among cultures and institutions. Literature is no longer a simple, discrete entity. It is an aspect of a larger system, one that includes not only texts and readers but the cultures that produce both. The study and teaching of literature have become more complex and, we imagine, actually and potentially more rewarding.

The second section, "Teachers' Voices," is composed of essays by those who responded to our invitation to tell us about their reaction—as teachers—to recent developments in critical theory. The writers in this section who attended one or both of the Myrtle Beach Institutes have written essays that can be read as responses to the arguments, perspectives, and materials they encountered at these meetings. Thus, some of the essays in this second part were spun off directly from one or more of the Institute sessions. Others began as written correspondence that evolved into essays, and a few came from teachers who did not attend either of the Institutes but who became engaged in conversations that began there. These are the teachers whose understanding of contemporary critical theory will inform reading lists, syllabi, writing assignments—pedagogical goals and strategies. These are the people whose students, and whose students' parents, read Bloom and Hirsch. The voices of these teachers remind us of this important truth: English is a discipline that is fundamentally connected to teaching in a way that the physical, natural, and social sciences are not. Literary theory must somehow relate to our teaching, or it dies—cut at the root. The teachers in this second section have re-theorized their practice in a variety of interesting and creative ways.

Steven Lynn begins this section by providing what many participants at the Institutes felt we should have provided but did not: a quick sense of how different critical perspectives might inform one's teaching of a single work. Later in this section, Irene Goldman tells us how women and feminist teachers can come to terms with the masculine presence in *Walden;* Warren Rosenberg describes to us the difficulty—and excitement—of bringing new works into his course in American literature; Jane Rose outlines the way in which cultural criticism helps us read, appreciate, and therefore teach Rebecca Harding Davis's "Life in the Iron-Mills"; Nancy Vogel describes the process she follows as she attempts to create a gender-balanced syllabus; and Lloyd Dendinger explains that he will, and should, continue to teach the traditional canon in his nineteenth-century American literature course. Walker Gibson and Joseph Dupras both integrate post-structuralist assumptions into their teaching, despite what Jane Tompkins has argued earlier—that you can't, really, "apply" post-structuralist criticism to literature. Gibson describes post-structuralist moves he makes as he teaches *Pride and Prejudice*—finding authority for these moves in the work of the Sophist Protagoras; and Dupras argues that "Porphyria's Lover" must be approached deconstructively, and that to do otherwise is to practice what he calls "texticide"—the teacher's appropriation, and stifling, of the text. Joel Wingard describes for us the dynamics of his move from a New Critical teaching stance to one that is founded upon reader-response and cultural criticism. Bobby Fong writes to us from the perspective of the liberal arts college, where English departments are small, course offerings are limited, and the "add-on" strategy available at large research institutions is not available. And Judy Arnold and Ben Howard write to us from the perspective of the teacher at the two-year college, where the study of literature is required but is often not well received.

The voices in this second section come from many different kinds of institutions: the two-year college, the small four-year liberal-arts college, the state college/university, and the "flagship" research campus. We are pleased and proud to have this measure of diversity represented here. It makes for a rich and lively conversation. We invite the readers to join the conversation as they read, as they write, and as they teach—and perhaps as participants in future Summer Institutes.

# I  Aspects of Contemporary Critical Theory

# 1 Literature and Authority

Myra Jehlen

Myra Jehlen is professor of English at the University of Pennsylvania, where she normally teaches two courses each semester—one graduate and one undergraduate. In both her teaching and scholarship, she examines the relation of literature and culture. Of her teaching and scholarship she writes, "My most recent direction has been backwards, through the colonial period in America and before that to the sixteenth century and the emergence of a European world empire, which is the context in which I think America is most fully seen."

Author of *Class and Character in Faulkner's South,* Professor Jehlen has recently published *American Incarnation: The Individual, the Nation and the Continent,* a study of the ways that assumptions about the nature of America and Americans inspire the form as well as the content of eighteenth- and nineteenth-century writings. Her current research is on the period of discovery and exploration.

Professor Jehlen's essay is a revision of the talk she gave as the opening of the first NCTE Summer Institute. As she began speaking, those of us who had planned the meetings knew, from our own reactions and those of the participants, that the Summer Institutes were going to be successful. Her talk, a cultural critique of our activity as teachers of literature (and organizers of institute programs!) generated a lively hour-long discussion that ended only because of the hour (10:30 p.m.) and because we had to prepare for Jane Tompkins's presentation at 8:30 the next morning.

The author thanks Houston Baker and Jane Tompkins, also speakers at the 1987 Institute, for their comments on her talk—comments that have contributed to the development of the essay published here.

The theme of this Institute might be put simply, it seems to me, as the exploration of other ways of reading, and of teaching others to read. Beyond this, by specifying three of these other ways, the Institute also projects a stance toward them, for it relativizes them and all but explicitly enjoins against adopting any one as a new orthodoxy in its turn. In exploring other ways, the Institute would appear, then, to be

7

making a general philosophical point about the value of such explorations in general, as a way of multiplying perspectives and of keeping them multiple. This seems all the more to be the intention in that each of the approaches by itself asserts that the meaning of literature arises out of multiplicity and the contemplation of otherness. Thus:

- Post-structuralism starts from the definition of an irreconcilable difference between word and object, of an uncloseable distance between self and other, as the very inspiration and engine of language.

- Reader-response theory focuses on the inevitable presence in every literary act of one other, or another group, equally engaged in the world of the text—its readers.

- Cultural criticism is inspired by the perception of the inescapable multiplicity of culture and its constitution precisely out of interactions.

By proposing these three methods of reading literature as newly enriching for both teacher and student, then, the Institute can be seen as projecting a notion of permanent otherness, a little like Trotsky's concept of permanent revolution, in that otherness and the perception of otherness are cast as permanently beneficial to society rather than as temporary disturbances to be overcome.

But of course there is nothing Bolshevik about the notion of permanent otherness. It is a perfectly solid liberal notion that might be summed up in the slogan "Everyone is different." Different and proud of it: my daughter's nursery school teacher tried once to reassure her that although she could not be the Princess in the class play but only a grape on a moreover silent bunch, this was of no moment because "everyone is special." At the age of four, however, few have the patience for paradox. My daughter wanted to be especially special and, refusing to try to be anyway the best grape she could, she sulked.

This was many years ago, before the lessons of the civil rights movement and the women's movement had altogether sunk in. Teachers probably soothe baby egos in other terms now, perhaps by promising them that "no one is special" since everyone is incomparably different. I doubt that solves the problem better, however: any four-year-old will see at once that all the same or all different, universal or unique, the problem is still who gets to be the Princess.

Not only nursery school tots but undergraduates as well can observe that in the world out there some different equals are more equal than others, and indeed less different. My purpose here is to question whether it may not be disingenuous to respond to this political common sense with examples of literary pluralism and demonstrations of the ways novels, poems, and plays subvert social hierarchy. In itself it is surely a good thing to recognize the complexity of literature's relation to established authorities and for students whose social identity does not permit them to identify with established authority to discover their nonauthorized ways and views encompassed by that complexity. But by itself this is as well a paradoxical thing. For in reassuring our students that literature, which they thought categorically beyond them, does encompass their experiences, and has often been written by people who shared these experiences, we may be implying more of equality than literary difference can quite bestow. Even with the spotlight upon her, is a grape ever a Princess? Current critical methods do seem particularly useful for changing students' relations to literature; it is certainly possible to translate the concepts of deconstruction, of reader-response theory, and of cultural historicism into empowering new ways of reading. But if some students go on sulking, complaining that literature is for others, meaning not for them precisely because they *are* "others," they may have a point.

Listen, for instance, to the objection of one very bright student who, led to believe that he was reading about life in a way that might help him in his, stopped cold when he found that the hero with whom he had identified was not after all his *semblable.* For when the Widow Douglas first read to Huckleberry Finn from the book about "Moses and the Bulrushers," he was "in a sweat to find out all about him." But "by-and-by she let it out that Moses had been dead a considerable long time"; so then, he explains, "I didn't care no more about him; because I don't take no stock in dead people."

Now, Huck was alienated from literature under conditions much like those we are planning here to create. The Widow Douglas was never a New Critic, and while a firm adherent of the canon, she read always in relation to history and life. She certainly encouraged Huck to interpret the text in the light of his own life, as he did the story of the baby Moses drifting helplessly down the stream. Indeed the success of the widow's teaching is evident later when her pupil turns out to be an astute critic of Emmeline Grangerford's poetry, the key to which he discerns, without benefit of Freud, is a luxuriant death-wish. For that matter, the best short critique extant of any work may well be Huck's reading of *Pilgrim's Progress,* which he sums up as a tale "about a man that left his family it didn't say why." Huck's perception of the excluded term in the story, the suppressed question which is in fact Bunyan's central assertion—namely that henceforth the individual will seek salvation individualistically and thus ontologically apart from family and community to whom he expressly does not owe explanations—reflects a powerful deconstructive capacity. Indeed Twain seems to grant Huck the ultimate critical power when he gives him control of the novel's language. In the terms I have been using, Huck Finn has appropriated literature and rewritten it in his own words. His interpretation works at such a basic level that the interpretation becomes the novel.

*Almost* becomes the novel. Let us look at a passage in which Huck appears in full command of his story, so that it seems to be fully *the* story. Dramatizing the reversal of authority, Huck is here describing exactly the type of characters who would conventionally be describing him:

> Col. Grangerford was a gentleman, you see. He was a gentleman all over; and so was his family. He was well born, as the saying is, and that's worth as much in a man as it is in a horse, so the Widow Douglas said, and nobody ever denied that she was of the first aristocracy in our town; and Pap he always said it, too, though he warn't no more quality than a mudcat himself.

It is possible to spend an entire class just on the "you see" in that wonderful sentence. This simple, friendly direct address to the reader accomplishes Twain's entire revolution: appropriating the Colonel as the object of Huck's conversation with the reader, it demotes him radically in the structure of the narration so that we look down on him. Without the "you see," Grangerford would have remained our superior as, following Huck's gaze, we (Huck and the reader) looked up. But Huck's interpolation, telling us instead to look across at *him,* creates a mutual space that is the new site of value and summons the Colonel onto this site for us to scrutinize. In short, the phrase "you see" frames values in the passage the way Huck's narrative voice frames the whole story. The demoting effect of the frame is evident in the next sentence as well as in Huck's insistence that the Colonel was a gentleman "all over" and so was his family, both additions actually subtracting from the Colonel's status. Finally, the expression "as the saying is" appended to the assurance that he is "well born" seals Huck's control while it reduces the cavalier to equine status: he is as good as a horse, not a jot less, and if you don't believe it ask the Widow Douglas and Pap, the two characters whose judgment the book values least.

Having established the principles of Grangerford's distinction, Huck proceeds to illustrate it:

Col. Grangerford was very tall and very slim, and had a darkish-paly complexion, not a sign of red in it anywheres; he was clean-shaved every morning all over this thin face, and he had the thinnest kind of lips, and the thinnest kind of nostrils, and a high nose, and heavy eyebrows, and the blackest kind of eyes, sunk so deep back that they seemed like they was looking out of caverns at you, as you may say. His forehead was high, and his hair was gray and straight and hung to his shoulders.

And so on . . . descending down the man in a parody of a top-to-bottom medieval portrait which buries the neo-feudal Grangerford by praising him. For the piled-on authorities of the first passage, Huck now substitutes his own detailed observations which work to the same effect. His scrupulous description of the Colonel's "darkish-paly complexion" entirely vitiates the traditional spiritual import of a "pale complexion" with the literalizing and materializing explanation that it had "not a sign of red in it anywheres." The incarnation of the cavalier convention, the Colonel is confirmed in every trait and in and by every trait debunked. Huck's common man's sense penetrates the pretenses of the master class and demystifies them: he explodes the genteel cultural hegemony; his is the point of view and the vision of the "other." In his mouth, conventional diction is made deconstructively self-reflexive to reveal its ideological artifice.

*But not to him.* Huck does not know that he is doing any of this, for he intends and believes the opposite. He admires the Colonel exceedingly and is only concerned that his description does not do the paragon justice. That the description does full justice to an absurd bully would much surprise and sadden Huck, who is entirely sincere in urging the reader to believe that Grangerford "was as kind as he could be." "You could feel that, you know [note the direct address again, as in "you see"], and so you had confidence." "Confidence" calls attention to the delicate machinery of the first-person narration whose ability to inspire confidence is crucial to the viability of the story. Now, we do have confidence in Huck; we are dazzled by the keenness of his observation, and we trust him always to tell the truth. But when here he seeks to realize that confidence in a community of judgment or an interpretive community, we realize that we have in fact no confidence in him at all—not, that is, in his conscious judgment, in his consciousness. At times Huck judges better than he knows, but what he knows is all too plainly wrong. Indeed the passages we have just been considering instruct us to reverse Huck's evaluation as completely as we accept his facts. The Colonel *appears* exactly the way Huck says, the passage tells us, but he *is* the opposite.

Huck sees right and understands wrong. Those familiar with the story will recall that the same conjunction operates a few pages earlier when Huck admires the splendors of the Grangerford parlor, which features among other display items a crockery cat and a crockery dog who squeaked "when you pressed down . . . but didn't open their mouths nor look different nor interested." This is because, Huck explains, "They squeaked through underneath." Another visitor to the plantation house would not have told us that, would not have penetrated to this level of the parlor/text. But if we therefore derive this insight from Huck, the admiration that inspires these exact observations is also the ground on which we reject his judgment. He is similarly impressed by a clock that will strike a hundred and fifty when particularly well-wound, as by plaster fruit "much redder and yellower and prettier than real ones is." Here again, he sees the difference between the real and the artificial with utter clarity, and unlike his betters he never conceals the line between them. In that sense we see through his eyes in opposition to the visions of the self-deluding and pretentious Grangerford. But the clearer Huck sees, the more clearly we perceive the errors of his cultural and aesthetic judgments.

In short, Huck has the power of sight but still lacks cultural and political power. He is not and could not be the author of the text that centers on him. He does not have final authority. The distinction between Huck Finn's sight and his judgment is a matter of authority, and this is also the theme of the Grangerford passage. The Colonel has but to knit his eyebrows for everyone to fall in. In the last sentence the planter's authority assumes even divine proportions: "When he turned into a cloud-bank it was awful dark for a half a minute and that was enough; there wouldn't nothing go wrong again for a week." Now, by the time we read that last sentence, in our eyes the Colonel has been, on the contrary, stripped of all authority. He has been made a figure of fun, an absurd mannequin of a grandee, a humbug. And this is the direct result of Huck's description: in that sense Huck has exposed the sham. But from Huck's perspective the passage ends not with Grangerford's exposure but with his triumph, almost his apotheosis.

Through a reversal that essentially negates the book's initial reversal of narrative power, Huck's granting of authority to the Colonel in turn strips Huck's authority. In the end, the authority of the passage rests neither on the upper-class Colonel nor on lower-class Huck, but on the author whose presence is realized in the reader. So that we end up reading *against* Huck—and in that sense not too differently from the way we would have read a conventionally narrated text, that is, a text narrated by a character of the class and culture of the author and reader. Huck's vernacular voice, which ostensibly articulates an alternative perspective—the perspective of an alternative class—actually serves as a way for the alienated middle-class author and reader to criticize their own class from within. Such criticism disputes rather than challenges authority; at any rate it does not constitute an alternative authority, for it represents dissent but not necessarily another perspective, let alone a revision.

There is perhaps nothing very surprising in a white middle-class male author confirming the authority of his kind even as he criticizes it. But the possibility that literature as such, even written by authors who not only describe others but are themselves other, confirms authority is more troubling. If different characters fail to achieve full narrative power in the works of writers like Emily Dickinson and Amiri Baraka—whose works this Institute studies—or like Frederick Douglass, the implications for a pluralistic criticism are truly disturbing.

In Douglass's *Narrative of the Life of Frederick Douglass,* the ability to read and write is directly the key to freedom, to autonomous selfhood. Yet in one often-cited passage at whose conclusion Douglass explicitly grasps a pen to tell the slave's own story—to tell his own slave story—the issue of linguistic authority remains at least ambiguous.

The passage describes Douglass's early childhood, thus taking up a conventional autobiographical issue in the emergence of personal identity. Slavery of course makes of the process a cruel parody:

> As to my own treatment while I lived on Colonel Lloyd's plantation, it was very similar to that of the other slave children. . . . I was seldom whipped by my old master, and suffered little from any thing else than hunger and cold. I suffered much from hunger, but much more from cold. In hottest summer and coldest winter, I was kept almost naked—no shoes, no stockings, no jacket, no trousers, nothing on but a coarse two linen shirt, reaching only to my knees. I had no bed. I must have perished with cold, but that, the coldest nights, I used to steal a bag which was used for carrying corn to the mill. I would crawl into this bag, and there sleep on the cold, damp, clay floor with my head in and feet out. My feet have been so cracked with frost, that the pen with which I am writing might be laid in the gashes.

In recalling his agonized childhood, Douglass strives for an objectivity somewhat like Huck's, the narrative stance of the reliable truth-teller. The tone of moderation throughout should lend authority to the boy Douglass's clearly different outlook on his society—were he able to communicate it. But consider the last two sentences of the passage, where structurally the description makes its culminating claim for a radically and catastrophically distinct vision. The slave child here described to an audience of authoritative persons assumes the posture of his abjection: prone on the floor, his head concealed and only his feet visible, he is asleep, unconscious of the readers' consciousness, which is, in the moment of reading, preternaturally heightened. There is a painful irony here: the unseeing and silent being in the flour bag draws our sympathy in a way that, if it does not confirm, does not challenge his slave status of object.

I do not mean to suggest that Douglass thus demeans slaves or his childhood self; on the contrary he scrupulously avoids the sort of projection that would appropriate the boy's consciousness and that way erase its difference. For how is the boy to be described as different when much of his difference consists of conditions of being that are not communicable in the language of the text? The boy is not only illiterate, he does not know that literacy exists. He does not even really comprehend what it is to be a slave: as Douglass describes it, perhaps the crux of slavery is not really knowing the conditions of one's being. How can the language of the text communicate the boy's vision of things from within, that is, as an act of authorship? Certainly slaves were depicted in literature, famously by Harriet Beecher Stowe only five years after the publication of the *Narrative*. But Stowe describes Tom from her perspective, not his. The boy Douglass obviously had a fully constituted language in which he expressed himself to his fellow slaves, but this language is not that of the *Narrative*. Indeed it is a language largely defined by its inaudibility in the frequencies of the dominant language.

Douglass goes far toward solving his problem in the last sentence of the paragraph: "My feet have been so cracked with the frost, that the pen with which I am writing might be laid in the gashes." From the perspective of his new identity, as no longer an illiterate slave but an educated freeman who, much to the point, is here writing in his persona as an abolitionist-sponsored lecturer to white audiences, he can become the translator, a mediator between the muteness of a being as other as the enslaved child he once was and the constrained eloquence of the free adult he is now. (Actually, the not-quite-free adult: historians have described Douglass as increasingly resentful of the limited role in which the abolitionists cast him, giving him as it were a script rather than admitting him to the company of the writers.) But even in the measure of his freedom, he remains less free as a writer to transmit this freedom to his slave character. He is constrained by history and society beyond any individual's ability to transcend.

It is not, or not only, because Mark Twain was not of Huck's class that he did not grant him the authority of his text. In a sense Frederick Douglass cannot fully appropriate the authority of his own text: the language in which both Twain and Douglass write will not let them give over authority to those whom that language has excluded from power. Even when the authors want to bestow their own authority on others, they cannot, or not beyond certain limits: Douglass can lay the pen with which he is writing in the gashes of the boy's feet; he cannot give the pen into the boy's hands.

For the boy's self-description exists, as it were, on the other side of the mirror. If we imagine literature as a mirror—which is not to say an objective camera but an engine for reflecting the life of society, and in the process reflecting upon it—if then we imagine literature as a mirror, we might describe the inspiration for the present Summer Institute as the recognition that mirrors face one way, into rooms. Not only do they not reflect what goes on outside the rooms, they deny that there is an outside. In that the room they mirror constitutes their entire universe, they project it as universal. But for every inside there is an outside, and for every insider an outcast. Less melodramatically, for every one there is an other, another person or class or race or gender or philosophy. The unifying aim of the diverse methods of criticism currently ascendant seems to me to be the desire to read not only the "one" but the "other," and this not only for the sake of the other but in order to understand the one more fully, to see it and its room in the context of the house and the street it inhabits.

But this excellent aim, which sounds entirely achievable in that it seems to incorporate fundamental liberal principles of pluralistic understanding, may be quite impossible to achieve. On the evidence of two children, one "white trash" and the other a "nigger," both thus named for their exclusion from the room of American culture, the dominant one may not be able to understand others, or at any rate others in their own terms. Consider what would happen were Huck Finn to control the paragraph we have been examining. On one hand we would finish reading admiring Colonel Grangerford; on the other we would find him entirely opaque, not only failing to see through him but not even seeing that there was anywhere to see through to. In Mark Twain's control, the meaning of the passage emerges precisely from the act of seeing through; it arises in the space between Huck's meanings and Mark Twain's. Huck admires the Colonel, Twain abhors him; by manipulating Huck's admiration, Twain transforms it into an irony that Huck ignores. The drama of Grangerford's exposure, therefore, is played out between Mark Twain and the Colonel. Any play between Huck and the Colonel would in fact negate this one precisely by removing its ground, the distance that does not exist for the quintessentially naive Huck, the distance between appearance and reality. Where would Mark Twain be without that distance? He would be out of the room: out of Huck's room, as Huck is out of Twain's.

Similarly the experience of the boy Douglass is for the adult Douglass an experience of unconsciousness (emblematically represented in the reversal of his body in the bag). That is, the essence of the boy's consciousness is for the adult its unconsciousness. From another perspective, the adult does not exist for the child, who therefore cannot represent the adult's *Narrative*.

I am suggesting, reluctantly, that otherness cannot be represented in its own terms in the voice, the language, the literature, of the dominant observer. An author is always an authority and can cease to be an authority (and thus cease to dominate those whom his or her authority controls) only by ceasing to be. This is admittedly a rather abstruse syllogism, but its interest is quite practical, having to do with the practice of criticism and the possibility of reading through to genuinely other perceptions of the world than those that currently dominate our culture. Still more practically, it has to do with how we represent literature to our students as it reflects their lives, life in general, and all possible worlds. In our desire to teach them to read more penetratingly and to see in literature—whether canonical or non-canonical—the expression of other visions, stressing the "other" as it might complicate their visions—whether dominant or marginal—do we imply a freer literature than we have or can have? Do we in our desire to empower our students conceal or anyway fail to reveal to them the reality of power? And do we fail to show them how authority works, so that, to return to the point of origin, we finally are obfuscating the nature of authority even as we urge our students to grasp their own?

An incident in my class several years ago has come retrospectively to seem more disturbing than I then thought it. I was teaching *Huckleberry Finn* and using its story line to represent the general nature of plots as meaningful, intentional constructions. Having discussed Huck's inferior social status as a device that enabled the novel to be radically critical of its society, I asked the class why Twain might have had Huck run away with Jim? Why not with Tom? Seeming a little embarrassed on my behalf, a student promptly offered to explain: "It was Jim that Huck met when he was leaving town. He didn't meet Tom."

That answer no longer seems as funny as it did at the time. Then it seemed evident that the student's unwitting wit lay in mistaking Twain's story for history. In that sense, her error would entail failure to recognize the authority of the story's inventor, and therefore the way the plot was his meaningful invention. It is doubtless important to correct such errors and to make clear the difference between fiction and reality. I would still try to teach that lesson, but perhaps with a more complicated sense of its import, for this particular instance of taking story for history involved as well taking one story for another, Huck's story for Twain's and Huck's authority for that of his author, so that Huck became autonomous and his novel an autobiography. Needless to say, the same student read the portrait of Colonel Grangerford as genuinely admiring and was both impressed and a little intimidated by that cartoon cavalier. Told that the description was ironic, she balked: Huck was too right to be so wrong; indeed he was for her the most trustworthy voice in the novel, and not only as observer but precisely as interpreter. She was sure that in Huck's place she would have seen things as he did. This is my question: what was I teaching her by insisting that this was not the way the *novel* saw things, that though it saw through Huck's eyes, it also looked through Huck?

To be sure I was trying to teach her that literature is a construction. But to the extent I succeeded, I also taught her that to read properly one has to identify with those who construct it, who are its real authors and authorities. I taught her simultaneously to understand what Huck and Jim stood for and that neither was to be listened to. In retrospect this seems to me a problematic and even a contradictory lesson if I intended also to teach her to listen to other voices and to see how literature contains many voices. A little teaching may be a dangerous thing, and the students who learn to discount Huck's values as they smartly distinguish his ideology from his innate powers of perception may be both empowered by this new skill and disempowered by it. They are disempowered by coming to trust Mark Twain's authority not only over Huck's but over their own authority as well, insofar as they recognize themselves rather in Huck than in his author (or in Twain's Huck-like aspects than in his empowered and established side).

What to do? One can hardly teach naïveté. Artists can be primitives, but teachers cannot. Besides, the power that emerges from an identification with Huck is dangerously illusory. But if we cannot go back, perhaps we can go forward. Forward would mean showing students not only how to discern Mark Twain's voice in *The Adventures of*

*Huckleberry Finn* but also how to hear the way the authorial voice, which invented Huck and in part projects itself into Huck's voice, also suppresses it—thus teaching them not to hear Huck's voice, which is inaudible, but to listen to its silence; to see not the other side of the mirror, which is invisible, but the opaqueness of this side. I am suggesting, in short, that while it is all to the good of our students and to our own good to become more and more sophisticated readers, it would be good also to become more aware of the limits of reading as they embody the limits of our culture, which in turn is defined not only by its possibilities but fully as much by its prohibitions. Moses began his journey as a helpless babe, but he ended it as the very type of the autocratic patriarch. It was not his first subjection but his later authority, the authority of "dead people," that the Widow Douglas invoked in her effort to "civilize" Huck. Huck's naive rejection of Moses could at the last rejoin the ultimate sophistication. When it comes to it, the operative difference between grapes and Princesses is that grapes speak very little if at all. This is common sense that no education should unteach.

# 2 A Short Course in Post-Structuralism

Jane Tompkins

Jane Tompkins is professor of English at Duke University. She is author of *Sensational Designs: The Cultural Work of American Fiction, 1790–1860,* and editor of *Reader-Response Criticism: From Formalism to Post-Structuralism.* In addition, she has written articles on a wide range of subjects, including canon formation, *Uncle Tom's Cabin,* the American Indian in history and literature, and the use of the personal voice in academic criticism.

She teaches courses in American literature, popular culture, and women's studies, and is now completing a book on the Western, seen from a feminist perspective. The book's title: *West of Everything: The Construction of Male Identity in American Popular Culture.*

Professor Tompkins's essay is a transcribed, edited version of the talk she gave at the 1987 NCTE Summer Institute. Those of us who were there remember this as a remarkable morning, one in which we were given the background we needed to begin to understand post-structuralist criticism.

We thank Lloyd Dendinger, whose essay is included later in this volume, for his foresight in recording Professor Tompkins' talk, and the editorial staff of *College English,* who edited the transcription of the tape. The essay is reprinted from the November 1988 *College English.*

## Introduction: The Post-Structuralist Challenge

Post-structuralism might be described as a challenge to the accepted model of reading and of criticism. The traditional "application" model of literary criticism puts in the number one spot the *reader;* in the number two spot, the *method,* or approach; in the number three spot the *text* (what we read); and in the fourth spot, the *reading* (or what comes out the other end). To give these terms somewhat different, more philosophical or exalted, names, we might call the reader the "subject" or the "self," the "I-who-reads"; the method could be called "the interpretive framework"; we could call the text "the object," so it sounds more philosophical and abstract; and we could call what comes out the other end, when the subject takes the framework and applies it to the object, the "interpretation." Such an understanding of reading, as a process of application, implies that critical modes can be assumed, applied, and then dropped: post-structuralism on Monday, reader-response criticism on Tuesday, cultural criticism on Wednesday. The reader is thus a dramatic *persona* who picks up each one of these systems, like a pair of eyeglasses, and looks through it at the text to filter the interpretation. In other words, there are four discrete entities: the reader, the method (post-structuralism, feminism, Marxism, psychoanalytic criticism, cultural studies, etc.), the text (*Heart of Darkness,* or whatever you happen to be reading), and what emerges as an interpretation.

Now, the significance of the post-structuralist model is that it collapses all four of these entities into a simultaneity, into a single, continuous act of interpretation so that, instead of four discrete items in a row—subject, method, object, interpretation—all are part of a single, evolving field of discourse. In effect, post-structuralism collapses position one (the reader) into position two (the critical stance), and then both into three—which is also four. It does this by asserting that we—you and I, the reader or subject and the "text," or any object "out there"—are not freestanding autonomous entities, but beings that are culturally constituted by interpretive frameworks or interpretive strategies that our culture makes available to us, and these strategies are the only way that we have of conceiving who we are, of thinking or of having a "self." The objects of our gaze are likewise constituted by these interpretive strategies. The things that we see, the things that are given to us, are already articulated according to some preexisting interpretive framework or system of differentiation.

This is the post-structuralist territory, more or less, for which we are headed, and it is necessary first to establish a way of talking that allows you to understand what it means to say things like "discourse reproducing itself," or "a reader who is constituted," or "objects that are constituted by an interpretive framework." In order to see how post-structuralism arrives at such a conclusion, I am going to read closely two texts: Saussure's *Course in General Linguistics* and Derrida's "Différance."

## *Ferdinand de Saussure's* Course in General Linguistics

Saussure is where post-structuralism starts; everything follows from his *Course in General Linguistics.* Saussure begins by laying down some general principles: "Some people regard language, when reduced to its

elements, as a naming-process only—a list of words, each corresponding
to a thing that it names" (1959, p. 65). For example, everybody assumes
that *tree* means something growing out there, just as *dog* refers to a
four-legged animal. This is the model of language that pretty much
everyone still carries around in their heads, whether they've been
studying post-structuralism for twenty years or have only begun to
study it today. We all act on the assumption that language is made up
of words, and words refer to things; the words are there, they are
perceptible, we know what they are and can point to them on the
page, and the things referred to are there too. You can indicate them:
tables, chairs, rugs, microphones, and so forth. This commonsense
understanding of what language is and what the world is like is the
one that we normally operate with, indeed, have to operate with.

It is this idea of things in themselves and words in themselves that
the *Course in General Linguistics* wants to undo. The founding principle
of Saussurean linguistics—the principle that acts as a wedge driven
into this commonsense idea and which, when driven far enough, will
break it up completely—is, as Saussure tells us very clearly, "the
arbitrary nature of the sign." The arbitrariness of the sign is the one
principle from which everything else in Saussure follows.

What is a sign? A sign as Saussure defines it is a concept (or what
he calls a "signified") plus a sound image (that is, the psychological
image of the sound that the word makes when we pronounce it, or the
"signifier"). When he talks about the arbitrariness of the sign, Saussure
means that there is no natural relationship between the concept and
the sound image—"the bond between the signified and the signifier is
arbitrary" (p. 67). He says,

> The word *arbitrary* . . . calls for comment. The term should not
> imply that the choice of the signifier is left entirely to the speaker
> (we shall see below that the individual does not have the power
> to change a sign in any way once it has become established in
> the linguistic community); I mean that it [the signifier] is un-
> motivated, i.e., arbitrary in that it actually has no natural con-
> nection with the signified. (pp. 68–69)

In other words, there is nothing about the tree that necessitates that it
be represented by t-r-e-e, as we well know, since in French it's *arbre,*
in Italian *albero,* and in Latin *arbor,* and so on. So there is no necessary
connection between the concept "tree" and the sound used to designate
that concept. The only connection between the signifier and the signified
is convention—not logic or rationality; there is no rule, no way to
deduce a binding method from anything. Rather, it's usage, tradition,
that connects the sound image to the concept.

However, this is not to suggest that the speaker can choose to assign freely any signifier-sound to any concept-signified:

> The signifier, though to all appearances freely chosen with respect to the idea that it represents, is fixed, not free, with respect to the linguistic community that uses it. The masses have no voice in the matter, and the signifier chosen by language could be replaced by no other. (p. 71)

That is, although the bond is unmotivated, arbitrary, and although there is no natural connection between the sound image and the concept, it is nevertheless fixed within an individual system of language.

From this initial observation, that the sign is arbitrary, Saussure takes a very important step. He talks about language as a system of pure values:

> This distinction has to be heeded by the linguists above all others, for language is a system of pure values which are determined by nothing except the momentary arrangement of its terms. A value— so long as it is somehow rooted in things and in their natural relations, as happens with economics (the value of a plot of ground, for instance, is related to its productivity)—can to some extent be traced in time. (p. 80)

Saussure contrasts what he calls a system of pure values, in which there is no necessary relation between the value of an item and anything else in the world—it's just defined by convention—with a natural concept of value, which he represents by the idea of a piece of ground having some value connected naturally to it by the extent to which it is productive. It is a very important distinction.†

In language, values are not natural in the sense that they are already implied in a pre-existing object; they come about only by convention, are stipulated from the start. Saussure gives some illustrations of what he means by arbitrary value in language when he talks about the way in which we, for instance, distinguish the singular from the plural. He talks about the way in which the plural of the word *foot* is formed. At one time the difference between *foot* (singular) and *feet* (plural) was indicated in the following way: "*fōt*: *\*fōti*" (p. 83). Over the course of time the singular comes to be distinguished from the plural in a different way: singular *fōt*, plural *fēt*, or what we now call *foot/feet*. This is an illustration of the arbitrary or unmotivated character of the sign in the sense that the opposition between *fōt* and *fōti* on the one hand, is no

---

† Later, post-structuralism will challenge the naturalness of the very distinction Saussure invokes to establish the character of the arbitrary or conventional (i.e., the nature-culture distinction), but this move presupposes and derives from the initial Saussurean insight.

better than the later *fōt* and *fēt* on the other, enabling us to distinguish the singular from the plural.

Thus there is no natural value of the plural built into a particular sound. It is only "the opposition of two terms [that] is needed to express plurality" (p. 85). Linguistic value is a matter, then, that is determined by the ways in which something can be distinguished from something else, and not by virtue of the particular character of the things examined. Saussure offers another example of exactly the same kind: the nominative singular in Czechoslovakian for woman is *žena,* the accusative singular is *ženu,* the nominative plural is *ženy,* and the genitive plural is *žen.* (The genitive plural of this word has a zero inflection; that is, there is no ending on the end.) Saussure comments: "We see then that a material sign is not necessary for the expression of an idea; language is satisfied with the opposition between something and nothing" (p. 86). So what it is that allows us to establish the value of the genitive plural, *žen,* is not anything that is there; rather, it is the difference between *žena* and *žen.* The nothing that is there, so to speak, allows us to distinguish the genitive plural from *žena.* The key concept here is opposition. Language works—gains meaning, carves things up, articulates the world—through opposition. Any opposition will do.

Part II of the *Course in General Linguistics,* "Synchronic Linguistics," is the essence of Saussure's theory. Saussure begins part II by reminding us that the sign is dual—it has two parts—and that it comes into being through the association of two things—the concept (signified) and the sound image (signifier). Sound images alone, just signifiers or "pure sound," in other words, are not language. Saussure believes that "a succession of sounds is linguistic only if it supports an idea" (p. 103). That is, in order for language to be language, it has to signify something.

The next Saussurean concept to be grasped is the question of linguistic identity, how a unit of language can be distinguished: "The linguistic mechanism is geared to differences and identities, the former being only the counterpart of the latter" (p. 108). Now, what is it that enables him to say this at this point? The way that the plural *feet* is distinguished from the singular *foot* depends on the difference in those two items, not on the essential nature of *feet* or *foot.* The identity of the plural in any case is a function of its difference from the singular, and *only* a function of its difference from the singular. In language, therefore, identity is a function of difference. Linguistic identity, in other words the signs, the words, the items of language that you perceive, does not exist independently, in and of itself, but only in relation to other such entities. And at this point Saussure gives perhaps his most effective illustration of the principle of linguistic identity, his notion that in language identity is only and always relational, with his great example of the 8:25 Geneva-to-Paris trains:

> For instance, we speak of the identity of two "8:25 p.m. Geneva-to-Paris" trains that leave at twenty-four hour intervals. We feel that it is the same train each day, yet everything—the locomotives, coaches, personnel—is probably different. Or if a street is demolished, then rebuilt, we say that it is the same street even though in a material sense, perhaps, nothing of the old one remains. Why can a street be completely rebuilt and still be the same? Because it does not constitute a purely material entity; it is based on certain conditions that are distinct from the materials that fit the conditions, e.g., its location with respect to other streets. (pp. 108–9)

In other words, the relationality of the street is what makes it the "street" and not the stones of the pavement. Saussure continues, "Similarly, what makes the express is its hour of departure, its route, and in general every circumstance that sets it apart from other trains" (p. 109). In other words, what identifies the express is its relationship within its system to other elements of that system. Saussure goes on, "Whenever the same conditions are fulfilled, the same entities are obtained. Still the entities are not abstract since we cannot conceive of a street or train outside its material realization" (p. 109). Keep in mind this notion of identity as exemplified in the illustration of the 8:25 Geneva-to-Paris train, which is the same every day even though there is a different locomotive and a different engineer, different passengers and different personnel. It is the same because it occupies the same position in a system of relationships. It differs in the same way from all other elements in the schedule.

In order to make this example even clearer, Saussure contrasts this to its opposite in an illustration of the way we normally conceive of identities either of words or things:

> Let us contrast the preceding examples with the completely different case of a suit which has been stolen from me and which I find in the window of a second-hand store. Here we have a material entity that consists solely of the inert substance—the cloth, its lining, its trimmings, etc. Another suit would not be mine regardless of its similarity to it. But linguistic identity is not that of the garment; it is that of the train and the street. (p. 109)

Linguistic identity does not reside in substance; it resides in relationality. It resides in position-in-relation-to-something, and that position is defined within some system. In the case of the train, the system is the equivalent of the train schedule, different hours of departure, different destinations, and different hours of arrival. Identity therefore is a function of positioning within its system. The train's timetable is a system which is itself organized, a principled way of making distinctions. So language, then, by analogy with the train schedule, is a domain of articulation, a way of dividing things up, a principled way of making distinctions. Linguistic identity or value does not depend upon substance or essence, on the sameness of the locomotive. It does not consist of the union of a particular concept with a particular sound; the particularity of the sound has nothing to do with it. The linguistic identity of a word doesn't depend on the "thing itself"; rather, it depends on its difference from all the other words in the language.

Saussure further demonstrates how value is constituted with another example, the game of chess:

> Take a knight, for instance. By itself is it an element in the game? ["By itself" means taken out of the game, carried in your pocket.] Certainly not, for by its material makeup—outside its square and the other conditions of the game—it means nothing to the player; it becomes a real concrete element only when endowed with value and wedded to it. (p. 110)

And how does something become endowed with value? When it is a part of the system within which it becomes articulated in relation to other elements in the system. So that when a knight is taken out of a game of chess, it loses its value as a piece in the game. But of course it could acquire another value, say, as a beautiful carving, in which case its value would not be self-starting or autonomous either, would not reside in the thing itself but in its relationship to other carvings within the game called art (a game which works by its own rules of differentiation). The point of the chessman example is that, pushed to its ultimate conclusion, everything has value, but the value of anything depends upon the particular framework or game within which it is being seen. That is, as long as it is part of the chess game, the knight has the value of a piece that moves forward one and over two or forward two and over one, and so forth. Taken out of the chess game and looked at next to some other carving, it then acquires its identity, its distinctness from other objects, according to the way we look at and judge and identify carvings, and so on.

Similarly, to go back to the game of chess: if, for example, a dog came and chewed up the knight, you could replace the knight with a piece of chalk. Or in a deck of cards, for example, if you lose the Jack of Hearts, you take the Joker and write on it with your pencil "J" and draw a heart. The piece of chalk and the Joker serve equally well as the knight or the Jack of Hearts. That is, identity has nothing to do with substance at all. Identity has to do rather with the stipulated position of something within a conventional system. Chalk, paper clips, buttons, a corn chip, whatever happens to be available, will do. Because what makes a knight a knight is its difference from the bishop, from the pawn, from the queen or king—a difference stipulated within a system like the game of chess.

One of the things that post-structuralism shows us is the conventionality of aesthetic value, the sense in which aesthetic value, literary value, the value of sculpture, the value of painting is conventional, constructed, traditional, habitual, not natural, not intrinsic. This doesn't mean that aesthetic value isn't "real"; this doesn't mean that in a particular kind of sculpture competition you wouldn't lose by entering a piece of chalk. But in another kind of competition you might win. The value of the carving is going to be judged according to the conventions for distinguishing value within a particular mode. You see how that is still another illustration of the point that, within the game of sculpture, there are different games being played, just as within literary criticism there are different games being played. If I submit an article to *Philological Quarterly* and submit the same article to *Representations,* it would be accepted or rejected depending upon the game that is being played within the editorial board of those two different quarterlies.

But there are objections to this assertion.

Say for instance we substitute a corn chip for the knight. Is there still not a whole set of associations with the knight which somehow cannot be replaced by the corn chip given any kind of change of context? Can I really replace the knight with the corn chip? In a momentary sense I can. Insofar as I am doing nothing but playing chess, replacing the one unit by the other doesn't essentially matter. I have only chess on my mind, and it is the only game I am playing (although in fact we are never in such a pure situation). However, for the sake of argument, in that case it makes absolutely no difference.

As human beings, though, we are in fact—even at this very moment—players in a number of games at once. And to the extent that we are players, the objects of our perception are defined multiply by our participation in one or more games at the same time. To that extent, you can't rule out associations. But the associations that will come along with the corn chip are themselves not grounded outside of games of a different kind. You haven't grounded the corn chip in something essential or natural by simply carrying some of the associations along; rather, those associations come from another context with another set of values, another system of differences, one that distinguishes a corn chip from a tortilla chip or a nacho. (Quite a complicated system of differences these days.)

Now, to recap. We started with the notion of the arbitrariness of the sign, of the unmotivated relationship between concept and sound image, and saw that a sign is not a thing in itself. Its identity does not spring from the it-ness of the sign; it springs from its differences from all of the signs that surround it, as in the case of the chessmen and the 8:25 Geneva-to-Paris train. And once something is isolated from the system, it "falls apart." Saussure reformulates the notion of linguistic value thus:

> The community is necessary if values that owe their existence solely to usage and general acceptance are to be set up; by himself the individual is incapable of fixing a single value.
>
> In addition, the idea of value, as defined, shows that to consider a term as simply the union of a certain sound with a certain concept is grossly misleading. To define it in this way would isolate the term from its system. It would mean assuming that one can start from the terms and construct the system by adding them together when, on the contrary, it is from the interdependent whole that one must start. (p. 113)

The notion of language, in a Saussurean way of talking, becomes a metaphor for understanding, or intelligibility itself. It happened that thinkers began to use a linguistic model as a way of understanding the process of knowledge, as a way of understanding perception. In order to speak of a "linguistically operating system," you don't need words necessarily. Words are just one example of the way sign systems work. A verbal system—a system of articulation involving words—is only one kind of system of intelligibility. But all systems of intelligibility operate according to the Saussurean principle; that is, they are systems of difference without positive terms.

### Derrida's "Différance"

It is the notion of a non-centered field of signification, spreading itself over the entire horizon, with which Derrida begins his essay "Différance." The first point Derrida makes in "Différance" is directly related to the Saussurean conception of language and differences. Derrida has been talking about this word *différance,* a word which doesn't exist in French spelled this way, a word which Derrida says he is only *provisionally* calling a word or concept. He observes that when you pronounce this word *différance,* there is no oral distinction between it and the pronunciation of *différence* (an actual existing word): "This graphic (*a* instead of *e*), this marked difference between two apparently vocal notations, between two vowels, remains purely graphic: it is read, or it is written, but it cannot be heard" (1982, p. 3). He concludes that, as this silent difference demonstrates, "contrary to a very widespread prejudice, there is no phonetic writing" (p. 3). On the basis of this simple observation, Derrida goes a long, long way. There is no such thing as phonetic writing, the conception of writing as a visual transcription of speech, a system of visual marks that represents discrete sounds. Derrida points out that writing involves lots of nonphonetic signs, like punctuation or spacing or capital lettering, or the *u* after *q*, for example. But more important, as he points out, "The play of difference, which, as Saussure reminded us, is the condition for the possibility and functioning of every sign, is in itself a silent play. Inaudible is the difference between two phonemes which alone permits them to be and to operate as such" (p. 5). The difference between *fōt* and *fōti* is silent. You can't hear the difference between *fōt* and *fōti*. The difference which makes either of these audible is itself inaudible. The same holds true with *cat* and *mat*. You don't hear the difference between *c* and *m;* what you hear are the *c* and the *m*. The difference is what enables us to tell the *c* from the *m*.

Rather than the differences themselves, you hear the words that the differences make available: "The inaudible opens up the apprehension of two present phonemes such as they present themselves. If there is no purely phonetic writing, it is that there is no purely phonetic *phone*" (p. 5). That is, the sounds of the *c* and the *m* come to us by virtue of the inaudible difference between them, and therefore are dependent upon that silent play of difference. The sound itself is in a sense constituted by a certain form of silence.

The meaning of these particular lines in the essay is more or less congruent with the way in which we have been learning to operate. The word *différance,* finally, is going to be not like anything seen before on land or sea. At this point in the essay, the idea is being put very simply. Visually we can't see the difference between the *c* and the *m,* or between the *e* and the *a* in *différance;* we can see the different letters, and recognize that they are dissimilar, but we can't see whatever it is that enables us to distinguish between the two. That we don't see. We can see the letters, hear the sounds, but the play of difference that distinguishes them is itself invisible, inaudible.

Derrida goes on to point out that *différance* (what allows us to tell the *e* from the *a*) doesn't belong to the realm of the sensible, that which can be apprehended with the senses. You can't see it, you can't hear it, you can't smell it, you can't touch it. But neither does it belong to the realm of intelligibility, since the concept of intelligibility is itself dependent upon the faculty of sensibility. As Alan Bass, Derrida's translator, notes here, "The very names by which we conceive of objective intelligibility are already in complicity with sensibility. *Theō-rein*—the Greek origin of 'theory'—literally means 'to look at,' to *see;* and the word Derrida uses for 'understanding' here is *entendement,* the noun form of *entendre,* to *hear*" (quoted in Derrida, f.n. 5). That is, there is no such thing as pure intelligibility without an anterior aspect. What is intelligible, is distinguishable, is distinct, articulated because it belongs to some system of signification (which as we remember is made up of two elements—a material sound element and a conceptual element).

*Différance* expresses the possibility of differentiation, the possibility of opposition, and so it doesn't belong to any realm that could be named as such. Why not? Because as soon as you want to assign it to a realm, say of the sensible or the intelligible, or of any two pairs, you have abrogated what *différance* itself is, that which makes any such opposition come into being. *Différance* is something that cannot ever actually be given a name because as soon as you name it, you have unnamed it.

*Différance* is what makes linguistics different. It is, as Derrida says, what allows us to speak each to the other. It is what allows us to understand one another: "If *différance* ⨉ (and I also cross out the 'is,') what makes possible the presentation of the being-present, it is never presented as such. It is never offered to the present" (p. 6). Now, don't be dismayed by the Heideggerian terminology of *present* and *being-present.* Don't be intimidated by that. We already know what this means, if we think of what Saussure has been talking about, of the nature of linguistic identity and the sign, in place of words like *presence* or *being.* Derrida is saying that *différance* is what makes possible the presentation of being-present, that is, the possibility of opposition. It nonetheless never enables us to see the difference between the *c* and the *m* and the *e* and the *a,* or to hear the difference between them; *différance* is not something that we can either see or hear. *Différance* analogously is that which allows us to think in terms of contrast/comparative relationships. It is the very possibility of thinking relationally and, therefore, it couldn't itself ever appear. It is what enables other things to appear.

And that idea then justifies Derrida in producing sentences like the following: "Reserving itself, not exposing itself, in a regular fashion it exceeds the order of truth at a certain precise point, but without dissimulating itself as something, as a mysterious being, in the occult of a nonknowledge or in a hole with indeterminable borders" (p. 6).

All Derrida is saying here is that as soon as we say that *différance,* because it is the very possibility of articulation, cannot itself be articulated, we are not then positing some sort of essential negativity. It is not that *différance* is the opposite of presence or being—absence or nonbeing. Now, why couldn't it be the opposite? What do opposites mean? Absence/presence, being/nonbeing. *Différance* couldn't be assigned to the negative pole, since assigning it to the negative pole is to make it what it is not. It can't be articulated in the domain of oppositions. Derrida explains that "in every exposition it would be exposed to disappearing as disappearance. It would risk appearing: disappearing" (p. 6).

As soon as we name the thing, as soon as it becomes the object of our attention, it no longer could be that which enabled us to see it. It would be something else. And that's why we can't name it. That's why as soon as it appears, it disappears. Because what it is, is the thing that allows things to appear.

That's why this essay is so damned hard to read! There is a principled reason for the maddening way in which Derrida writes. He is trying to talk about something that all our forms of language and thought prevent us from saying. And that's why he has to put himself, and us, through such contortions as "disappearing as disappearance." Yet it's that very sort of acrobatic attempt that makes this so exciting. Once you begin, you've got to go with it. And it's also why, at least for me, I can never go over these materials too many times. Because the habits of my mind, and the habits of everybody's mind in our culture, are so against what he is talking about that we have to constantly practice undoing those habits in order to somehow come close to the mental way of going that he is trying to convey. So my job here is to try to establish what it is we are talking about in the first place.

Let me just go back to something that I didn't say anything about, which is the *is* that Derrida crossed out. "If *différance* ~~is~~"—why did he cross *is* out? Because *différance* does not exist in the sense that *is* exists for us. One of the questions to ask yourself when you feel you are getting rusty is: Why did he cross out *is*? Now, why can't you have a sentence beginning "*Différance* is"; why do you have to say, "Uh oh" and then cross it out? It appears a little bit, it is not erased, it still shows through the *X*. That's exactly the kind of thing that we're talking about here. Just as you can't see or hear the difference between *e* and *a, différance* with an *a* exceeds the order of truth. It exceeds the order of truth because it is not an assertion, but nor is it a negation either. It goes beyond assertion or positivity, and calls it into question. At the same time, it's not absence/nonbeing either because it's what makes possible the thought of such opposition (present/absent, being/nonbeing).

The whole essay in a sense is about why you can't define *différance*. If you succeed in defining it, you fail. It disappears. That is also why the essay proceeds in a series of maddening stops and starts, beginning over and over again. Why? Because there is no place to begin. *Différance* and the Saussurean tradition of language as a system of differences abrogate precisely this notion of some logical place to begin, some sort of absolute starting point, precisely that notion of having an absolute starting point. The notion of *différance* cannot be built up systematically, because there is no foundation on which such a logical systematic structure could rest. Another name for post-structuralism is antifoundationalism. As Derrida says,

> There is nowhere to begin to trace the sheaf or the graphics of *différance*. For what is put into question is precisely the quest for a rightful beginning, an absolute point of departure, a principal responsibility. The problematic of writing is opened by putting into question the value *arkhe* ["The Greek *arkhe* combines the values of a founding principle and of government by a controlling principle" (Translator's Note 6)]. What I will propose here will not be elaborated simply as a philosophical discourse operating according to principles, postulates, axioms or definitions, and proceeding along the discursive lines of a linear order of reasons. In the lineation of *différance* everything is strategic and adventurous. Strategic because no transcendent truth present outside the field of writing can govern theologically the totality of the field. (pp. 6–7)

There is no point to begin. There is nothing that is solid and firm from which we could then somehow move to an understanding of *différance*, because any such thing that we could conceive of would be itself already an effect of *différance*. For the same reason, what Derrida will be explaining here has no goal; there is no transcendent truth present outside the field which governs the field in its totality because such a goal, some final master principle, would have to be thought within language and so would always be at stake, rather than governed. The idea of a ground, insofar as it is the opposite of something that is not on the ground, something floating or hovering up there, has already then come into the domain of articulation, of oppositions, and therefore is ruled out as a ground. Anything that you could point to as a firm ground will, by virtue of being pointable to, be automatically within the system of differentiation, will already have been produced through some system of oppositions and therefore will not be able to function as some sort of ground of that system. Everything you can think of is an effect of *différance:* nothing can finally delimit it, and it itself can't be grounded because it is what enables apprehension.

So, as Derrida says, "By means of this solely strategic justification, I wish to underline that the efficacity of the thematic of *différance* may very well, indeed must, one day be superseded, lending itself if not to its own replacement, at least to enmeshing itself in a chain that in truth it never will have governed" (p. 7). What he is saying here is that right now this notion, *différance,* is a way into understanding, a conveniently elusive term that enables us to do a certain kind of intellectual work but which may some day lose that efficacity; it may, in fact, appear. That is, it may itself be taken up within some other more satisfactory way of understanding what's going on, a way whose basis would be just as unavailable to us as *différance* is unavailable now.

At this point, Derrida sort of steps back, starts over again, and begins to talk about the buried meanings that are floating around inside the words he has made up for the occasion. He points to the fact that in French the verb *différer* means both to tell things apart from one another in space, i.e., "to distinguish" or "differ," and "to defer," or to postpone or delay. It implies difference both in spatial and in temporal terms, so that you're working with two different axes of differentiation in this word *différance.* The word hovers between a noun form and a verb form: the "*ance*" is reminiscent of the participle *ant,* which implies action, which implies agency, but the fact that it is a noun implies some sort of state or condition. So the word *différance* hovers also between being an agent and being a product or an effect, between activity and passivity, the act of doing and what is done.

Derrida next shows us how the notion of deferral—temporization, of putting off, of differentiation in time (this is the thing that Saussure was not dealing with; he was dealing purely with spatial or simultaneous time)—how the fact that language functions in time is essential to our understanding of the sign. The sign, he says, stands for what is absent: "The sign represents the present in its absence. It takes the place of the present. When we cannot grasp or show the thing, state the present, the being-present, when the present cannot be presented, we signify, we go through the detour of the sign. . . . The sign, in this sense, is deferred presence" (p. 9). The sign defers, puts off, postpones the moment in which we can encounter the thing itself. Now, on this basis it would seem that we are dealing here with that scientific definition of language that Barthes spoke of, that is, language as secondary or provisional, merely a place marker standing in until presence can arrive (see Barthes 1970).

But Derrida turns this notion upside down by reminding us at this crucial moment of Saussure. He brilliantly reviews all of Saussure in a nutshell, by reminding us one more time that signs are arbitrary and differential, and that they are only there by virtue of differences. And the fact that there are no positive terms is a function of their arbitrariness. As he puts it here, in a really elegant formulation of Saussure, "The elements of signification function due not to the compact force of their nuclei but rather to the network of oppositions that distinguishes them, and then relates them to one another" (p. 10). This is saying exactly what we were saying about Saussure all the way through our reading above. Derrida quotes Saussure as saying,

> Whether we take the signified or the signifier, language has neither ideas nor sounds that existed before the linguistic system, but only conceptual and phonic differences that have issued from the system. The idea or phonic substance that a sign contains is of less importance than the other signs that surround it. (Derrida, p. 11; Saussure, *Course,* pp. 117–18)

Instead of a bunch of objects where presence is deferred, a group of objects being represented by a group of words that are temporarily standing in for them, we have the play of differences which produces concepts, objects, words, all forms of positivity, of presence, of everything, which are not really present but are effects of difference. In other words, what Saussure says about the nonpositivity of words, which also means the nonpositivity of objects, means that these objects, too, are produced through systems of articulation. There is then no difference between language and objects because objects are at play in a system of differences, too. It is not that language or a word is taking the place of something; it's that anything that is perceptible is dependent for its being there upon its position within a system, and there isn't anything else for which to wait. The sign, the thing that is articulated by the system of differences, is all that there is, and, therefore, language is not secondary, is not provisional, is not just marking time or keeping a place until the thing itself arrives because things themselves are linguistically constituted. And the world itself is a discourse.

Next comes the hardest passage of all:

> It is because of *différance* that the movement of signification is possible only if each so-called "present" element [that is, the sign], each element appearing on the scene of presence, is related to something other than itself, thereby keeping within itself the mark of the past element, and already letting itself be vitiated by the mark of its relation to the future element, this trace being related no less to what is called the future than to what is called

> the past, and constituting what is called the present by means of
> this very relation to what it is not: what it absolutely is not, not
> even a past or a future as a modified present. (p. 13)

Okay, this is really only a philosophical and happy way of talking about
the difference between *žena* and *žen*. That is, *žen* as plural is present
to us because we know it by what it is not. Derrida is radicalizing the
force of that idea by saying that whatever is present is there only
because of its relation to all the things that it is not. It is radically
dependent for its identity on what is not itself. A linguistic unit is
definable only by its dissimilarities to other beings, which are in turn
dependent for their identities on their dissimilarities to other beings.
So there are no positive terms, only differences. Just so, Derrida is
saying, the present is constituted only by virtue of its relation to what
it is not itself, i.e., the past, the future; its identity rests on what is
non-identical to itself. It is radically constituted by what it is not. To
read on:

> An interval must separate the present from what it is not in order
> for the present to be itself, but this interval that constitutes it as
> present must, by the same token, divide the present in and of
> itself, thereby also dividing, along with the present, everything
> that is thought on the basis of the present, that is, in our
> metaphysical language every being and singularly substance or
> the subject. (p. 13)

What's going on here? The present itself is divided by virtue of its
radical dependence on the other—the past, the future—which is necessarily implied; there is no present without past and future; therefore,
it is radically dependent on those things which it is not. For its very
existence it depends on things that it is not and, therefore, if it is
divided within itself, it is not whole, it is not unitary. What it is, it is
only by virtue of what it is not, and, therefore, it does not have a kind
of unitary being: it is split. Everything that is thought on the basis of
the present, which is to say, everything, but in particular substance
(which is to say, objects) and subject (that is to say, selves), is similarly
self-divided. We are effects of *différance* and are inscribed in a chain
of signification that is always being reborn, insofar as language is always
being spoken and beings are always being produced, and it is the same
for the "object" that we "perceive."

Here Derrida is really driving the Saussurean notion of language as
a system of differences without positive terms to its furthest limit. That
is, insofar as anything that is, is by virtue of *différance*, by being
different from what it is not; insofar as it exists, it represents the
cleavage between itself and what it is not and, therefore, is, in a sense,

divided within itself. Anything that can be thought of—his great example is the present—anything that we can think of, we always think of as in the present, as existing in time, being right there. Insofar as there is no present in and of itself, there is no "right there" that isn't constituted by a relation to a past and a future; just so, anything that can be thought of on the basis of the present, such as "object," such as "self," is similarly self-divided, similarly radically constituted by what it is not.

Let me quote from another passage, where Derrida focuses on the subject—that is, on the reader, on the self, on us, whoever we are:

> The subject (in its identity with itself, or eventually in its consciousness of its identity with itself, its self-consciousness) is inscribed in language, is a "function" of language, becomes a *speaking* subject only by making its speech conform—even in so-called "creation," or in so-called "transgression" to the system of the rules of language as a system of differences, or at very least by conforming to the general law of *différance.* (p. 15)

Insofar as we think of ourselves, as we can have any notion of ourselves, that notion is itself, of course, inscribed in language, is an effect, always produced and at stake in the game of *différance.* Insofar as you can think of yourself or be aware of yourself, you are aware of yourself from within some particular way of thinking about yourself, the way that our culture happens to make available to us one particular way (a way which we happen to know now has been changing over the centuries).

People's conceptions of what it means to be a "self," to be a person or an individual—even the word *individual*—have a particular loaded quality. That is an historical notion, a notion which has been changing in the course of history, just as our ways of dividing up the world, of articulating the world, have changed. And so our very selves are at stake in this game of language, are vulnerable to the play of differences that make possible our apprehending anything, including anything that we apprehend about ourselves, including "ourselves."

Derrida then answers the objection "But isn't there a self before language, isn't there something there that is going on inside our heads that is independent of words?"

> Such a question therefore supposes that, prior to the sign and outside it, excluding any trace and any *différance,* something like consciousness is possible. And that consciousness, before distributing its signs in space and in the world, can gather itself into its presence. But what is consciousness? What does "consciousness" mean? Most often, in the very form of meaning, in all its

> modifications, consciousness offers itself to thought only as self-
> presence, as the perception of self in presence. (p. 15)

In other words, I think "consciousness" by thinking that I am in
some way present to my "self":

> Thus one comes to posit presence—and specifically consciousness,
> the being beside itself of consciousness—no longer as the abso-
> lutely central form of Being but as a "determination" and as an
> "effect." (p. 16)

## Conclusion: Returning to the Beginning

This returns us to my introduction. The point I want to make here is
that you can't apply post-structuralism to literary texts. Why not?
Because to talk about applying post-structuralism to literary texts
assumes the following things: (1) that we have freestanding subjects,
(2) that we have freestanding objects of investigation, (3) that there are
freestanding methods, and (4) that what results when we apply reader
to method and method to text is a freestanding interpretation. This
series of assumptions revokes everything that Derrida is getting at in
"Différance," and that is implicit in Saussure's theory of language.
Once you've acknowledged that language is a system of differences and
that all articulation proceeds on a model of language, the substantiality
of the self and of the object it perceives dissolves. Instead of the self
and/or the object of perception, you have effects of language, language
which is always in process, always modifying itself. The self and its
percepts, its objects, are simultaneous products of discourse, embedded
in and articulated by systems of differences that are culturally specific,
that is, by the thousands of rules that tell us how to tell an *e* from an
*a, foot* from *feet.* These are all learned, not natural but given to us by
our culture.

As we read literary texts, then, "we" are not applying a "method";
we are acting as an extension of the interpretive code, of those systems
of difference that constitute us and the objects of our perception
simultaneously. We don't have access to the codes that constitute us,
to the whatever it is, *différance,* that enables us to tell an *a* from an *e*
and a *c* from an *m.* Remember, that which enables us to see opposition
is itself not visible. What enables us to hear the difference between *c*
and *m, e* and *a,* is not audible, is not available to us; we can't see it,
much less apply it. We are extensions of it. As soon as you unearth
the interpretive system, the system of differences that has governed
your perception of something, that has made you able to see something,

it no longer does. You are now able to see it by virtue of some other system of differences, which is what makes you able to see this one in front of you.

And that is why you can't "*apply* post-structuralism." You are being constituted by some system of articulation, or some other code that now allows you to see the one that you've just uncovered. If you self-consciously apply a method to a literary text, both the text and the method have already been constituted by you, by the systems of difference that allowed you to be aware of them in the first place. They are already the product of interpretation before you have even begun to apply the one to the other. So is the "you" who does the applying, insofar as you are the object of your own thought. It is in that sense that we have ended up by collapsing reader, method, text, and interpretation into a continuous act in which discourse reproduces itself.

## References

Barthes, Roland. 1970. "Science vs. Literature." In *Introduction to Structuralism,* edited by Michael Lane. New York: Basic Books, 410–16.

Derrida, Jacques. 1982. "Différance." In *Margins of Philosophy,* translated by Alan Bass, 3–27. Chicago: University of Chicago Press.

Saussure, Ferdinand de. 1959. *Course in General Linguistics,* translated by Wade Baskin and edited by Charles Bally and Albert Sechehaye. New York: Philosophical Library.

# 3 The Turns of Reader-Response Criticism

Steven Mailloux

Steven Mailloux is professor of English at Syracuse University, where he has just completed a three-year term as chair of the English Department. During his tenure, the department established a new undergraduate major in English and Textual Studies, one that reconceptualizes the literary studies curriculum as a "culture studies" program.

He is the author of *Interpretive Conventions: The Reader in the Study of American Fiction; Rhetorical Power;* and *Interpreting Law and Literature: A Hermeneutic Reader.* At Syracuse he teaches a freshman course called "Reading and Interpretation: From Language to Discourse," and upper-division courses such as "American Cultural Rhetoric" and "Studies in Hermeneutics." At the graduate level he teaches a course titled "Contemporary Rhetoric: Theory, Interpretation, Politics."

The essay that follows is an expansion and a deepening of the materials Professor Mailloux presented at the NCTE Summer Institute in 1987, where he accomplished a wonderfully lucid review of reader-response criticism in a three-hour morning lecture/workshop.

The goal of reader-response criticism is to talk more about readers than about authors and texts. During the last twenty years such talk has involved a diversity of tropes and arguments within the institutional activities of literary criticism, history, theory, and pedagogy. In this brief essay I analyze early forms of this diversity in the 1970s and suggest some new turns reader-response criticism has taken in the 1980s.

Rhetoric as trope (figurative language) and as argument (persuasion) provides the framework for my discussion of reader-oriented criticism. Rhetoric presents a useful conceptual bridge from the linguistic and philosophical topics of post-structuralism to the material and political concerns of cultural criticism. That is, the rhetorical tradition has returned again and again to the very questions that now preoccupy such discourses as deconstruction and ideology critique, having often focused on the former's questions about the grounds of knowledge claims and the role of tropes in the communication (or troubling) of textual meaning, and the latter's questions about the grounds of political action and the role of persuasion in a text's ideological effects. It is precisely these rhetorical concerns with tropology and anti-foundationalism and with ideology and politics that seem lacking in most reader-response criticism of the 1970s. Instead, the predominant rhetorical focus of most reader criticism was the issue of how the literary text did or did not directly affect its readers during or after the reading process. In retrospect, this rhetorical focus appears to have accomplished three things within academic literary study: it provided a decade of intense arguments about a limited number of theoretical topics; it extended without radically altering the practice of close reading within literary criticism; and it presented a renewed institutional justification for a student-centered pedagogy.

## The Old Rhetoric of Reader Talk

The easiest way into reader-response criticism is to view it within the rhetorical context of American literary criticism in the late 1960s. At that time, despite various foreign and domestic challenges, New Critical formalism continued to provide the most influential tropes for critical practice and theory: the literary work was figured as an organic unity, a well-wrought urn, or a verbal icon, and criticism was equated with close reading or objective analysis of this artifact. In most versions of New Critical formalism, such metaphors for literature and definitions of criticism focused attention on the text in and of itself, emphasizing the objective meaning contained in the work and rejecting as evidence for correct interpretation historical background, the testimony of authors, or any response statements by readers.

In fact, the discourses placed under the banner of "New Criticism" differed in many important respects, but such diversity counted for little within the rhetorical context of academic criticism in the late sixties. Reader-response approaches, like other challenges to formalist orthodoxy, treated New Criticism monolithically and picked out of its theoretical manifestos a limited number of doctrines that it then used strategically to position itself as a "new" approach to academic literary study. Chief among these foregrounded doctrines was the New Critical rejection of the "Affective Fallacy."

In the opening sentences of their influential 1949 essay, Monroe Beardsley and W. K. Wimsatt summarized their formalist fears about "obstacles to objective criticism" (Wimsatt and Beardsley 1954, p. 21).

First, there was the danger of the "Intentional Fallacy," defined as "a confusion between the poem and its origins," and then there was the "Affective Fallacy... a confusion between the poem and its *results* (what it *is* and what it *does*)." It was exactly this rhetorical topic— what a text does to a reader—that reader-response criticism came to take as central to its critical project. But, according to New Criticism, any approach that interpreted literature in terms of its effects on readers committed the Affective Fallacy, which inevitably led to critical "impressionism and relativism." Indeed, Wimsatt and Beardsley claimed, the outcome of both fallacies is "that the poem itself, as an object of specifically critical judgment, tends to disappear." These anxieties about disappearing texts and unconstrained interpretations were constitutive of the rhetorical context of literary theory when a new focus on readers reading began to be promoted in the late sixties.

The most vital theoretical phase of this reader-response criticism extended from about 1970 through 1980, from the initial impact of a new reader-oriented criticism through publication of the retrospective collection *Reader-Response Criticism: From Formalism to Post-Structuralism* (1980b), edited by Jane Tompkins. The theoretical debates of this period were defined ahead of time by a rhetorical situation in which New Criticism, under attack for years, still defined the terms of theorizing about literature for most professors of English. And most telling for the arguments of reader-response theory was the New Critical designation of the Affective Fallacy as "a special case of epistemological skepticism" (Wimsatt and Beardsley, p. 21). As we will see, the most prominent reader-response critics of the 1970s felt it necessary to respond to the latter charge of relativism as they promoted specific kinds of reader talk in literary study.

But the rhetorical context of the early seventies was not constituted simply by what was explicitly foregrounded in theoretical debates. Equally important was what remained excluded and forgotten. Reader-response criticism of this early period acknowledged some precursors to its focus on readers reading, but it strangely overlooked one of the most influential reader critics of the previous thirty years: Louise Rosenblatt. It will be my speculative argument here that Rosenblatt's work and its implicit neo-pragmatism had to be "forgotten" in order for the new reader-response criticism to establish its theoretical ethos and carry out a decade of intense theoretical debate over the question of its "epistemological skepticism." Put most simply: Rosenblatt's prior dismantling of the reader/text distinction had to be ignored in order for a certain kind of theoretical work to be done, and that theoretical work needed to be done, it was thought, in order to provide a foundation for reader talk in criticism and pedagogy.

*Literature as Exploration* first appeared in 1938. Thirty years later, immediately before the rise of a new reader-oriented criticism, Rosenblatt published a revised version, in which she explicitly adopted the transactional vocabulary of John Dewey and Arthur F. Bentley's *Knowing and the Known* (1949). In a footnote citing this pragmatist text, Rosenblatt explains that "The usual terminology—e.g., 'the reaction of the reader to the literary work,' 'the interaction between the reader and the work,' or references to 'the poem itself'—tends to obscure the view of the literary experience presented here. . . . In various disciplines *transaction* is replacing *interaction,* which suggests the impact of distinct and fixed entities. *Transaction* is used above in the way that one might refer to the interrelationship between the *knower* and what is *known. The poem* is the transaction that goes on between reader and text" (Rosenblatt 1968, p. 27n). Here Rosenblatt allies her reading theory with the pragmatist rejection of traditional epistemology and the separation of the knower from the known, the subject from the object. Figuring the poem as a transactive event, Rosenblatt set aside beforehand the very question that fueled the next decade of reader-response critical theory: is it the reader or the text that determines interpretation?

This question assumes that the reader and the text are "distinct and fixed entities" and that the job of reader-response theory is to figure out which is in control. To ask this question is to accept Wimsatt and Beardsley's foundationalist concern over "epistemological skepticism." It is precisely such foundationalism that pragmatism refuses to take seriously. More exactly, pragmatism denies the subject-object split and rejects the notion that there needs to be a theory of knowledge that regulates the relationship between a knower and an object known. In explaining their transactional framework, Dewey and Bentley define "self-action" as the view that things act under their own powers, and "inter-action" as the view that "thing is balanced against thing in causal interconnection." They then replace both views with a notion of *transaction,* "where systems of description and naming are employed to deal with aspects and phases of action, without final attribution to 'elements' or other presumptively detachable or independent 'entities,' 'essences,' or 'realities,' and without isolation of presumptively detachable 'relations' from such detachable 'elements' " (1949, p. 108). In another place the authors define transaction as the "knowing-known taken as one process in cases in which in older discussions the knowings and knowns are separated and viewed as in interaction" (p. 304).

In an appendix to *Knower and the Known,* Dewey observes that separating the subject and the object has led to a long tradition of epistemological controversy over the relation of the knower to the known, a controversy in which "the problem of problems was to determine some method of harmonizing the status of one with the status of the other with respect to the possibility and nature of knowledge." Dewey suggests that the debate has reached a deadend: "It is . . . as if it had been discovered that the competing theories of the various kinds of realism, idealism, and dualism had finally so covered the ground that nothing more could be found to say" (p. 322). Dewey and Bentley tried to displace such foundationalist theorizing with their transactional argument for not separating subject and object, and Bentley observed with pleasure in a 20 April 1950 letter to Dewey that Rosenblatt was "all excited about applications of *Knowing and the Known* to literature" (see Rosenblatt 1978, p. xiv). But such anti-foundationalist theorizing certainly didn't convince everybody. Wimsatt and Beardsley published "The Affective Fallacy"—with its foundation-alist worry over "epistemological skepticism"—in the same year as *Knowing and the Known,* and twenty years later reader-response theorists were to spend a decade arguing over the same problem. All these new theorists seemed oblivious to Rosenblatt's neo-pragmatist attempt to dissolve the problem by refusing to separate the reader and the text.

## A Review of Reader-Response Criticism

The canon of reader-response criticism was established by a series of retrospective collections, overviews, and reading lists of the early 1980s. The texts most often included in this canon were authored by David Bleich, Norman Holland, Wolfgang Iser, Stanley Fish, and Jonathan Culler. As we will see, these five critics varied widely in their different theoretical assumptions, critical strategies, and pedagogical practices; but because in varying degrees they all explicitly rejected New Critical formalism, they were grouped together under the rubric of "reader-response criticism." This naming process is, in fact, a very important aspect of how institutional practices get modified within academic literary studies. As with the label "New Criticism" decades earlier, "reader-response criticism" covered over many differences among critics but gave a certain kind of institutional leverage and rhetorical power to an array of new theories and methods. During the seventies it was more important that reader-response critics rejected the "Affective Fallacy" than it was that they did so in sometimes contradictory ways.

In an overview (*Interpretive Conventions*) published in 1982, I presented a chart that attempted to map out the similarities and differences among the most important reader-response critics. A version of this chart (Fig. 1) is still useful, I believe, not only for its intended purposes but because it stands as an emblem for the exclusions alluded to above: tropology, anti-foundationalism, ideology, politics, and Rosenblatt's transactional theory. Each of these exclusions enables a certain kind of theorizing to continue, a kind quite important to the reader talk of the seventies. In my reuse of the chart here I mention in passing how each of these exclusions functioned to enable the rhetoric of reader-response theory and practice. In what follows I will not do full justice to the complexity and sophistication of these reader-response critics, and I will only gesture toward how some of them have revised their approaches in the 1980s. My main goal is simply to provide an introduction to reader-response criticism by describing in schematic form the rhetorical context of reader talk in recent literary studies.

## Subjectivism

We can begin with David Bleich's subjective criticism. In books such as *Readings and Feelings* (1975) and *Subjective Criticism* (1978), Bleich insisted that teachers and critics should start their talk about literature with the individual reader's response. He argued again and again that the literary text exerts no constraints on the individual reader and that there is no such thing as an objectively correct interpretation. The worst fears of the New Critics were realized in Bleich's theorizing: "The poem itself, as an object of specifically critical judgment, tends to disappear" (Wimsatt 1954, p. 21). Bleich rejected the formalist worry over impressionism and relativism by embracing with glee these dual dangers of the Affective Fallacy. However, despite this radical rejection of formalism, Bleich still accepted the foundationalist alternatives of New Criticism: his subjectivism simply reversed its objectivism. Rather than displacing the reader/text framework entirely, as Rosenblatt often did, Bleich made one of its poles—the reader—completely dominant, mirroring in his theorizing the New Critical move to give complete dominance to the opposite pole—the text.

Bleich's early theory of reading elaborates a three-step process. First you have the original individual reading experience, which he calls "symbolization." Then there's the reader's attempt to articulate that reading experience in the act of "resymbolization." In the classroom situation, this resymbolization involves the writing of response statements by individual student-readers. It is this aspect of Bleich's theory

| PSYCHOLOGICAL MODEL | | INTERSUBJECTIVE MODEL | | SOCIAL MODEL | |
| --- | --- | --- | --- | --- | --- |
| David Bleich's subjective criticism | Norman Holland's transactive criticism | Wolfgang Iser's phenomeno-logical criticism | Stanley Fish's affective stylistics | Jonathan Culler's structuralist poetics | Stanley Fish's theory of interpretive strategies |
| primacy of subjectivity | transaction between reader and text within reader's identity theme | inter-action between reader and text | text's manipu-lation of reader | reading conventions | authority of interpretive communities |

Figure 1. Similar in some ways, different in others, the theorizing of reader-response critics in the seventies enabled the rhetoric of reader-response theory and practice. (Reprinted from Steven Mailloux: *Interpretive Conventions*. Copyright © 1982 by Cornell University. Used by permission of the publisher, Cornell University Press.)

that has been most influential. Literature teachers at many levels have cited Bleich's work as a justification for less authoritarian, more student-centered pedagogy.

The third and final stage in Bleich's model is the sharing of individual response statements in a process he calls "negotiation." I have previously questioned this move from symbolization to negotiation because I found it difficult to understand how radically subjective responses could be in any sense rhetorically "negotiated" (Mailloux 1982, pp. 32–37). If a process of negotiation means some kind of interpretive give-and-take, on what shared basis would such a process take place if there were nothing but individual responses to appeal to as a basis for judgment? If in a particular rhetorical context no hierarchies of criteria or shared interpretive conventions for valid readings were even temporarily in place, how could a negotiation (a give-and-take rather than a show-and-tell) ever come about? Furthermore, wouldn't the radical subjectivism of the theory imply that for every response statement to be negotiated there would be as many different subjective responses to *that* document as to the original literary text? I am now less concerned with these theoretical contradictions than with the pedagogical conse-quences of Bleich's theory. Throughout the 1970s and 1980s his work was adapted and used to empower many teachers in their revisions of traditional classroom practices.

On my chart, I grouped Bleich's subjective criticism with the theory of another psychological critic, Norman Holland. The rhetoric of Holland's transactive criticism develops out of the arguments of ego-psychology combined with at least one significant trope from New Critical formalism. Rather than the text determining interpretation, Holland sees the reader's "identity theme" producing a text's meaning. Thus, disagreements over a text's interpretation derive from readers' different identity themes employed in reading. Identity themes are, in turn, located by reading a certain unity into the varied acts and attributes of a person. In fact, Holland draws an explicit parallel between his troping of the reader as a unity and formalism's troping of the text: "*Identity* is the *unity* I find in a *self* if I look at it as though it were a *text*" (Holland 1975c, p. 815). For Holland the identity of a reader is unique to that reader, just as for a New Critic the unity of a poem was unique to that poem.

Armed with this assumption, Holland's transactive criticism has always done a good job explaining differences in interpretations: dif-ferent identity themes lead to the construction of different meanings (see, for example, *5 Readers Reading*). But, as with Bleich's subjectivist theory, interpretive agreement has always presented Holland's transactive criticism with a problem. Once you build radical difference into your reading theory at its foundations, it is extremely difficult to arrive at a persuasive account of shared meanings and interpretive agreements.

Bleich's and Holland's psychological reader-response criticism has had a very uneven effect on the discipline of literary studies. In each of the activities of theory, criticism, and pedagogy, their psychological models have exerted different levels of rhetorical influence. Quite understandably, in the discourse of literary criticism, they have found few imitators. In "*Hamlet*—My Greatest Creation," Holland (1975b) describes the way his identity theme transacted Shakespeare's text as his own. This is an entertaining performance but one that few others could or would want to bring off. New Critical admonitions against impressionism and relativism remain very powerful, and traditional and avant-garde critics continue to resist letting the text disappear entirely as they rely upon many formalist assumptions about what counts as a convincing interpretation in today's rhetorical context. In discourses of contemporary theory the situation is slightly different. Psychological reader-response theory has persuaded many to take its work seriously, especially groups of theorists devoted to exploring the problems of reading and interpretation. However, it has had much less influence than one might have thought, probably because its assumption of a unified reader with self-presence contradicts widely influential post-structuralist assumptions about a decentered self and rejections of the myth of presence. It is not that every literary theorist now agrees with Lacanian psychoanalysis or Derridean deconstruction; it is simply that critiques of the unified self have a particularly strong rhetorical purchase at the present moment, and psychological reader-response criticism does not appear to respond forcefully to this critique of its most basic assumptions and enabling metaphors. Finally, Holland and especially Bleich have achieved a significant effect in the area of pedagogy. Whatever one might say about their theories and critical projects, psychological reader-response critics have provided influential arguments for teachers at all levels who are attempting to move their classroom practices toward more student-centered methods and goals. In this way, Bleich and Holland are continuing the pedagogical emphasis that has always distinguished the work of Louise Rosenblatt. Such classroom effectivity remains an important accomplishment for any literary theorist.

## The Intersubjective Model

More influential than psychological reader-response theorists are reader critics who base their work on an intersubjective model of reading. On my chart (see Fig. 1) I grouped the early work of Wolfgang Iser and Stanley Fish in this category of reader talk. Iser borrows from Ingarden's phenomenology and Gadamer's hermeneutics to propose a theory of reading that attempts to avoid the extremes of readerly subjectivity and textual objectivity. He often figures the reader as a creative gap-filler. The reader fills textual gaps of various kinds: for example, the facial features left out of a character description, or a moral judgment implied but not explicitly stated after a particular juxtaposition of plot events. The presence of these gaps in the text requires that the reader be active, not passive, during the temporal reading process. As Iser (1974) puts it, "the unwritten aspects" of fictional scenes

> not only draw the reader into the action but also lead him to shade in the many outlines suggested by the given situations, so that these take on a reality of their own. But as the reader's imagination animates these 'outlines,' they in turn will influence the effect of the written part of the text. (p. 276)

In *The Implied Reader* (1974) and *The Act of Reading* (1978), Iser provides detailed phenomenological analyses of the reader's literary experience.

In describing this reading process, Iser often sounds much like Rosenblatt:

> The convergence of text and reader brings the literary work into existence, and this convergence can never be precisely pinpointed, but must always remain virtual, as it is not to be identified either with the reality of the text or with the individual disposition of the reader. (1974, p. 275)

However, Iser's theory soon turns away from claims like those of Rosenblatt's neo-pragmatism, and instead of talking about the *trans-action* between entities that are not distinct and fixed, he talks in great detail about "the *interaction* between text and reader" (1974, p. 276, my emphasis). The features of the text are pre-given, and it is those pre-given features that constrain the reader's creative activity. Thus, instead of setting aside the problems of foundationalist theories of correct interpretation, he takes up their claims and skillfully crafts a theory that avoids the charges of "impressionism and relativism" and justifies the large amount of reader talk in his critical interpretations.

Particularly telling is Iser's theoretical attempt to negotiate his way around Wimsatt and Beardsley's criticism of the Affective Fallacy. He basically accepts their point that a focus on the results of the work is not the job of the literary critic or theorist. "Where their criticism is justified is in the fact that they regard the disappearance of the work in its result as a problem—in this case—of psychology and not of aesthetics." Iser argues that granting this formalist point does not mean a prohibition on talk about the reader. He claims that his theory of reading does not focus on results but on how those results are at least potentially prestructured by the literary text itself. "It follows that the reproach of the 'Affective Fallacy' cannot be applied to a theory of aesthetic response because such a theory is concerned with the structure of the 'performance' which precedes the effect" (1978, pp. 26–27). Not only does Iser assume fixed entities that interact; he also provides a detailed description of the textual structures that guide the reader's performance. Here the neo-pragmatism seen in Rosenblatt's work is left far behind indeed.

Whatever its theoretical underpinnings, Iser's readerly interpretations of fiction exerted a strong influence on many critics. Jane Tompkins (1980a) and others have pointed out a significant institutional reason for this influence and the similar persuasive force of Fish's early "affective stylistics." Unlike the reader talk of Bleich and Holland, that of Iser and Fish enabled the continuation of the formalist practice of close reading. Through a vocabulary focused on a text's manipulation of readers, Fish was especially effective in extending and diversifying the formalist practices that continued business as usual within literary criticism. In his detailed interpretations, he constructed intricate narratives of how a text guides its reader step-by-step through the syntax of sentences and the turns of longer passages. He described how a text's rhetoric creates a temporal pattern of responses with puzzles, revelations, corrections, lessons, surprises, and a wealth of other effects often passed over by critical perspectives focusing on holistic meanings.

What such reader-response criticism claims to make visible is the temporal reading process, in which meaning is the product of the interaction of reader and text. What becomes *invisible* in many such readings is the sociopolitical context constituting the reception of a text at particular historical moments. This form of reader criticism often assumed an ideal reader unencumbered by particular characteristics of class, occupation, race, nationality, gender, and age. When the question was asked, "Whose reading experience does affective stylistics describe?" The answer came back, "That of the informed reader." Such a response could have opened up reader-response criticism to an array of questions about the reading subject: how was what counted as "informed" for a particular text determined by sociopolitical coordinates? How were readers positioned by the ideologies of their historical moments in reading a literary work?

## Structuralism and the Social Model

Such questions as the above were usually ignored by reader-response critics in the seventies. Instead, questions about the informed or ideal reader were answered by exclusively literary answers. The most powerful version of this response came from Jonathan Culler, who challenged Fish to provide a full-blown description of the informed reader. In his 1970 essay, "Literature in the Reader: Affective Stylistics," Fish had explained that the informed reader was the person with the linguistic and literary competencies assumed by the text (1980b, p. 48). Culler called Fish to account for not describing in detail the reader's literary competence (1981, p. 125). In *Structuralist Poetics* (1975) Culler himself attempted to use recent semiotic and structuralist theory to elaborate such an account of reading conventions for the lyric poem and the novel. According to Culler, reading conventions are the shared strategies used for making sense of literary texts, strategies such as viewing a text in a specific genre, organizing meaning around a central theme, and relating metaphors to each other. The set of reading conventions that enabled the understanding of poems and novels constituted what Culler called "literary competence." Though not exclusively so, Culler's readerly project focused on conventions of intelligibility for making sense of *literary* texts. He tended to treat literary competence somewhat monolithically, pushing to the background the political stakes of competing literary competencies. He did not emphasize how the literary competence he described was embedded within larger social formations and traversed by political ideologies extending beyond the academy. Moreover, Culler did not question the whole linguistic project of formally describing what he posited as an integrated, coherent system of conventions.

At least one of the reasons for backgrounding these issues is once again the old foundationalist fear of epistemological skepticism. In *Structuralist Poetics* Culler was especially interested in describing how his view of reading conventions did not lead to extreme relativism or interpretive freeplay. He argued against certain versions of post-structuralism, claiming that in opening up interpretation to the play of signification, some post-structuralists depend on but refuse to acknowledge the shared conventions of reading. Culler suggested that such post-structuralist projects collapse two very different semiological activities: descriptions of the "implicit rules which enable readers to make sense of texts" and attempts "to change those rules" (p. 249). Failing to recognize this distinction, some post-structuralists appear to think that they can change ways of reading all at once without relying on conventions already in place. "But by the very nature of things they can proceed only step-by-step, relying on the procedures which readers actually use, frustrating some of these so that some new ways of producing meaning are developed, and only then dispensing with others" (p. 253).

Culler noted that one of the goals of such a reading revolution is to set free the "text of infinite possibilities," the "geno-text" with its hidden traces of all past, present, and future meanings. When a post-structuralist emphasizes that texts are open to this unending play of signification, Culler claimed, they create a problem for the activity of criticism: if no reading conventions are recognized as limiting the play of meanings, then there "is no standpoint from which a proposal could be rejected" (p. 247). And since post-structuralists "would not want to claim that their analyses are no better than any other" (p. 252), they must reject their own calls for interpretive freeplay and accept the fact that they must work within the present conventions even as they attempt to change them.

This argument near the end of *Structuralist Poetics* points in two directions at once: backwards to formalist worries about relativism and epistemological skepticism and forward to a rhetorical understanding of interpretation. In the former turn, Culler seems to be at one with Fish's early claims about the "objectivity" of reader talk. Reader-response criticism is more objective than New Criticism because reader-oriented theory and practice include what is truly objective about "the *activity* of reading" and focus attention on "the meaning experience" and "the active and activating consciousness of the reader" (Fish 1980b, p. 44). Reader-response criticism describes this reading process, and its theory guarantees that the reading described is the correct one. Its theory claims to provide constraints on what counts as a correct reading—thus avoiding relativism—by positing an informed reader with literary competence. Culler in turn takes this competence as the object of his theory and in one place justifies his enterprise by arguing that if such competence did not exist, then literature professors would have no justification for their teaching:

> The time and effort devoted to literary education by generations of students and teachers creates a strong presumption that there is something to be learned, and teachers do not hesitate to judge their pupil's progress towards a general literary competence. (1975, p. 121)

But the content of a "general literary competence" is often exactly what is at stake among competing perspectives in literary theory and criticism. Is what counts as a valid interpretation for a Jungian usually acceptable to most traditional or postmodern Marxists? Still, there is another way to turn Culler's preoccupation with reading conventions. Often in *Structuralist Poetics* Culler's reader talk is as much about readers' talking as it is about readers' reading. That is, reading conventions are often described as the available rhetorical moves that interpreters use in convincing someone else to accept their interpretations. In this sense, "literary competence" points not only to accepted practices of understanding texts but to "certain standards of argument and plausibility" in debates about textual meaning (1975, p. 253). "Indeed, the possibility of critical argument depends on shared notions of the acceptable and the unacceptable, a common ground which is nothing other than the procedures of reading" (p. 124). Here "reading" refers not just to a relation between a reader and a text but to the discussion of texts among interpreters.

## New Reader Talk about Rhetoric

In the 1980s reader-response critics addressed many of the issues I have raised. For example, in *The Double Perspective: Language, Literacy, and Social Relations* (1988), David Bleich raises political questions about reading and gender and provides a wide-ranging discussion of literacy and intersubjectivity. In *On Deconstruction: Theory and Criticism after Structuralism* (1982), Jonathan Culler gives up his project of describing a monolithic set of reading conventions and analyzes the rhetorical reading of textual tropes by deconstruction. In *Is There a Text in This Class?* (1980a), Stanley Fish rejects the objectivist claims of affective stylistics and takes an explicit turn toward a hermeneutic theory of rhetoric as persuasion, a turn more fully developed in the anti-foundationalist arguments of *Doing What Comes Naturally: Change, Rhetoric, and the Practice of Theory in Literary and Legal Studies* (1989). And Louise Rosenblatt's transactional approach finally seems to be getting the attention in literary theory circles that it has long had among compositionists, educational reading theorists, and teachers of teachers. Rosenblatt's own assessment of the changed rhetorical context can be found in her preface to the fourth edition of *Literature as Exploration* (1983), in which she notes that the book "is being cited as the first empirically based theoretical statement of the importance of the reader's contribution" (p. xiv). The publication of Rosenblatt's *The Reader, the Text, the Poem* in the late seventies gave additional impetus in the eighties to theoretical reconsideration of her transactional approach to the literary work. In that book Rosenblatt provides a more systematic presentation of her theory, distinguising between aesthetic and nonaesthetic reading activities and entering into current debates over interpretation and evaluation.

If the new turns of reader-response criticism do not actually signal the end of a kind of reader talk that is distinguishable from other kinds of theories, they certainly do point to a new stage in the critical conversation. One way of characterizing this stage is to see reader talk as participating in the widely acknowledged return of rhetoric. To say that, however, is to say very little. The real question is "*How* does rhetoric return in the latest phase of reader-response criticism?" I will conclude with a couple of answers to this question, answers that develop out of the rhetorical tradition of reader-oriented criticism and theory.

A turn to rhetoric can be seen as the culmination of two related but separate trajectories of early reader-response criticism. In certain versions of such theories, the preoccupation with establishing the objectivity or, conversely, the subjectivity of reader-response criticism has given way to a questioning of the importance of the New Critical anxiety over epistemological skepticism. Paralleling the neo-pragmatist critique of foundationalism in philosophy, such a post-structuralist questioning of grounds among reader-oriented theorists has led to what I have elsewhere called a rhetorical hermeneutics, an attempt to put aside the foundationalist question "Is it the reader or the text that determines interpretation?" (see Mailloux 1989, ch. 1). A rhetorical hermeneutics tries to change the subject of interpretive theory from talk about readers approximating texts to talk about interpreters arguing over meanings. Such a change of subject entails a re-understanding of sophistic rhetoric, not as the embodiment of relativism and subjectivism, but as the tradition of critiques of foundationalist philosophy. A rhetorical hermeneutics joins neo-pragmatism in collapsing the reader-text distinction in that it claims there is no way of theoretically describing the correct reader-text relation in general. From this point of view, a rhetorical hermeneutics is always therapeutic, attempting to avoid the problems of foundationalist theories that claim to regulate interpretation outside the agonistic context of rhetorical assertion and challenge.

But the more positive aspect of rhetorical hermeneutics involves turning therapeutic theory into rhetorical history. Such histories construct narrative and analytical accounts of culturally situated acts of interpretation. Instead of claiming to specify how reading and interpretation work in general, rhetorical hermeneutics turns to how specific interpretive practices function within sociopolitical contexts of persuasion. These contexts involve tropes and arguments within the cultural conversation at specific historical moments. To do such rhetorical histories means to provide a fine-grained description of a particular interpretive act in a particular institutional setting, within a particular cultural politics, involving agents and audiences traversed by ideologies of a particular social formation. To be concerned with such questions *as a hermeneutic theorist* means to become a practitioner of reception aesthetics and cultural critique. In this review, then, the next turn of contemporary reader-response criticism is toward neo-pragmatism and histories of cultural reception. The rhetoric of reader talk finally turns into talk about readers as rhetors.

## References

Bleich, David. 1988. *The Double Perspective: Language, Literacy, and Social Relations.* New York: Oxford University Press.

————. 1975. *Readings and Feelings: An Introduction to Subjective Criticism.* Urbana, Ill.: National Council of Teachers of English.

————. 1978. *Subjective Criticism.* Baltimore: Johns Hopkins University Press.

Culler, Jonathan. 1982. *On Deconstruction: Theory and Criticism after Structuralism.* Ithaca, N.Y.: Cornell University Press.

————. 1981. *The Pursuit of Signs: Semiotics, Literature, Deconstruction.* Ithaca, N.Y.: Cornell University Press.

————. 1975. *Structuralist Poetics: Structuralism, Linguistics, and the Study of Literature.* Ithaca, N.Y.: Cornell University Press.

Dewey, John, and Arthur F. Bentley. 1949. *Knowing and the Known.* Boston: Beacon Press.

Fish, Stanley. 1989. *Doing What Comes Naturally: Change, Rhetoric, and the Practice of Theory in Literary and Legal Studies.* Durham, N.C.: Duke University Press.

————. 1980a. *Is There a Text in This Class? The Authority of Interpretive Communities.* Cambridge: Harvard University Press.

————. 1980b. "Literature in the Reader: Affective Stylistics." In *Is There a Text in This Class?*, edited by Stanley Fish. Cambridge: Harvard University Press. (Reprinted from *New Literary History* 2 [Autumn 1970].)

Holland, Norman. 1975a. *5 Readers Reading.* New Haven: Yale University Press.

————. 1975b. "*Hamlet*—My Greatest Creation." *Journal of the American Academy of Psychoanalysis* 3: 419–27.

————. 1975c. "Unity Identity Text Self." *PMLA* 90 (October): 813–22.

Iser, Wolfgang. 1978. *The Act of Reading: A Theory of Aesthetic Response.* Baltimore: Johns Hopkins University Press.

————. 1974. *The Implied Reader: Patterns of Communication in Prose Fiction from Bunyan to Beckett.* Baltimore: Johns Hopkins University Press.

Mailloux, Steven. 1982. *Interpretive Conventions: The Reader in the Study of American Fiction.* Ithaca, N.Y.: Cornell University Press.

———. 1989. *Rhetorical Power.* Ithaca, N.Y.: Cornell University Press.

Rosenblatt, Louise M. 1968. *Literature as Exploration.* Rev. ed. New York: Noble and Noble.

———. 1983. Preface. *Literature as Exploration.* 4th ed. New York: Modern Language Association.

———. 1978. *The Reader, the Text, the Poem: The Transactional Theory of the Literary Work.* Carbondale: Southern Illinois University Press.

Tompkins, Jane P. 1980a. "The Reader in History: The Changing Shape of Literary Response." In *Reader-Response Criticism,* edited by Jane P. Tompkins. Baltimore: Johns Hopkins University Press.

———, ed. 1980b. *Reader-Response Criticism: From Formalism to Post-Structuralism.* Baltimore: Johns Hopkins University Press.

Wimsatt, W. K., Jr., and Monroe C. Beardsley. 1954. "The Affective Fallacy." In *The Verbal Icon: Studies in the Meaning of Poetry,* edited by W. K. Wimsatt, Jr. Lexington: University Press of Kentucky. (Reprinted from *Sewanee Review* 57 [1949].)

# 4 The Master's Pieces: On Canon Formation and the Afro-American Tradition

Henry Louis Gates, Jr.

Henry Louis Gates, Jr. is W.E.B. DuBois Professor of Literature at Cornell University. His involvement in Afro-American studies and issues of the canon there and elsewhere made him an ideal choice as a speaker for the second Summer Institute. The essay that follows re-creates in large part Professor Gates's introductory talk but not the questions and discussion that it provoked, which included an illuminating reinterpretation of Zora Neale Hurston's *Her Eyes Were Watching God*—one that brought contemporary literary theory to the teaching of the text.

Professor Gates's book *The Signifying Monkey: Towards a Theory of Afro-American Literary Criticism* was published just before the Institute, and the thirty-volume *Schomberg Library of Nineteenth-Century Black Women Writers,* which he edited, was published just after. Those publications add to his already distinguished work on Zora Neale Hurston, Wole Soyinka, Jean Toomer, Frederick Douglass, and Phillis Wheatley. For the past several years, he has been working as general editor for the forthcoming *Norton Anthology of Afro-American Literature.*

At Cornell, Professor Gates teaches a series of graduate and undergraduate courses on such topics as Afro-American Women and Their Fictions, The African-American Literary Tradition, Autobiography, The Harlem Renaissance, and African-American Literature in the Nineteenth Century. In 1983, he received the Yale Afro-American Cultural Center Faculty Prize.

The following essay by Professor Gates was published, in part, in the 26 February 1989 *New York Times Book Review* as "Whose Canon Is It, Anyway?" (copyright © 1989 by The New York Times Company; reprinted by permission). The entire essay was published in the Winter 1990 issue of the *South Atlantic Quarterly,* and is reprinted here with permission.

William Bennett and Allan Bloom, the dynamic duo of the new cultural right, have become the easy targets of the cultural left—which I am defining here loosely and generously as that uneasy, shifting set of alliances formed by feminist critics, critics of so-called minority discourse, and Marxist and post-structuralist critics generally—in short, the Rainbow Coalition of contemporary critical theory. These two men (one a former United States secretary of education and now President Bush's "drug czar," the other a professor at the University of Chicago and author of *The Closing of the American Mind*) symbolize the nostalgic return to what I think of as the "antebellum aesthetic position," when men were men, and men were white, when scholar-critics were white men, and when women and persons of color were voiceless, faceless servants and laborers, pouring tea and filling brandy snifters in the boardrooms of old boys' clubs. Inevitably, these two men have come to play the roles that George Wallace and Orville Faubus played for the civil rights movement, or that Nixon and Kissinger played during Vietnam—the "feel good" targets whom, despite internal differences and contradictions, the cultural left loves to hate.

And how tempting it is to juxtapose their "civilizing mission" to the racial violence that has swept through our campuses since 1986—at traditionally liberal Northern institutions such as the University of Massachusetts at Amherst, Mount Holyoke College, Smith College, the University of Chicago, Columbia, the University of Pennsylvania, and at Southern institutions such as the University of Alabama, the University of Texas, and the Citadel. Add to this the fact that affirmative action programs on campus have meanwhile become window-dressing operations, necessary "evils" maintained to preserve the fiction of racial fairness and openness but deprived of the power to enforce their stated principles. When unemployment among black youth is 40 percent, when 44 percent of black Americans can't read the front page of a newspaper, when less than 2 percent of the faculty on campuses is black, well, you look for targets close at hand.

And yet there's a real danger of localizing our grievances; of the easy personification, assigning celebrated faces to the forces of reaction and so giving too much credit to a few men who are really asymptomatic of a larger political current. Maybe our eagerness to do so reflects a certain vanity that academic cultural critics are prone to. We make dire predictions, and when they come true, we think we've changed the world.

It's a tendency that puts me in mind of my father's favorite story about Father Divine, that historic con-man of the cloth, a man who made Al Sharpton look like someone out of *Paper Moon*. In the 1930s he was put on trial for using the mails to defraud, I think, and convicted. At sentencing, Father Divine stood up and told the judge, "I'm warning you, you send me to jail, something terrible is going to happen to you." Father Divine, of course, was sent to prison, and a week later, by sheer coincidence, the judge had a heart attack and died. When the warden and the guards found out about it in the middle of the night, they raced to Father Divine's cell and woke him up. "Father Divine," they said, "your judge just dropped dead of a heart attack." Without missing a beat, Father Divine lifted his head and told them, "I *hated* to do it."

As writers, teachers, or intellectuals, most of us would like to claim greater efficacy for our labors than we're entitled to. These days, literary criticism likes to think of itself as "war by other means." But it should start to wonder: have its victories come too easily? The recent turn toward politics and history in literary studies has turned the analysis of texts into a marionette theater of the political, to which we bring all the passions of our real-world commitments. And that's why it is sometimes necessary to remind ourselves of the distance from the classroom to the streets. Academic critics write essays, "readings" of literature, where the bad guys (for example, racism or patriarchy) lose, where the forces of oppression are subverted by the boundless powers of irony and allegory that no prison can contain, and we glow with hard-won triumph. We pay homage to the marginalized and demonized, and it feels almost as if we've righted a real-world injustice. Academic battles are so fierce—the received wisdom has it—because so little is truly at stake. I always think about the folktale about the fellow who killed seven with one blow: flies, not giants.

Ours was a generation that took over buildings in the late 1960s and demanded the creation of black and women's studies programs and now, like the return of the repressed, has come back to challenge the traditional curriculum. And some of us are even attempting to redefine the canon by editing anthologies. Yet it sometimes seems that blacks are doing better in the college curriculum than they are in the streets. This is not a defeatist moan, but an acknowledgment that the relationship between our critical postures and the social struggles they reflect is far from transparent. That doesn't mean there's no relationship, of course, but that it's a highly mediated one. We need to be clear about when we've swatted a fly and when we've toppled a giant.

In the swaddling-clothes of our academic complacencies, few of us are prepared when we bump against something hard—which, sooner or later, we do. One of the first talks I ever gave was to a packed audience at the Howard University Honors Seminar. This was one of those mistakes you don't make twice. Fresh out of graduate school, immersed in the arcane technicalities of contemporary literary theory, I was going to deliver a crunchy structuralist analysis of a slave narrative by Frederick Douglass, tracing the intricate play of its "binary oppositions." Everything was neatly schematized, formalized, analyzed; this was my Sunday-best structuralism: crisp white shirt and shiny black shoes. And it wasn't playing. If you've seen an audience glaze over, this was double glazing. Bravely, I finished my talk and, of course, asked for questions. Long silence. Finally, a young man in the very back of the room stood up and said, "Yeah, brother, all we want to know is, was Booker T. a Tom or not?"

This was an interesting question, a lot more interesting than my talk. While I didn't exactly appreciate it at the time, the exchange drew my attention, a little rudely perhaps, to the yawning chasm between our critical discourse and the traditions they discourse on. You know—"Is there a canon in this class?" People often like to represent the High Canonical texts as the reading matter of the power elite. I mean, you have to try to imagine James Baker curling up with the "Pisan Cantos," Dan Quayle leafing through the *Princess Cassimassima*. I suppose this is the vision. What is wrong with this picture? Louis L'Amour or Ian Fleming, possibly. But that carries us a ways from the High Canonical.

When I think back to that Howard talk, I think back to why I went into literature in the first place. I suppose the literary canon is, in no very grand sense, the commonplace book of our shared culture, the archive of those texts and titles we want to remember. And how else did those of us who teach literature fall in love with our subject than through our very own commonplace books, in which we inscribed, secretly and privately, as we might do in a diary, those passages of books that named for us what we had for long deeply felt but could not say? I kept mine from the age of twelve, turning to it to repeat those marvelous passages that named me in some private way. From H. H. Munro and O. Henry—some of the popular literature we had on the shelves at home—to Dickens and Austen, to Hugo and de Maupassant, I found resonant passages that I had inscribed in my book. Finding James Baldwin and writing him down at an Episcopal church camp during the Watts riots in 1965 (I was fifteen) probably determined the direction of my intellectual life more than did any other single factor. I wrote and rewrote verbatim his elegantly framed paragraphs, full of sentences that were at once somehow Henry Jamesian and King Jamesian, yet clothed in the cadences and figures of the spirituals. I try to remind my graduate students that each of us turned to literature through literal or figurative commonplace books, a fact that we tend to forget once we adopt the alienating strategies of formal analysis. The passages in my commonplace book formed my own canon, just as I imagine each of yours did for you. And a canon, as it has functioned in every literary tradition, has served as the commonplace book of our shared culture.

### Defining a Black Canon

But the question I want to turn to now is this: how does the debate over canon formation affect the development of Afro-American literature as a subject of instruction in the American academy?

Curiously enough, the very first use of the word *canon* in relation to the Afro-American literary tradition occurs in 1846, in a speech delivered by Theodore Parker. Parker was a theologian, a Unitarian clergyman, and a publicist for ideas whom Perry Miller described eloquently as "the man who next only to Emerson . . . was to give shape and meaning to the Transcendental movement in America" (1967, p. 226). In a speech on "The Power of the Merchant Class" delivered in 1846, Parker laments the sad state of "American" letters:

> Literature, science, and art are mainly in [poor men's] hands, yet are controlled by the prevalent spirit of the nation. . . . In England, the national literature favors the church, the crown, the nobility, the prevailing class. Another literature is rising, but is not yet national, *still less canonized* [my italics]. We have no American literature which is permanent. Our scholarly books are only an imitation of a foreign type; they do not reflect our morals, manners, politics, or religion, not even our rivers, mountains, sky. They have not the smell of our ground in their breath. (pp. 148–49)

Parker, to say the least, was not especially pleased with American letters and their identity with the English tradition. Did Parker find any evidence of a truly American literature?

> The American literature is found only in newspapers and speeches, perhaps in some novel, hot, passionate, but poor and extemporaneous. That is our national literature. Does that favor man— represent man? Certainly not. All is the reflection of this most powerful class. The truths that are told are for them, and the lies. Therein the prevailing sentiment is getting into the form of thought. (p. 149)

Parker's analysis, we see plainly, turns upon an implicit reflection theory of base and superstructure. It is the occasional literature, "poor and extemporaneous," wherein American literature dwells, but that literature, like English literature, reflects the interests and ideologies of the upper classes.

Three years later, in his major oration on "The American Scholar," Parker had at last found an entirely original genre of American literature:

> Yet, there is one portion of our permanent literature, if literature it may be called, which is wholly indigenous and original . . . [W]e have one series of literary productions that could be written by

> none but Americans, and only here; I mean the Lives of Fugitive
> Slaves. But as these are not the work of the men of superior
> culture they hardly help to pay the scholar's debt. Yet all the
> original romance of Americans is in them, not in the white man's
> novel. (p. 37)

Parker was right about the originality, the peculiarly *American* quality,
of the slave narratives. But he was wrong about their inherent inability
to pay the scholar's debt; scholars had only to learn to *read* the
narratives for their debt to be paid in full, indeed many times over.
Parker was put off by the language of the slave narratives. He would
have done well to heed the admonition that Emerson had made in his
1844 speech, "Emancipation in the British West Indies": "Language,"
Emerson said, "must be raked, the secrets of slaughter-houses and
infamous holes that cannot front the day, must be ransacked, to tell
what negro-slavery has been" (p. 5). The narratives, for Parker, were
not instances of greater literature, but they were the prime site of
America's "original romance." As Charles Sumner said in 1852, the
fugitive slaves and their narratives "are among the heroes of our age.
Romance has no stories of more thrilling interest than theirs. Classical
antiquity has preserved no examples of adventurous trial more worthy
of renown" (quoted in Osofsky 1969, p. 29). Parker's and Sumner's
divergent views reveal that the popularity of the narratives in antebellum
America most certainly did not reflect any sort of common critical
agreement about their nature and status as art. Still, the implications
of these observations upon black canon formation would not be lost
upon those who would soon seek to free the black slave, or to elevate
the ex-slave, through the agency of literary production. (Herder's ideas
of the "living spirit of a language" were brought to bear with a vengeance
upon eighteenth- and nineteenth-century considerations of the place
in nature of the black.)

   The relationship between the social and political subjectivity of the
Negro and the production of art had been discussed by a host of
commentators, including Hume, Hegel, and Kant, ever since Morgan
Godwin wondered aloud about it in 1684. It was probably Emerson's
comments that generated our earliest efforts at canon formation. As
Emerson said, again in his speech on "Emancipation in the West
Indies,"

> If [racial groups] are rude and foolish, down they must go. When
> at last in a race a new principle appears, an idea—*that* conserves
> it; ideas only save races. If the black man is feeble and not
> important to the existing races, not on a parity with the best race,
> the black man must serve, and be exterminated. But if the black

> man carries in his bosom an indispensable element of a new and coming civilization, for the sake of that element, no wrong, nor strength, nor circumstance, can hurt him; he will survive and play his part. . . . now let [the blacks] emerge, clothed and in their own form. (pp. 31–32)

The forms in which they would be clothed would be those of literature, registered in anthologies that established the canon of Black American literature.

The first attempt to define a black canon that I have found is that by Armand Lanusse, who edited *Les Cenelles,* an anthology of black French verse published at New Orleans in 1845—the first black anthology, I believe, ever published. Lanusse's "Introduction" is a defense of poetry as an enterprise for black people in their larger efforts to defend the race against "les traits lancés contre nous par le dédain ou par la calomnie." The target for these "spiteful and calumnious arrows" was defined as the collective black intellect (p. 10). Despite this stated political intention, these poems imitate the styles and themes of the French Romantics, and never engage directly the social and political experiences of black Creoles in New Orleans in the 1840s. *Les Cenelles* argues for a political effect—that is, the end of racism—by publishing apolitical poems, poems which share as silent second texts the poetry written by Frenchmen three thousand miles away. We are just like the French—so, treat us like Frenchmen, not like blacks. So an apolitical art is put to uses most political.

Four years later, in 1849, William G. Allen published an anthology in which he canonized Phillis Wheatley and George Moses Horton. Like Lanusse, Allen sought to refute intellectual racism by the act of canon formation. "The African is called inferior," he writes. "But what race ever displayed intellect more exalted, or character more sublime?" (p. 3). Pointing to the achievements of Pushkin, Placido, and Augustine as the great African tradition to which Afro-Americans are heir, Allen claims Wheatley and Horton as the exemplars of this tradition, Horton being "decidedly the superior genius"—no doubt because of his explicitly racial themes, a judgment quite unlike that which propelled Armand Lanusse into canon formation. As Allen puts it, with the publication of their anthology,

> Who will now say that the African is incapable of attaining to intellectual or moral greatness? What he now is, degrading circumstances have made him? What he is capable of becoming, the past clearly evinces. The African is strong, tough and hardy. Hundreds of years of oppression have not subdued his spirit, and though Church and State have combined to enslave and degrade

him, in spite of them all, he is increasing in strength and power,
and in the respect of the entire world. (p.7)

Here, then, we see the poles of black canon formation, established
firmly by 1849: is "black" poetry racial in theme, or is black poetry
any sort of poetry written by black people? This question has been at
play in the tradition ever since.

I will not trace in detail the history of this tension over definitions
of the Afro-American canon and the direct relation between the
production of black poetry and the end of white racism. Suffice it to
point to such seminal attempts at canon formation in the twenties as
James Weldon Johnson's *The Book of American Negro Poetry* (1922),
Alain Locke's *The New Negro* (1925), and V. F. Calverton's *Anthology
of American Negro Literature* (1929), each of which defined as its goal
the demonstration of the existence of the black tradition as a political
defense of the racial self against racism. As Johnson put it so clearly,

> A people may be great through many means, but there is only
> one measure by which its greatness is recognized and acknowl-
> edged. The final measure of the greatness of all peoples is the
> amount and standard of the literature and art they have produced.
> The world does not know that a people is great until that people
> produces great literature and art. No people that has produced
> great literature and art has ever been looked upon by the world
> as distinctly inferior.
> The status of the Negro in the United States is more a question
> of national mental attitude toward the race than of actual con-
> ditions. And nothing will do more to change that mental attitude
> and raise his status than a demonstration of intellectual parity by
> the Negro through the production of literature and art. (pp. 9–
> 10)

Johnson, here, was echoing racialist arguments that had been used
against blacks since the eighteenth century, especially those by Hume,
Kant, Jefferson, and Hegel, which equated our access to natural rights
with our production of literary classics. The Harlem Renaissance, in
fact, can be thought of as a sustained attempt to combat racism through
the very *production* of black art and literature.

Johnson's and Calverton's anthologies "frame" the Renaissance
period, thus making a comparison between their ideological concerns
useful. Calverton's anthology made two significant departures from
Johnson's model, both of which are worth considering, if only briefly.
Calverton's was the first attempt at black canon formation to provide
for the influence and presence of black vernacular literature in a major
way. "Spirituals," "Blues," and "Labor Songs" each comprises a genre
of black literature for him. We all understand the importance of this

gesture, and we recognize the influence it had upon the editors of *The Negro Caravan* (1941). Calverton, whose real name was George Goetz, announces in his introductory essay, "The Growth of Negro Literature," that his selection principles have been determined by his sense of the history of black literary *forms,* leading him to make selections because of their formal "representative value," as he puts it (p. vii). These forms, he continues, are *Negro* forms, virtually self-contained in a hermetic black tradition, especially in the vernacular tradition, where artistic American originality was to be found:

> [I]t is no exaggeration whatsoever to contend that [the Negro's contributions to American art and literature] are more striking and singular in substance and structure than any contributions that have been made by the white man to American culture. In fact, they constitute America's chief claim to originality in its cultural history.... The white man in America has continued, and in an inferior manner, a culture of European origin. He has not developed a culture that is definitely and unequivocally American. In respect of originality, then, the Negro is more important in the growth of American culture than the white man.... While the white man has gone to Europe for his models, and is seeking still an European approval of his artistic endeavors, the Negro in his art forms has never sought the acclaim of any culture other than his own. This is particularly true of those forms of Negro art that come directly from the people. (pp. 3–5)

And note that Calverton couched his argument in just that rhetoric of nationalism, of American exceptionalism, that had long been used to exclude, or anyway occlude, the contribution of the Negro. In an audacious reversal, it turns out that *only* the Negro is really American, the white man being a pale imitation of his European forebears.

If Calverton's stress upon the black vernacular heavily influenced the shaping of *The Negro Caravan*—certainly one of the most important anthologies in the tradition—his sense of the black canon as a formal, self-contained entity most certainly did not. As the editors put it in the introduction to the volume:

> [We]... do not believe that the expression "Negro literature" is an accurate one, and... have avoided using it. "Negro literature" has no application if it means structural peculiarity, or a Negro school of writing. The Negro writes in the forms evolved in English and American literature.... The editors consider Negro writers to be American writers, and literature by American Negroes to be a segment of American literature....
>
> The chief cause for objection to the term is that "Negro literature" is too easily placed by certain critics, white and Negro, in an alcove apart. The next step is a double standard of judgment,

which is dangerous for the future of Negro writers. "A Negro novel," thought of as a separate form, is too often condoned as "good enough for a Negro." That Negroes in America have had a hard time, and that inside stories of Negro life often present unusual and attractive reading matter are incontrovertible facts; but when they enter literary criticism these facts do damage to both the critics and the artists. (p. 7)

Yet immediately following this stern admonition, we're told the editors haven't been absolutely concerned with maintaining "an even level of literary excellence," because the tradition is defined by both form and content:

> Literature by Negro authors about Negro experience . . . must be considered as significant, not only because of a body of established masterpieces, but also because of the illumination it sheds upon a social reality. (p. 7)

And later, in the introduction to the section entitled "The Novel," the editors elaborate upon this idea by complaining about the relation of revision between Frances Harper's *Iola Le Roy* (1892) and William Wells Brown's *Clotel* (1853), a relation of the sort central to Calverton's canon, but here defined most disapprovingly: "There are repetitions of situations from Brown's *Clotel,* something of a forecast of a sort of literary inbreeding which causes Negro writers to be influenced by other Negroes more than should ordinarily be expected" (p. 139). The black canon, for these editors, was that literature which most eloquently refuted white racist stereotypes (p. 5) and which embodied the shared "theme of struggle that is present in so much Negro expression" (p. 6). Theirs, in other words, was a canon that was unified thematically by self-defense against racist literary conventions, and by the expression of what the editors called "strokes of freedom" (p. 6). The formal bond that Calverton had claimed was of no academic or political use for these editors, precisely because they wished to project an integrated canon of American literature. As the editors put it,

> In spite of such unifying bonds as a common rejection of the popular stereotypes and a common "racial" cause, writings by Negroes do not seem to the editors to fall into a unique cultural pattern. Negro writers have adopted the literary traditions that seemed useful for their purposes. . . . While Frederick Douglass brought more personal knowledge and bitterness into his anti-slavery agitation than William Lloyd Garrison and Theodore Parker, he is much closer to them in spirit and form than to Phillis Wheatley, his predecessor, and Booker T. Washington, his successor. . . . The bonds of literary tradition seem to be stronger than race. (pp. 6–7)

Form, then, or the community of structure and sensibility, was called upon to reveal the sheer arbitrariness of American "racial" classifications, and their irrelevance to American canon formation. Above all else, these editors sought to expose the essentialism at the center of racialized subdivisions of the American literary tradition. If we recall that this anthology appears just thirteen years before *Brown v. Board,* we should not be surprised by the "integrationist" thrust of the poetics espoused here. Ideological desire and artistic premise were one. "Afro-American literature," then, is a misnomer; "American literature written by Negroes" more aptly designates this body of writing. So much for a definition of the Afro-American tradition based on formal relationships of revision, text to text.

At the opposite extreme in black canon formation is the canon defined by Amiri Baraka and Larry Neal in *Black Fire,* published in 1968, an anthology so very familiar to us all. This canon, the blackest canon of all, was defined by both formal innovations and by themes: formally, individual selections tend to aspire to the vernacular or to black music, or to performance; theoretically, each selection reinforces the urge toward black liberation, toward "freedom now" with an up-against-the-wall subtext. The hero, the valorized presence, in this volume is the black vernacular: no longer summoned or invoked through familiar and comfortable rubrics such as "The Spirituals" and "The Blues," but *embodied, assumed, presupposed,* in a marvelous act of formal bonding often obscured by the stridency of the political message the anthology meant to announce. Absent completely is a desire to "prove" our common humanity with white people by demonstrating our power of intellect. One mode of essentialism—African essentialism—was used to critique the essentialism implicit in notions of a common or universal American heritage. No, in *Black Fire,* art and act were one.

## A New Attempt at Canon Formation

I have been thinking about these strains in black canon formation because a group of us will be editing still another anthology which will constitute still another attempt at canon formation. I am pleased to confirm that W. W. Norton will be publishing the *Norton Anthology of Afro-American Literature.* As some of you know, the editing of this anthology has been a great dream of mine for a long time. After a year of reader's reports, market surveys, and draft proposals, Norton has enthusiastically embarked upon the publishing of our anthology.

I think that I am most excited about the fact that we have at our disposal the means to edit an anthology which will define a canon of Afro-American literature for instructors and students at any institution which desires to teach a course in Afro-American literature. Once our anthology is published, no one will ever again be able to use the unavailability of black texts as an excuse not to teach our literature. A well-marketed anthology—particularly a Norton anthology—functions in the academy to *create* a tradition, as well as to define and preserve it. A Norton anthology opens up a literary tradition as simply as opening the cover of a carefully edited and ample book.

I am not unaware of the politics and ironies of our canon formation. The canon that we define will be "our" canon, one possible set of selections among several possible sets of selections. In part to be as eclectic and as democratically "representative" as possible, most other editors of black anthologies have tried to include as many authors and selections (especially excerpts) as possible, in order to preserve and "resurrect" the tradition. I call this the Sears & Roebuck approach, the "dream book" of black literature. We have all benefited from this approach to collection. Indeed, many of our authors have only managed to survive because an enterprising editor was determined to marshal as much evidence as she or he could to show that the black literary tradition existed. While we must be deeply appreciative of that approach and its results, our task will be a different one. Our task will be to bring together the "essential" texts of the canon, the "crucially central" authors, those whom we feel to be indispensable to an understanding of the shape, and shaping, of the tradition. A canon is often represented as the "essence" of the tradition, indeed, as the marrow of tradition: the connection between the texts of the canon is meant to reveal the tradition's inherent, or veiled, logic—its internal rationale.

None of us is naive enough to believe that "the canonical" is self-evident, absolute, or neutral. It is a commonplace of contemporary criticism to say that scholars make canons. But, just as often, writers make canons, too, both by critical revaluation and by reclamation through revision. Keenly aware of this—and, quite frankly, aware of my own biases—I have attempted to bring together as period editors a group of scholar-critics (five black women, five black men, one white man), each of whom combines great expertise in her or his period with her or his own approach to the teaching and analyzing of Afro-American literature. I have attempted, in other words, to bring together scholars whose notions of the black canon might not necessarily agree with my own, or with each other's. I have tried to bring together a diverse array of ideological, methodological, and theoretical perspectives, so that we together might produce an anthology that most fully represents the various definitions of what it means to speak of the Afro-American literary tradition, and what it means to *teach* that tradition. And while we are in the early stages of organization, I can say that my own biases toward canon formation are to stress the formal relationships that obtain among texts in the black tradition—relations of revision, echo, call and response, antiphony—and to stress the vernacular roots of the tradition. For the vernacular, or oral literature, in my tradition, has a canon of its own.

Accordingly, our anthology includes a major innovation in anthology production. Because of the strong oral and vernacular base of so very much of our literature, we will sell a cassette tape along with the anthology—precisely *because* the vernacular has a canon of its own, one which has always in its turn informed the written works of our tradition. I am ecstatic about this aspect of our project. This means that each period will include both the printed and spoken text of oral and musical selections of black vernacular culture: sermons, blues, spirituals, R & B, poets reading their own "dialect" poems, speeches—whatever! Imagine having Bessie Smith and Billie Holliday singing the blues; Langston Hughes reading "I Have Known Rivers"; Sterling Brown reading "Ma Rainey"; James Weldon Johnson, "The Creation"; C. L. Franklin, "The Sermon of the Dry Bones"; Martin speaking "I Have a Dream"; Sonia Sanchez, "Talking in Tongues"—the list of possibilities is endless, and exhilarating. We will change fundamentally not only the way that our literature is taught, but the way in which any literary tradition is even conceived. So much of our literature seems dead on the page when compared to its performance. We will incorporate performance and the black and human voice into our anthology.

## Canon Formation and the Political Debate

My pursuit of this project has required me to negotiate a position between those on the cultural right who claim that black people can have no canon, no masterpieces, and, on the other hand, those on the cultural left who wonder why anyone wants to establish the existence of a canon, any canon, in the first place. On the right hand, we face the outraged reactions of those custodians of Western culture who protest that the canon, that transparent decanter of Western values, may become—breathe the word—*politicized.* That people can maintain a straight face while they protest the irruption of politics into something that has always been political from the beginning—well, it says something about how remarkably successful official literary histories have been in presenting themselves as natural objects, untainted by worldly interests.

I agree with those conservatives who have raised the alarm about our students' ignorance of history. But part of the history we need to teach has to be the history of the very idea of the canon, which involves (though it's hardly exhausted by) the history both of literary pedagogy and of the very institution of the school. Once we understand how canons evolve, we no longer see them as *objets trouvés* washed up on the beach of history. And we can begin to appreciate their ever-changing configuration in relation to a distinctive institutional history.

Universal education in this country was justified by the argument that schooling made good citizens, good American citizens; and when American literature started to be taught in our schools, part of the aim was to show what it was to be an American. As Richard Brodhead, a leading scholar of American literature, has observed, "No past lives without cultural mediation. The past, however worthy, does not survive by its own intrinsic power" (1986, p. 6). One function of "literary history" is, then, to disguise that mediation, to conceal all connections between institutionalized interests and the literature we remember. "Pay no attention to the man behind the curtain," booms the Great Oz of literary history.

Cynthia Ozick once chastised feminists by warning that strategies become institutions. But isn't that really another way of warning that their strategies, heaven forfend, may *succeed*? Here we approach the scruples of those on the cultural left who worry about, well, the price of success. "Who's co-opting whom?" might be their slogan. To them, the very idea of the canon is hierarchical, patriarchal, and otherwise politically suspect. They'd like us to disavow it altogether.

But history and its institutions are not just something we study; they are also something we live, and live through. And how effective and how durable our interventions in contemporary cultural politics will be depends upon our ability to mobilize the institutions that buttress and reproduce that culture. The choice is not between institutions and no institutions. The choice is always, "What kind of institutions shall there be?" Fearing that our strategies will become institutions, we could seclude ourselves from the real world and keep our hands clean, free from the taint of history. But that is to pay obeisance to the status quo, to the entrenched arsenal of sexual and racial authority, to say that things should not change, become something other, and, let's hope, better, than they are now.

Indeed, this is one case where we have to borrow a leaf from the right, which is powerfully aware of the role of education in the reproduction of values. We must engage in this sort of canon deformation precisely because Mr. Bennett is correct: the teaching of literature *is* the teaching of values—not inherently, no, but contingently, yes; it is—it has become—the teaching of an aesthetic and political order in which no women or people of color were ever able to discover the reflection or representation of their images, or hear the resonance of their cultural voices. The return of "the" canon, the high canon of Western masterpieces, represents the return of an order in which my people were the subjugated: the voiceless, the invisible, the unrepresented and the unrepresentable. Who would return us to that medieval never-never land?

## Constituting Ourselves as Discursive Subjects

The classic critique of our attempts to reconstitute our own subjectivity, as women, as blacks, etc., is that of Derrida, who says somewhere, "This is the risk. The effect of Law is to build a structure of the subject, and as soon as you say, 'Well, the woman is a subject and this subject deserves equal right,' and so on—then you are caught in the logic of phallo-centricism and you have rebuilt the empire of Law." To expressions such as this, made by a critic whose stands on sexism and racism have been exemplary, we must respond that the Western male subject has long been constituted historically for himself and in himself. And, while we readily accept, acknowledge, and partake of the critique of *this* subject as transcendent, to deny us the process of exploring and reclaiming our subjectivity before we critique it is the critical version of the grandfather clause, the double privileging of categories that happen to be *preconstituted.* Such a position leaves us nowhere, invisible, and voiceless, in the republic of Western letters. Consider the irony: precisely when we (and other Third World peoples) obtain the complex wherewithal to define our black subjectivity in the republic of Western letters, our theoretical colleagues declare that there ain't no such thing as a subject, so why should we be bothered with that? In this way, those of us in feminist criticism or Afro-American criticism who are engaged in the necessary work of canon deformation and reformation confront the skepticism even of those who are allies on other fronts over this matter of the death of the subject and our own discursive subjectivity.

So far I've been talking about social identity and political agency as if they were logically connected. I think they are. And that has a lot to do with what I think the task of the Afro-American critic today must be. Simone de Beauvoir wrote that one is not born a woman; no, and one is not born a Negro; but then, as Donna Haraway has pointed out, one isn't even born an organism. Lord knows that black art has been attacked for well over a century as being "not universal," though no one ever says quite what this might mean. If this means an attack against *self-identification,* then I must confess that I am opposed to "universality." This line of argument is an echo from the political right. As Allan Bloom writes,

> [T]he substantial human contact, indifferent to race, soul to soul, that prevails in all other aspects of student life simply does not usually exist between the two races. There are exceptions, perfectly integrated black students, but they are rare and in a difficult position. I do not believe this somber situation is the fault of the white students, who are rather straightforward in such matters and frequently embarrassingly eager to prove their liberal credentials in the one area where Americans are especially sensitive to a history of past injustice. . . . Thus, just at the moment when everyone else has become "a person," blacks have become blacks. . . . "They stick together" was a phrase once used by the prejudiced about this or that distinctive group, but it has become true, by and large, of the black students. (pp. 91–92)

Self-identification proves a condition for agency, for social change. And to benefit from such collective agency, we need to construct ourselves, just as the nation was constructed, just as the class was, just as *all* the furniture in the social universe was. It is utopian to think we can now disavow our social identities; there's not another one to take its place. You can't opt out of a Form of Life. We can't become one of those bodiless vapor-trails of sentience portrayed on a "Star Trek" episode, though often it seems like the universalists want us to be just that. You can't opt out of history. History may be a nightmare, as Joyce suggested, but it's time to stop pinching ourselves.

There is a treacherous non sequitur here, however, from "socially constructed" to "essentially unreal." I suppose there's a lurking positivism in the belief that social facts are unreal compared to putatively biological ones. We go from "constructed" to "unstable," which is one non sequitur; or to "changeable by will," which is a bigger problem still, since the "will" is yet another construction.

And theory is conducive to these slippages, however illegitimate, because of the real ascendancy of the paradigm of dismantlement. Reversals don't work, we're told: dismantle the scheme of difference altogether. And I don't deny the importance, on the level of theory, of the project; it's important to remember that "race" is *only* a sociopolitical category, nothing more. At the same time—in terms of its practical performative force—that doesn't help me when I'm trying to get a taxi on the corner of 125th and Lenox Avenue. ("Please, sire, it's only a metaphor.")

Maybe the most important thing, here, is the tension between the imperatives of an agency and the rhetoric of dismantlement. An example: Foucault says, and let's take him at his word, that the "homosexual" as life form was invented sometime in the mid-nineteenth century. Now, if there's no such thing as a homosexual, then homophobia, at least as directed toward people rather than acts, loses its rationale. But you can't respond to the discrimination against gay people by saying, "I'm sorry, I don't exist; you've got the wrong guy." The simple historical fact is that Stonewall was necessary: concerted action was necessary to take action against the very structure that, as it were, called the homosexual into being, that subjected certain people to this imaginary identity. To reverse Audre Lorde, *only* the master's tools will ever dismantle the master's house.

Let me be specific. Those of us working in my own tradition confront the hegemony of the Western tradition, generally, and of the larger American tradition, more locally, as we theorize about our tradition and engage in attempts at canon formation. Long after white American literature has been anthologized and canonized, and recanonized, our attempts to define a black American canon—foregrounded on its own against a white backdrop—are often decried as racist, separatist, nationalist, or "essentialist" (my favorite term of all). Attempts to derive theories about our literary tradition from the black tradition—a tradition, I might add, that must include black vernacular forms as well as written literary forms—are often greeted by our colleagues in traditional literature departments as misguided attempts to secede from a union which only recently, and with considerable kicking and screaming, has been forged. "What is *wrong* with you people?" our friends ask us in genuine passion and concern. "After all, aren't we all just citizens of literature here?"

Well, yes and no. Every black American text must confess to a complex ancestry, one high and low (i.e., literary and vernacular), but also one white and black. There can be no doubt that white texts inform and influence black texts (and vice versa), so that a thoroughly integrated canon of American literature is not only politically sound, it is *intellectually* sound as well. But the attempts of scholars such as Arnold Rampersad, Houston Baker, M. H. Washington, Nellie McKay, and others to define a black canon, and to derive indigenous theories of interpretation from within this canon, are not meant to refute the soundness of these gestures of integration. Rather, it is a question of perspective, a question of emphasis. Just as we can and must cite a black text within the larger American tradition, we can and must cite it within its own tradition, a tradition not defined by a pseudo-science of racial biology, or a mystically shared essence called blackness, but by the repetition and revision of shared themes, topoi, and tropes, a process that binds the signal texts of the black tradition into a canon just as surely as separate links bind together into a chain. It is no more, or less, essentialist to make this claim than it is to claim the existence of French, English, German, Russian, or American literature—as long as we proceed inductively, from the texts to the theory. For anyone to deny us the right to engage in attempts to constitute ourselves as discursive subjects is for them to engage in the double privileging of categories that happen to be pre constituted.

In our attempts at canon formation we are demanding a return to history in a manner scarcely conceived of by the New Historicists. Nor can we opt out of our own private histories, which Houston Baker calls the Afro-American autobiographical moment, and which I call auto-critography. Let me end, as I began, with an anecdote, one that I had forgotten until just recently.

Earlier this year at Cornell I was listening to Hortense Spillers, the great black feminist critic, read her important essay, "Mama's Baby, Papa's Maybe." Her delivery, as usual, was flawless, compelling, inimitable. And although I read this essay in manuscript, I had never before felt—or heard—the following lines:

> The African-American male has been touched, therefore, by the *mother, handed* by her in ways that he cannot escape, and in ways that the white American male is allowed to temporize by a fatherly reprieve. This human and historic development—the text that has been inscribed on the benighted heart of the continent—takes us to the center of an inexorable difference in the depths of American women's community: the African-American woman, the mother, the daughter, becomes historically the powerful and shadowy evocation of a cultural synthesis long evaporated—the law of the Mother—only and precisely because legal enslavement removed the African-American male not so much from sight as from *mimetic* view as a partner in the prevailing social fiction of the Father's name, the Father's law.
>
> Therefore, the female, in this order of things, breaks in upon the imagination with the forcefulness that marks both a denial and an "illegitimacy." Because of this peculiar American denial, the black American male embodies the *only* American community of males which has had the specific occasion to learn *who* the

female is within itself, the infant child who bears the life against
the could-be fateful gamble, against the odds of pulverization and
murder, including her own. It is the heritage of the *mother* that
the African-American male must regain as an aspect of his own
personhood—the power of "yes" to the "female" within. (1987,
p. 80)

How curious a figure—men, and especially black men, gaining their
voices through the black mother. Precisely when some committed
feminists or some committed black nationalists would essentialize all
"others" out of their critical endeavor, Hortense Spillers rejects that
glib and easy solution, calling for a revoicing of the master's discourse
in the cadences and timbres of the black mother's voice.

As I sat there before her, I recalled, to my own astonishment, my
own first public performance, when I was a child of four years. My
mom attended a small black Methodist Church in Piedmont, West
Virginia, just as her mom had done for the past fifty years. I was a fat
little kid, a condition that my mom defended as "plump." I remember
that I had just been given a brand new gray suit for the occasion, and
a black stingy-brim Dobbs hat, so it must have been Easter, because
my brother and I always got new hats for Easter, just like my dad and
mom did.

At any rate, the day came to deliver my Piece. What is a Piece? A
Piece is what people in our church called a religious recitation. I don't
know what the folk etymology might be, but I think it reflects the
belief that each of the fragments of our praise songs, taken together,
amounts to a Master Text. And each of us, during a religious program,
was called upon to say our Piece. Mine, if you can believe it, was
"Jesus was a boy like me, and like Him I want to be." That was it—
I *was* only four. So, after weeks of practice in elocution, hair pressed
and greased down, shirt starched and pants pressed, I was ready to give
my Piece.

I remember skipping along to the church with all of the other kids,
driving everyone crazy, saying over and over, "Jesus was a boy like
me, and like Him I want to be." "Will you shut up!" my friends
demanded. Just jealous, I thought. They probably don't even know
their Pieces.

Finally, we made it to the church, and it was packed—bulging and
glistening with black people, eager to hear Pieces, despite the fact that
they had heard all of the Pieces already, year after year, like bits and
fragments of a repeated Master Text.

Because I was the youngest child on the program, I was the first to
go. Miss Sarah Russell (whom we called Sister Holy Ghost—behind

her back, of course) started the program with a prayer, and then asked if Little Skippy Gates would step forward. I did so.

And then the worst happened: I completely forgot the words of my Piece. Standing there, pressed and starched, just as clean as I could be, in front of just about everybody in our part of town, I could not for the life of me remember one word of that Piece.

After standing there I don't know how long, struck dumb and captivated by all of those staring eyes, I heard a voice from near the back of the church proclaim, "Jesus was a boy like me, and like Him I want to be."

And my mother, having arisen to find my voice, smoothed her dress and sat down again. The congregation's applause lasted as long as its laughter, and I crawled back to my seat.

For me, I realized as Hortense Spillers spoke, much of my scholarly and critical work has been an attempt to learn how to speak in the strong, compelling cadences of my mother's voice. To reform core curricula, to account for the comparable eloquence of the African, the Asian, and the Middle-Eastern traditions, is to begin to prepare our students for their roles as citizens of a world culture, educated through a truly human notion of "the Humanities," rather than—as Bennett and Bloom would have it—as guardians at the last frontier outpost of white male Western culture, the Keepers of the Master's Pieces.

And for us scholar-critics, learning to speak in the voice of the black female is perhaps the ultimate challenge of producing a discourse of the critical other.

## References

Allen, William G. 1970. *Wheatley, Banneker, and Horton; with Selections from the Poetical Works of Wheatley and Horton.* Freeport, N.Y.: Books for Libraries Press.

Bloom, Allan. 1987. *The Closing of the American Mind.* New York: Simon and Schuster.

Brodhead, Richard H. 1986. *The School of Hawthorne.* New York: Oxford University Press.

Brown, Sterling A., Arthur P. Davis, and Ulysses Lee, eds. 1969. *The Negro Caravan.* 2nd ed. New York: Arno Press.

Baraka, Imamu Amiri, and Larry Neal, eds. 1968. *Black Fire: An Anthology of Afro-American Writing.* New York: William Morrow.

Calverton, V. F., ed. 1929. *Anthology of American Negro Literature.* New York: Random House.

Emerson, Ralph Waldo. 1844. "An Address Delivered in the Court-House in Concord, Massachusetts, on 1st August, 1844 on the Anniversary of the

Emancipation of the Negroes in the British West Indies." Boston: James Monroe and Co.

Johnson, James Weldon. 1931. *The Book of American Negro Poetry.* Rev. ed. New York: Harcourt, Brace.

Lanusse, Armand, ed. 1845. *Les Cenelles. Choix de Poesies indigenes.* New Orleans: H. Lauve et Compagnie.

Miller, Perry. 1967. *The Transcendentalists: An Anthology.* Cambridge: Harvard University Press.

Osofsky, Gilbert, ed. 1969. *Puttin' On Ole Massa: The Slave Narratives of Henry Bibb, William Wells Brown, and Solomon Northrup.* New York: Harper Torchbooks.

Parker, Theodore. 1907. *The American Scholar,* edited and with notes by George Willis Cooke. Boston: American Unitarian Association.

———. 1960 [1846]. "The Power of the Merchant Class." In *Theodore Parker: An Anthology*, edited by Henry Steele Commager, 148–49. Boston: Beacon Press.

Spillers, Hortense J. 1987. "Mama's Baby, Papa's Maybe: An American Grammar Book." *Diacritics* 17, no. 2: 80.

# 5 Authority, Desire, and Canons: Tendentious Meditations on Cultural Literacy

James C. Raymond

James Raymond, a seminar leader at both the 1987 and 1988 Institutes, is professor of English and director of freshman English at the University of Alabama. He is also editor of *College English,* the official journal of the College Section of NCTE. In addition to numerous articles and reviews, he has published a composition textbook, *Writing (Is an Unnatural Act),* coauthored a book on legal writing (*Clear Understandings,* with Ronald L. Goldfarb), edited a collection of essays on literacy (*Literacy as a Human Problem*), and coedited a collection of essays on linguistics (*James B. McMillan: Essays in Linguistics by His Friends and Colleagues,* with I. Willis Russell). His latest publication, "Rhetoric as Bricolage: Theory and Its Limits in Legal and Other Kinds of Writing," appears in W*orlds of Writing: Teaching and Learning in a Variety of Discourse Communities,* edited by Carolyn Matalene.

Professor Raymond teaches graduate seminars in rhetoric and conducts an annual practicum in teaching composition as part of the training program for new graduate assistants and instructors. Away from home he enjoys teaching judges and attorneys how to write prose that ordinary mortals can understand.

I cannot tell if it is the result of post-structuralism or the effect of middle age, but I find myself less and less inclined to attempt an argument that would convert those of other persuasions or leave them vanquished like the bad guys in cowboy movies (to borrow an image Jane Tompkins has been exploring). Because all belief and all rhetoric (which I regard as the study of the social construction of belief) is rooted in assumptions that elude rigorous verification, I cannot imagine that proponents of a pedagogy I perceive as reductive or of a canon I perceive as constrained would be converted or vanquished by a discourse that is neither more nor less grounded in the unprovable than their own. Point out to bestselling scholars like E. D. Hirsch and Allan Bloom or to former secretary of education William Bennett that their most cherished assumptions are merely political and esthetic preferences and they could validly counter "*tu quoque*; so are yours." That they seem not to recognize the ineluctable subjectivity of all our judgments, theirs and mine, is of course a problem more profound than the particularities of their preferences. But that is another issue.

What follows, then, is less an argument than a pair of meditations, one on authority and desire, the other on canons. They are, admittedly, tendentious meditations, but their tendency is not merely to indict Bloom and Hirsch and Bennett; it is to recognize their practice concealed in our own. I suspect that we who do not identify with the educational right resent it not so much for what it does, but for the way it does what we prefer doing ourselves.

## Authority and Desire

In chapter four of *Jane Eyre,* the following exchange takes place between Jane, then nine years old, and the redoubtable Mr. Brocklehurst, severe patron of the school to which Jane is about to be sent.

> "Do you read your Bible?" [asks Brocklehurst]
> "Sometimes."
> "With pleasure? Are you fond of it?"
> "I like Revelations, and the book of Daniel, and Genesis and Samuel, and a little bit of Exodus, and some parts of Kings and Chronicles, and Job and Jonah."

Now that's a response that should warm a teacher's heart, but of course it does not satisfy Brocklehurst, who continues in this fashion:

> "And the Psalms? I hope you like them?"
> "No, sir."
> "No? oh, shocking! I have a little boy, younger than you, who knows six Psalms by heart: and when you ask him which he would rather have, a ginger-bread nut to eat, or a verse of a Psalm to learn, he says: 'Oh! the verse of a Psalm! angels sing Psalms;' says he, 'I wish to be a little angel here below;' he then gets two nuts in recompense for his infant piety."
> "Psalms are not interesting," I [Jane] remarked.
> "That proves you have a wicked heart . . . "

It would take little imagination to read this dialogue as a parable of current conservative tendencies in education—the imposition of taste, the assumption that alternative interests imply a moral or intellectual deficit, and the system's vulnerability to exploitation by self-serving conformists. It would be easy to substitute Hirsch's name, or Bennett's, or Bloom's for Brocklehurst's, and to see the little psalm learner as an emblem of students who memorize what they are told to respect instead of developing the sort of critical distance and individuality of preferences that might enable them to actively engage a tradition.

Read as a parable, or even as a parody, the passage implies its own norms, according to which Brocklehurst's program—or its modern counterparts—are judged fatuous. But the very phrase "read as a parable" raises an even more fundamental question about the nature of reading: if the passage can be read as a parable, it can be read in lots of other ways as well. If it can be said that this passage is about anything other than the relationship between a particular fictional schoolmaster and a particular fictional student, then the act of reading and the task of enabling students to read are infinitely more complex than defenders of the tradition seem to think they are.

The program E. D. Hirsch proposes in *Cultural Literacy* (1988), for example, though admirable in its recognition that students cannot make sense of a text unless they recognize its allusions (would anyone think otherwise?) does not seem to recognize how small a part the recognition of allusions plays in reading. It is an obvious and essential part, but a small part nonetheless. Hirsch would argue, if I understand him properly, that a reader who fails to recognize the list of biblical titles cited in our passage from *Jane Eyre* cannot understand the passage. That's true enough. But while recognition of the allusions is a necessary condition for enjoying the passage, it is far from a sufficient condition. The pleasure that experienced readers derive from this passage requires not only a recognition of the titles, but an awareness of the genre (a novel) and of the subtle tropes the novelist employs to distinguish this narrative from a series of uninterpreted events, giving it not just meaning, but meanings, rendering it significant in different ways for different readers, even significant in different ways for an individual reader at various stages of her or his life. Readers trained by modern-day Brocklehursts might approach this passage with a complete command of its allusions, and yet still manage to miss both the pleasure(s) and the point(s).

Even an elementary reading of this passage calls into question one of the assumptions governing Allan Bloom's *The Closing of the American Mind* (1988)—the assumption that reading is a more or less simple act of seeing what is there on the page. Of course it is not, and no one remotely familiar with contemporary reading theory would pretend otherwise. As an example, I would imagine that *if* Bloom were to agree with my reading of *Jane Eyre,* at least to the extent that I think Brontë expects us to prefer Jane to Brocklehurst and his favorite pupil, he would imagine that the norms from which we derive this preference are in the text itself, objectively observable by any literate reader. I would argue (not with any great originality, I confess) that these norms are *not* entirely in the text, nor are they entirely in the reader. Rather, they are a function of a relationship between what is on the page and the particular set of values and life experiences that readers bring to the text, allowing them to judge the events and enjoy the narrative in the way they suspect Brontë wanted them to be judged and enjoyed. It is easy to imagine readers who would regard the passage as a criticism of Jane rather than of Brocklehurst (imagine, for example, a real-life Brocklehurst reading this passage) because they would assume, just as we all do, that Brontë, being a wise and established author, shares the same values and assumptions that they themselves find reasonable. *We* "know" that this reading is wrong; but we would be hard-pressed to find conclusive evidence on the page because in fact our own reading is based upon information and assumptions, even literary gossip, that the text is presumed to presume.

It is easy to imagine students who understand the passage "literally" (if that term has meaning any more), yet who are not equipped to make the readerly moves that would enable them to recognize Brocklehurst's insistence on the Psalms as finicky and rigid, to see Jane's list of preferred books as a simple preference for narrative to lyric, to see that Brocklehurst is duped by a clever gamin who knows how to double his cookie supply by feigning piety, to understand the whole passage as ironic commentary on the sort of abuse of authority in education that they themselves (these hapless students of ours) may have encountered and even revered in their own lives, and who therefore miss what might make reading *Jane Eyre* a pleasure rather than a duty. The tough part of teaching reading is not the recognition of allusions, but the readerly moves that turn recognition into insight and pleasure.

The currently popular notion of "cultural literacy" seems to me to be misguided, not just because of the bias with which it defines *culture,* but more importantly because of the reductiveness of its implicit definition of reading. Hirsch's program strikes me as merely one step beyond what Roland Barthes calls "the inaugural stage" of reading (1986a, p. 35)—by which Barthes seems to mean the ability merely to speak the words on the page. Hirsch would move beyond recognition of words to recognition of their significance in the culture. But far beyond that is the ability to recognize their significance in a particular text. The allusions are merely the tokens with which the game is played; true cultural literacy would require a knowledge of the thousands of subtle rules by which experienced readers play, often without the slightest conscious reflection. That sort of knowledge cannot be reduced to lists; and without that sort of knowledge lists are merely instruments of torture for adolescent minds. Reading's essential pleasure occurs far beyond the level of cognition; and it is precisely this pleasure that is ignored in Hirsch's program, which is, for all its earnestness, a Gradgrindian exercise in duty.

Knowing what the Psalms are, or what the Book of Daniel is, is not the same as knowing what they mean in a passage from a particular novel. This sort of knowledge must contend with the dizzying abyss of readings—the sort of limitless possibilities that enable us to impose/recover significance on/from texts, and to understand them differently on each reading, as a child might derive pleasure from *Jane Eyre* in the sixth grade and other pleasures on reading it again and again in later years, each time discovering that it is a different book because each reading does in fact constitute a different book.

The distinction between duty and pleasure has pedagogical and political consequences. We are all aware of the discipline we endured to become the readers we are: the hours spent, for example, reading required texts we did not particularly enjoy. We are always more conscious of self-discipline than of that other, more fundamental drive, desire, which motivates most of our reading and even our submission to discipline, but over which we have little control and for which we can take little credit. On other occasions I have drawn what seems to be a valid distinction between the French word for *desire* and the English. In English, desire is something that you can have or lack. Coaches may fault athletes for lacking desire, and expect them to develop it. In French, *le désir* is something that has *you,* and therein lies an important difference. What we do from *désir* we find more pleasant to do than to avoid.

The most extraordinary learning of our lives—learning our first language—is, if current psychoanalytic theory is correct, motivated by a desire so profound that we do not perceive any labor in the effort. No discipline. No duty. And fundamentally it is *désir,* not discipline, that accounts for our being English professors today, rather than physicists or accountants.

What is missing from Hirsch's program, then, is what Barthes calls the "eroticism" of reading (1986a, p. 38). Whether eros of this kind, or any other, is a subject that can be taught is a moot question, but it seems unlikely that memorizing lists will inflame passion of any sort. Our own love affairs with literature, I suspect, were started neither by duty nor instruction. More than likely, as Shirley Brice Heath (1982) has demonstrated, they began in the not incidentally sensuous setting of bedtime stories. However it occurred for us individually, it is hard to imagine that Hirsch or anyone else who loves reading was moved to love it by the discipline of memorizing discrete bits of knowledge.

By neglecting pleasure and emphasizing discipline, by letting us believe that our own achievements are the result of duty rather than of desire, Hirsch's book offers a program in which the usual suspects—students born into the margins of the economy and the culture of books—will fail, just as they always do. And, oddly enough, it will not be just the political right who will feel justified in attributing these students' failure to their lack of discipline, their lack of intelligence, or even their lack of desire—as if this last quality were attainable by choice. It will be ordinary mainstream teachers and voters who, by virtue of their unwitting indoctrination into American culture, really believe that individual failure, educational or economic, is generally attributable to choices not made, to discipline not embraced—in other words an ethical failure within the old Puritan creed, one for which we need feel no guilt since the individuals who fail are "evil."

Much more interesting than Hirsch's analysis (which is popular, I think, because it seems so commonsensical, makes the problem seem so manageable, and persuades its readers that they are culturally literate if they can recognize most of the trivia in his lists)—more interesting than this sort of analysis is the sort of investigations begun by Shirley Brice Heath (1983) to determine how families of predictably poor achievers behave in ways that make their children less likely to succeed in school. Or to put the blame elsewhere, it would be much more interesting to determine whether children fail because of certain operational assumptions considered normal in the schools, such as the assumption that differences in performance among children in the early grades reflect differences in innate ability, rather than differences in habits, attitudes, and predispositions developed at home and rewarded, not without bias, in school.

Changing pedagogy to accommodate those students who perceive themselves from the earliest grades as aliens in an indifferent land is, of course, a much more problematic enterprise than developing lists of information to be conveyed. It requires, more fundamentally, an understanding of desire. It requires acknowledging that only some students bring with them on the first day of school those desires that school is designed to satisfy and reward, and that the alienation experienced by those other children, those destined to fail, is caused by habits and attitudes that they and their families are powerless to change.

The psychological dynamics of desire are bewildering, but we can begin to understand them by examining our own experiences, remembering, for example, that while desire can be courted it can never be compelled, and that desire even for abstractions like knowledge or skill is often developed in connection with people we love, and for whom we imagine our knowledge or skill will make us more pleasing. Desire is affect; it is not the sort of thing that lends itself to behavioral models of teaching and learning or to positivistic methods of testing and measuring. The bedtime story cannot be literally institutionalized, but the pleasure of that experience might be—might be paradigmatic of all successful pedagogy. We all learned best from teachers we loved—particularly in our earliest years, which are as crucial to the acquisition of cultural literacy as they are to the acquisition of language itself.

## Canons

One specific way of including the alienated is, of course, to broaden the scope of literature to include representations of the cultures in which these students find themselves at home. This was the topic of a conference sponsored by NCTE at Myrtle Beach in the summer of 1988. The main speakers were Sandra Gilbert and Susan Gubar, editors of the *Norton Anthology of Literature by Women*, and Henry Louis Gates, editor of a Norton anthology of Afro-American literature. There was an extraordinary harmony in the group; questions from the floor often implied that the speakers and the audience agreed completely about the need to expand the canon, if only effective means could be found to persuade the reactionary forces back home. The only hint of discord came from voices in favor of including other literature traditionally marginalized: literature by Hispanic Americans, by Native Americans, by gays and lesbians. Even this discord, though, was effectively absorbed by a universal and, I think, proper attitude that all human experience can be a worthy subject of literature, and that our traditional exclusions merely impoverish ourselves and our students.

What was disturbing about this accord was the absence of a radical critique of canonicity. It seemed assumed that if Norton were to add still other literatures to its list, the balance of the official canon would be achieved. Each group seemed to want only an equitable piece of the action; only a few participants seemed bothered by the fact it is manifestly impossible to have Norton anthologies of everything ("What about Canadian literature?" someone next to me asked—or, for that matter, what about Caribbean literature, or Commonwealth literature, or literature in translation; and why should literature be defined so exclusively as to exclude the news media, the cinema, oral traditions, . . . ).

Anthologies obviously provide a valuable service by making disparate texts conveniently available, and, more recently, by extending the range of what might be conveniently taught. And the anthologies discussed at Myrtle Beach are particularly welcome, because they make available two universes of literature whose absence in traditional curricula imply that the realm of literature is much more limited than it really is, resulting in a sense of alienation, of otherness, of secondariness to be experienced by students who are neither white nor male, and a false sense of normalcy to be experienced by those who are.

Yet I would question the argument made by the anthologizers that the canons implicit in their work are less reprehensible than those in earlier anthologies because they, the new ones, result from a catholic and inclusive motive rather than an ideology of exclusion. Even a Norton anthology can contain only so many pages, so that every act of inclusion must necessarily be an act of exclusion as well. And while it may be unfair to expect anthologizers to foreground the principles and biases that guide their selections and omissions (one suspects that it boils down to a selection of what the editors perceive to be the most interesting, important, and affordable works within their ken and within their page limitations), it is indispensable for us as teachers to help our students infer and examine those principles and biases and to resist the inherent tendency of anthologies to canonize their contents.

One might begin, for example, with the subtitle of Gilbert and Gubar's anthology: *The Tradition in English*. Obviously what is included in the book is not *the* tradition, but selections reflecting the taste and judgment of two remarkable but not infallible scholars who are at times limited by external constraints (time, money, and space, for example) not entirely under their control. Nor is it a tradition in the sense that the more recent writers included were necessarily influenced by the earlier writers in the collection. Some, no doubt, were. But to claim a tradition, to suggest a sorority or matriarchy of influence is really to invent ex post facto a state of affairs that we all know did not exist. It strikes me that it would be better for students to come to grips with the political and cultural forces that made such a matriarchy or sorority unlikely than to suggest to them that it actually occurred; and then, perhaps, better for them to wonder whether and to what extent a tradition limited to a single gender is either possible or desirable. These are key questions, it seems to me, and I hope that raising them does not seem ungenerous. It's not that this anthology errs in a way that might have been avoided; it's that all anthologies are necessarily constructions based upon what particular editors consider important and interesting, and cannot be mere reflections of a tradition existing transcendentally out there on its own. There is always and necessarily an element of cultural and political aggression in every anthology.

Underlying the proliferation of specialized anthologies is the myth of coverage, the *reductio ad absurdum* of Hirsch's and Bennett's and Bloom's arguments that the ills of American education might be cured by the infusion of content, the supposition that a balanced representation of all human experience is achievable, when in fact we are all doomed by limits of time and taste to enjoy only fragments. Many English departments institutionalize the myth of coverage in the form of comprehensive exams on monumental or even unlimited reading lists. The inhumanity of these ordeals, the useless anguish they cause serious students, is as cruel as any abuse imagined in *Jane Eyre.* This myth also undergirds the pretense that potential for graduate work is properly assessed by GRE exams based in part upon someone's notion of what counts as important literature—a canon which the profession as a whole seems to accept as unproblematic, proper, and true. At all levels, from grade school through graduate school, there seems to be an operational dichotomy between formalism and content; or to put it more plainly, between practices that neglect coverage in order to emphasize intellectual skills of one kind or another, and those that focus on mastery of content rather than skills. It would be trite to say that neither skills nor content are of much value without the other, but given the popularity of Hirsch's and Bloom's books, perhaps this trite observation needs to be made: Hirsch's facts without critical skills are deadly, and Bloom's authoritarian reading of works in a fairly narrow canon amounts to a secular superstition, not a liberal education.

Also at stake in these practices is whatever the opposite of anxiety about influence might be—the dread of originality perhaps, the fear that our values and insights will be ignored by others, particularly by the next generation. It is a well-founded dread, since the best scholars of every generation are always those who successfully challenge their predecessors, and among the worst are always those who merely accept what they have been taught. I don't know why we resist the inevitable independence of our students—the fact that, regardless of our influence, they will analyze, evaluate, and sometimes even reject what we ourselves love, just as we have analyzed, evaluated, and sometimes rejected what our teachers loved. This is the same gesture by which Charlotte Brontë establishes Jane Eyre's right to dislike the Psalms if she desires to gives all of us, our students included, the right to dislike whatever we choose—even to dislike *Jane Eyre,* if we find its language artificially elevated, its heroine a trifle provincial, her virtue at times callous and insensitive, and the happy ending contrived.

The Ignatian tradition of meditation generally concludes with a series of resolutions—the Jesuits having distinguished themselves from the contemplative orders by their commitment to action. My list of resolutions would *not* include a call to resist superficial notions of reading and culture, because the comeditators I imagine are already, for reasons of their own, inhospitable to these notions. I would, however, propose some other resolutions.

One would be that as individual teachers, we develop our own varieties of what Barthes called a "peaceable speech" (1986b, p. 330), a discourse in which our authority to choose and interpret texts is not abdicated, but tempered by negotiation, so that the desire that motivates all genuine learning can be nurtured.

Another would be that as influential members of English departments, we hasten to dismantle all testing procedures that expose graduate students or undergraduates to harassment based upon the myth of coverage or the dread of originality. GRE subject exams, for example, are necessarily biased in their coverage, and comprehensive exams at many graduate institutions still purvey the myth that graduate students ought to remember absolutely every work in the field the exam covers, even though the students may have been required to prepare four or five fields. Would it not be more honest and more effective to have students, with the help of their professors, propose questions of their own (thus allowing the element of desire to play its natural role in their preparation), and for professors, on the day of the examination, to choose a few questions to be answered from the list prepared by the students?

A third resolution would be that a professional organization such as MLA or NCTE commission a study of the GRE exams, which even ETS tells us are the worst single predictors of success in graduate school, to determine whether they can be made free of linguistic and canonical biases.

Jane Eyre, incidentally, does not escape the centripetal pull of class bias and ethnocentricity to which we are all subject. She is remarkably unappreciative of Adele, her pupil, whose language (French), religion (Catholicism), and talent (theatrical) she regards not as just different from her own, but inferior. And when she finally has a school of her own, she clearly prefers the students who are most like herself and regards the others as uneducable, as if their resistance to learning were a fact of nature rather than a construct of the social order. If we can forgive Jane Eyre her condescension, it is because she is, after all, a provincial Quaker girl, and despite her modest achievements, not overly bright. And her potential for exercising cultural tyranny over others is nothing compared to the power wielded by a modern secretary of education, or a distinguished chair holder—or even an ordinary professor of English.

## References

Barthes, Roland. 1986a. "On Reading." In *The Rustle of Language,* translated by Richard Howard, 33–43. New York: Hill and Wang.

———. 1986b. "Writers, Intellectuals, Teachers." In *The Rustle of Language,* translated by Richard Howard, 309–31. New York: Hill and Wang.

Bloom, Allan. 1988. *The Closing of the American Mind.* New York: Simon and Schuster.

Heath, Shirley Brice. 1983. *Ways with Words.* Cambridge, England: Cambridge University Press.

———. 1982. "What No Bedtime Story Means: Narrative Skills at Home and School." *Language in Society* 2: 49–76.

Hirsch, E. D., Jr. 1988. *Cultural Literacy: What Every American Needs to Know.* New York: Random House.

# 6 Our Missing Theory

Janet Emig

Janet Emig, president of NCTE in 1989, is University Professor of English Education at Rutgers University. She is the author of *The Composing Processes of Twelfth Graders; The Web of Meaning: Essays on Writing, Teaching, Learning, and Thinking;* and articles and poems in a broad range of scholarly journals. She is cofounder of the New Jersey Writing Project, and a recipient of the MLA's Mina Shaughnessy Award.

She attended the 1988 NCTE Summer Institute in her capacity as the Council's president-elect. During the Institute, she raised what we feel is an inevitable question: why is it that in our contemporary enthusiasm for "theory" we exclude *learning theory* from our field of attention? By implication, are we not ignoring the student reader and, despite our apparent intention to do otherwise, re-privileging the text, particularly those texts we deem worthy of the name "literature"?

In the opening of her essay, Professor Emig re-creates the scene we remember so well: the intellectual excitement of the morning session, the asking of the question, and the quiet shock we felt as we understood: learning theory somehow did not belong here—an odd situation, for we were, all of us, teachers.

A throbbing recent conference on the teaching of literature. One of the most productive, scholarly, and eloquent of our feminists. The lecture shot from the canon's mouth—fresh, witty—with a triple somersault into a curtsy at the end. The discussion period. Some skewed, intriguing insights into Stowe, Chopin, Plath. Then a question: "What you've been talking about this afternoon is a feminist transformation of our tradition. Will transforming our tradition also transform our teaching?" Pause. Then, "Are you talking about chairs in a circle and all that touchy, feely stuff of the sixties?" No; that was not what the questioner—what I—was talking about. I was asking a question about feminist theory, about its marrow, by which I meant "How does feminist theory enter your classroom, inform your teaching, and stay?" I persisted; I asked about Carol Gilligan, about women's ways of knowing (Belenky et al. 1986)—growing visibly angry, as friends told me who were too far across the room to tug me back into my chair. Her reply? "I'm not a psychologist."

Here was a woman seemingly willing to entertain every possibility about theory but one: that there could be embedded in her theory requisite implications for how she conducted her classes. Or perhaps, more, that there could be theory concerning learning and teaching as vivid and explanatory as any attempting to characterize the nature of textuality and of language. Not that she is alone. In most departments of English there is, I believe, a terrifying naïveté, a proud and boastful absence of any such theory. In my own department, for example, theories of learning and of teaching are regularly dismissed as matters of "mere affect."

A second encounter: at the beginning of the English Coalition Conference, that unique 1987 professional conversation among elementary, secondary, and college teachers of English, an almost immediate confrontation about theory. The elementary and secondary teacher participants challenged the college participants' steady citing of theory to make their arguments. Actually, the teachers first classed *theory,* along with other terms such as *privileged* and *situated,* as jargon to which they took exception. What emerged, once a brokered definition was finally formulated, was not that the college participants were theoried and the precollegiate participants were not. Rather, that both groups were theoried, but theoried differently, drawing upon different theoretical traditions. If the elementary teachers were hearing for the first time such names as Lacan and Derrida, many of the college participants were hearing, also for the first time, such names as Clay, Donaldson, Luria, and even Vygotsky.

To overgeneralize, the theories that the college participants knew attempted to characterize universals of textuality and of language; the theories the public school teachers, particularly the elementary school teachers, knew attempted to characterize the developmental dimension of learning and of teaching, the dimension that suggests that all of us evolve through phases, stages, episodes, periods (various theorists have their favorite metaphor) as we mature as doers and thinkers.

This essay makes two claims: the first is that most of us in English studies do not know these crucial learning and teaching theories. The second is that if we do not soon come to learn these theories and allow them to enter our classrooms, English studies will continue to lose its constituency, the possible future English major, and continue to fail the general student population, thus contributing, ironically—that is, unintentionally, but formidably—to the literacy crisis in higher education.

What can learning about learning contribute to a transformation of English studies? First, it offers a redefinition of theory that organically brings our students into the dialogue. Second, it offers explanations for the failures we are experiencing in our attempts to introduce and to sustain the teaching of literary critical theory in our classrooms. Third, more positively, a developmental perspective provides the foundations for far greater success, representing for our students the possibility of becoming the very theorists we want them to become.

The view of theory many of us currently hold is that it represents an explanatory matrix of some phenomenon or phenomena, formulated, preferably, with formality, power, and elegance. If asked where we acquired such a definition of theory, most of us would confess that we developed it over a significant period of time—often many years— as the result of inculcation through our undergraduate courses but more likely our graduate courses and seminars in critical theory. There, as Robert Parker notes in a recent essay, "Theories of Writing Instruction," theories were "treated as public objects, proposed by expert scholars in the field" (p. 19), with students getting theories "by selecting them from the public arena of professional discourse. More accurately, in most departments of English, of having these theories selected for them."

We came then to regard serious theory as an entity to be transmitted by professors and to be received by students, by us. Many of the theories we thus came to know were literally remote, observing stringent geographic and linguistic requirements, with *far* viewed as superior to *near,* arriving from across oceans and from continents beyond those oceans; and, if not actually in other languages, or requiring active translation, at least heavily accented.

Not surprisingly, then, when many of us began to teach critical theory in our classes, we followed the models provided by our graduate professors, though often without explicitly noting the features of their selection and presentation noted above. And without remembering our own responses (for "responses," read *uncertainties, confusions,* and *vulnerabilities*) as novice theorists along the way.

Some of us—do we remember?—demonstrated awesome negative or protean capabilities. At conferences we attended, after hearing as the keynote a compelling Marxist reading of *The Cat in the Hat,* we thought "Yes, I really am a Marxist." Then, in the first session, a Rosenblattian conducted a beautifully modulated orchestration of our responses to *Under the Lilacs*: "Obviously, I am even theoretically a reader-responder." Next followed a tautly eloquent feminist reading of *The Little Prince* and a new response: "Only a feminist perspective provides the insights I require." Finally, we were introduced to the basic tenets of post-structuralism: "Now logic compels me to deconstruct my universe, and the universe of my students." Locally, we may have noticed that while we heatedly espoused one theory of textuality over lunch, we enacted another after lunch in our blurred genre class, and wrote yet a third after we arrived home in that article we hoped to submit to *College English.*

Some of us experienced the opposite reaction. We found one theory that to our favorite professor and perhaps even to us illuminated vividly and inclusively all essences of the acts of reading and writing; and we settled down on that theory like a brooding hen. Perhaps our acceptance even hardened into an implacable and possibly ossifying allegiance that we required of those who would be our colleagues and those who had no choice but to be our students, with the irrational outcome that we were asking our freshmen and sophomores to be at eighteen and nineteen where we were, theoretically and developmentally, at thirty or forty or even fifty.

By not knowing developmental theory, we do not appreciate that most of the major critical theories make stringent developmental demands. William Perry (1970) and other developmentalists suggest that the capability for a "full relativism" (the term is, I think, self-explanatory) represents a late cognitive development; and yet comprehension of most variants of deconstruction, Marxism, and feminism requires such relativism. As an example, let us examine the demands of deconstruction.

## Deconstruction

In his introduction to Sharon Crowley's (1989) valuable *Teacher's Introduction to Deconstruction,* W. Ross Winterowd provides this definition:

> In bare essence, the project of deconstruction is to obliterate the doctrine of presence in Western metaphysics—that is, to deconstruct the all-pervasive notion that behind the words is *a* truth that the words express. ... Deconstruction, then, razes determinate meaning and from the rubble constructs the indeterminate text, behind which or within which there is no simple, unvarying meaning. (p. x)

The most telling way we can imagine the cognitive shock with which unsteady and naive eighteen- and nineteen-year-old readers would greet such epistemological unendings would be to try to imagine how we as freshmen and sophomores would have responded to that news. If we had learned reading as it was/is taught in most secondary schools, early on we would have regularly been expected to answer such text and teacher questions as "Why did the author write this story?" or "What is the author's purpose in this essay?"—questions that clearly assume determinate meanings and determinate texts. We were programmed to expect a one-to-one correspondence, not a one-to-many correlation. Suddenly we must consider that the text has many meanings, many of which are equally legitimate? The author's purpose is but *one* factor, if it exists or counts at all, in our interpretation of the text? Our readings create the text? More than relativistic, it is quite possible that we would have regarded such a state of affairs as chaotic, and we may have responded with high anxiety, even anger.

The linguist C. Jan Swearingen rebukes colleagues who ask freshmen and sophomores to become instant deconstructionists. In an essay succinctly titled "Bloomsday for Literacy: How Reactionaries and Relativists Alike Undermine Literacy while Seeming to Promote It" (1988), she claims that for such students "the bullies of the left and the bullies of the right are bullies in equal measure." The essentials of her argument against the bullies of the right—Hirsch, Bloom, Bennett— are now as well-worn as the hall carpet. Her case against what she calls "the left wing critical theory mandarinate" is newer, with what she calls its "scandalous disregard for those entering the entry-level courses in college":

> How can students who have not yet learned to read as "naive" or "sentimental" readers jump in at the level of problematizing such reading? How can anyone learn to problematize something that has not yet been known or imparted? Do we impart traditional modes of reading and writing only to hastily—and cruelly—snatch them away? Our writing classes are full of students whose self is mute because they have never come into contact with the cultural conventions of post-Cartesian, post-Enlightenment, or post-Romantic conceptions and practices as self and voice. To tell such students that there is no such thing as accurate reference because there is no reality is—many feel—a pathologically arrogant act. (pp. 4–5)

Is there then no theory that will not make insuperable cognitive demands? I believe that what is more appropriate, sensible, helpful, and developmentally valid is to sponsor initially among our undergraduates, particularly our entry-level students, a constructivist point of view.

## Constructivism

Here is a graceful definition of constructivism by my late colleague at Rutgers, Marianne Amarel (1988):

> The keystones of a constructivist view seem to me related to two qualities of the human mind: the predisposition to seek order, and derive meaning from experiences; and its corollary, that cognition has an intentional, purposive quality. [It is obvious that we are in the presence of a theory with tenets antithetical to deconstruction.] Applied to learning, such a view implies an active learner who does not passively inhale and retain knowledge as encountered but instead attends to and interprets experience actively, selectively. It is in this sense that knowledge is con- structed—individuals perceive, organize and retain their experi- ence in a unique fashion.

Note here that theory becomes a personal construct—but ours, not someone else's. Theorizing is acknowledged as an inevitable human activity. As Donald Graves once said to me, "You can't get up in the morning without one." Theory becomes, as Louise Phelps (1988) suggests, "a form of intelligibility that the theorist tries to give to personal dilemmas, deeply felt . . . a way to make sense of life. For oneself, for others" (p. viii).

According to this theory, all of us hold, if only tacitly and unsys- tematically, constructs about the nature of learning. What it means, too, is that our students come to us with constructs about reading and writing. Through their private and their school encounters with text, their creation, comprehension, and interpretation, our students have built constructs about what reading and writing are and about what roles these processes serve, or do not serve, in their lives.

Where theory contemplation begins, then, is with our attempting as instructors to elicit *our students'* constructs—not ours; not a noted theorist's—about the nature of literacy. Because our students' constructs are probably tacit, we must devise and enact methods for eliciting their sets of beliefs and values. In a graduate seminar I teach on developing a theory of English studies, students move through a sequence of activities from tacit to explicit, from terse to elaborated. They are asked to make a one-sentence metaphor about their construct for reading. Even before that, they have the option of either drawing their view of reading and writing or of bringing in a photograph or a montage that represents how they define the processes. Even before that, honoring Bruner's and Piaget's cognitive sequencing, I have asked them to express their views through movement or dance. (But why do I feel that I have just lost some of you, dear, inhibited readers?)

Later, the students are asked to write a fable or story about their views; to make, literally, a model of those views; to write a letter to anyone living or dead about how they regard literacy; and to set forth as a geometry with proposition and corollaries their set of beliefs. The last follows the mode in which the psychologist George Kelly, whom they read, sets out his theory in *A Theory of Personality* (1963). (Kelly and his followers devised ingenious ways of ascertaining such constructs through what they called Repertory Grids, but these are possibly too psychometrically complex for our purposes.) The instructor participates, by the way, often by doing her own assignments.

What emerges in the classroom are at once remarkably similar and remarkably diverse views of just what reading is and how it can or cannot serve the reader. Theory then becomes a vivid matter of setting out the beliefs we hold against the beliefs of others, an occasion for making more coherent to others, and—quite as important—to ourselves, just what it is we believe, and why. Since, as Perry notes, we evolve intellectually only if our notions must confront contrasting notions, perhaps after examining their own theories of reading, students can turn to the established theories of noted literary critics more openly and comprehendingly.

In the report *The English Coalition Conference: Democracy through Language* (1989), after describing a year-long entry-level course focusing on "how language shapes and is shaped by the self, by communities, and by society," the participants in the college strand note:

> Such a sequence would require designing the freshman English course around three basic principles: investigation or critical inquiry, collaboration, and conscious theorizing. The principle of critical inquiry suggests that students are in active control of their learning—using, analyzing, and evaluating language within different contexts. The collaborative model suggests that the teacher acts as an informed and challenging coach, offering multiple perspectives, while students practice and experience the kind of cooperation all citizens increasingly need.

And finally, to our purposes,

> The concept of conscious theorizing about their learning and about how language works (and to what ends it works in various contexts) allows students to understand the principles they follow and so enables them to transfer what they learn. (p. 28)

If we candidly remember our own intellectual, our own theoretical histories, we will acknowledge that we were not born Marxists or feminists; that we evolved, often tortuously, to whatever current sets of beliefs and theories we now hold. Consequently, we must not merely permit, we must actively sponsor those textual and classroom encounters that will allow our students to begin their own odysseys toward their own theoretical maturity.

## References

Amarel, Marianne. October 1988. Memo to Teacher Education Committee, Graduate School of Education, Rutgers–The State University.

Belenky, Mary Field, Blythe McVicker Clinchy, Nancy Rule Goldberger, and Jill Mattuck Tarule. 1986. *Women's Ways of Knowing: The Development of Self, Voice, and Mind.* New York: Basic Books.

Kelly, George A. 1963. *A Theory of Personality: The Psychology of Personal Constructs.* New York: Norton.

Lloyd-Jones, Richard, and Andrea Lunsford, eds. 1989. *The English Coalition Conference: Democracy through Language.* Urbana, Ill.: National Council of Teachers of English.

Parker, Robert P., Jr. 1988. "Theories of Writing Instruction." *English Education* 20, no. 1: 18–40.

Perry, William G. 1970. *Forms of Intellectual and Ethical Development in the College Years.* New York: Holt, Rinehart & Winston.

Phelps, Louise W. 1988. *Composition as a Human Science.* New York: Oxford University Press.

Swearingen, C. Jan. 1988. "Bloomsday for Literacy: How Reactionaries and Relativists Alike Undermine Literacy while Seeming to Promote It." *Freshman English News* 17 (Fall): 1–5.

Winterowd, W. Ross. 1989. Introduction to *A Teacher's Introduction to Deconstruction,* by Sharon Crowley. Urbana, Ill.: National Council of Teachers of English.

## Learning: Selected Readings

Bannister, D., and F. Fransella. 1971. *Inquiring Man: The Theory of Personal Constructs.* Baltimore: Penguin.

Barnes, Douglas, and D. Shemilt. 1974. "Transmission and Interpretation." *Educational Review* 26 (3): 213–28.

Belenky, Mary Field, Blythe McVicker Clinchy, Nancy Rule Goldberger, and Jill Mattuck Tarule. 1986. *Women's Ways of Knowing: The Development of Self, Voice, and Mind.* New York: Basic Books.

Britton, J. 1970. *Language and Learning.* Baltimore: Penguin.

Bruner, J. 1971. *The Relevance of Education.* New York: Norton.

———. 1986. *Actual Minds, Possible Worlds.* Cambridge: Harvard University Press.

Dewey, J. 1938. *Experience and Education.* New York: Macmillan.

Donaldson, M. 1978. *Children's Minds.* New York: Norton.

Emig, J. 1983. "Writing as a Mode of Learning" and "Non-Magical Thinking." In *The Web of Meaning,* edited by M. Butler and D. Goswami. Montclair, N.J.: Boynton/Cook.

Flavell, J. P. 1963. *The Developmental Psychology of Jean Piaget.* New York: Van Nostrand Reinhold.

Fodor, A. 1983. *The Modularity of Mind.* Cambridge: MIT Press.

Friere, P. 1970. *Pedagogy of the Oppressed.* New York: Continuum.

Furth, Hans. 1970. *Piaget for Teachers.* New York: Prentice-Hall.

Gardner, H. 1981. *The Quest for Mind: Piaget, Levi-Strauss, and the Structuralist Movement.* Chicago: University of Chicago Press.

————. 1983. *Frames of Mind: The Theory of Multiple Intelligences.* New York: Basic Books.

————. 1985. *The Mind's New Science: A History of the Cognitive Revolution.* New York: Basic Books.

Gilligan, Carol. 1982. *In a Different Voice: Psychological Theory and Women's Development.* Cambridge: Harvard University Press.

Goodman, N. 1978. *Ways of Worldmaking.* Hassocks, Sussex: Harvester Press.

Greene, M. 1978. *Landscapes of Learning.* New York: Teachers College Press.

————. 1988. *Dialectic of Freedom.* New York: Teachers College Press.

Hunt, M. 1982. *The Universe Within: A New Science Explores the Human Mind.* New York: Simon and Schuster.

John-Steiner, V. 1985. *Notebooks of the Mind: Explorations of Thinking.* Albuquerque: University of New Mexico.

Kelly, G. 1963. *A Theory of Personality.* New York: Norton.

Langer, J., and A. Applebee. 1987. *How Writing Shapes Thinking: A Study of Teaching and Learning.* Urbana, Ill.: National Council of Teachers of English.

Luria, A. R. 1976. *Cognitive Development: Its Cultural and Social Foundations.* Cambridge: Harvard University Press.

Mead, G. H. 1934. *Mind, Self, and Society.* Chicago: University of Chicago Press.

Olson, D. 1970. *Cognitive Development.* New York: Academic Press.

Perry, W. G. 1970. *Forms of Intellectual and Ethical Development in the College Years.* New York: Holt, Rinehart & Winston.

Piaget, J. 1977. *The Essential Piaget,* edited by H. Gruber and J. Voneche. New York: Basic Books.

Polanyi, M. 1958. *Personal Knowledge: Towards a Post-Critical Philosophy.* Chicago: University of Chicago Press.

Polya, G. 1957. *How to Solve It: A New Aspect of Mathematical Method.* New York: Anchor Books.

Ryle, G. 1940. *The Concept of Mind.* London: Hutchinson.

Schwebel, M., and J. Raph, eds. 1973. *Piaget for the Classroom.* New York: Basic Books.

Smith, F. 1971. *Understanding Reading.* New York: Holt, Rinehart & Winston.

Von Glasenfeld, E. 1984. "An Introduction to Radical Constructivism." In *The Invented Reality,* edited by Paul Watzlawick. New York: Norton.

Vygotsky, L. 1962. *Thought and Language.* Cambridge: MIT Press.

————. 1978. *Mind in Society: The Development of Higher Psychological Processes,* edited by S. Scribner et al. Cambridge: Harvard University Press.

# II  Teachers' Voices

# 7 A Passage into Critical Theory

Steven Lynn

Steven Lynn is associate professor of English at the University of South Carolina–Columbia, a large research university enrolling 15,000 undergraduate and graduate students. He has taught there for seven years, having taught previously at the universities of Texas and Alabama. Professor Lynn teaches courses in writing, in the history of rhetoric, in eighteenth-century literature, and in critical theory. In addition to his teaching, he directs the university's Writing Center.

Having written his dissertation—soon to become a book—on the rhetoric of Samuel Johnson's *Rambler* essays, Professor Lynn sees himself as "a hybrid—a composition/rhetoric person (I studied with Kinneavy) and a 'literature person' in one. My interest in theory helps pull the two areas together." His essay in this collection is also a synthesis, not only of theory and practice, literary criticism and pedagogy, but also of many of the theoretical perspectives represented in the two Summer Institutes. In the year following the first Myrtle Beach meeting, he designed and led a three-week teacher-training institute on contemporary theory, an experience which he describes in the opening of his essay.

Professor Lynn's essays have been published in journals as various and distinguished as *Eighteenth Century Studies, The Journal of Developmental Education,* and *The Journal of Technical Writing and Communication.* The following was originally prepared for inclusion in this volume, but appeared in somewhat different form in the March 1990 *College English.*

She might have deplored the sentiment had it come from one of her students. "What we need," she was saying, "is a short cut, a simple guide, a kind of recipe for each of these theories, telling us step by step how to make a particular reading." It was the second week of a three-week institute dedicated to the proposition that all teachers were created equal, and therefore all should share in the excitement and challenge of the ongoing transformation of literary criticism. But these teachers, it was clear, were on the verge of saying, "Let's just pretend that nothing important has happened since, oh, 1967." I had whipped them into an evangelistic fever at the outset of the institute, ready to receive the spirit of critical theory; and they had read so much and worked so hard. But I nodded. She was right. They were mired in complexity and subtleties. I realized, of course, that no one whose loaf was fully sliced would seriously attempt an overview of recent critical theory in a few pages. But they needed to get their bearings. Once they did, the confusion would subside. So I came up with the briefest of guides to some of the recent critical theory, an overview that would succeed when its users began to understand its limitations.

My strategy was to show how a single passage might be treated by a handful of different critical theories. Although multiple readings of the same work are easy to assemble, and useful, my effort not only had the virtue of a calculated simplicity and brevity; it also displayed the same reader attempting to act as the extension of various different interpretive codes. The passage I chose, an excerpt from Brendan Gill's *Here at the New Yorker* (1975), is itself brief, but also rich. In offering these notes I am assuming that my reader, like those teachers, knows enough about recent critical theory to be confused. Obviously, my theorizing will be alarmingly reductive, and the examples will not illustrate what any student at any level can produce, given a sketch of this or that theory. They illustrate only what I can do to provide in a very small space an example of a particular kind of critical behavior. But my teacher/students, as well as my student/students, have found these discussion/examples helpful, and so I will proceed immediately to Gill's text and then mine:

Here's Gill's text:*

> When I started at *The New Yorker,* I felt an unshakable confidence in my talent and intelligence. I revelled in them openly, like a dolphin diving skyward out of the sea. After almost forty years, my assurance is less than it was; the revellings, such as they are, take place in becoming seclusion. This steady progress downward in the amount of one's confidence is a commonplace at the magazine—one might almost call it a tradition. Again and again, some writer who has made a name for himself in the world will begin to write for us and will discover as if for the first time how difficult writing is. The machinery of benign skepticism that surrounds and besets him in the form of editors, copy editors, and checkers, to say nothing of fellow-writers, digs a yawning pit an inch or so beyond his desk. He hears it repeated as gospel that there are not three people in all America who can set down a simple declarative sentence correctly; what are the odds against his being one of this tiny elect?

* From *Here at the New Yorker,* by Brendan Gill. Copyright © 1975 by Brendan Gill. Reprinted by permission of Random House, Inc.

In some cases, the pressure of all those doubting eyes upon his copy is more than the writer can bear. When the galleys of a piece are placed in front of him, covered with scores, perhaps hundreds, of pencilled hen-tracks of inquiry, suggestion, and correction, he may sense not the glory of creation but the threat of being stung to death by an army of gnats. Upon which he may think of nothing better to do than lower his head onto his blotter and burst into tears. Thanks to the hen-tracks and their consequences, the piece will be much improved, but the author of it will be pitched into a state of graver self-doubt than ever. Poor devil, he will type out his name on a sheet of paper and stare at it long and long, with dumb uncertainty. It looks—oh, Christ!— his name looks as if it could stand some working on.

As I was writing the above, Gardner Botsford, the editor who, among other duties, handles copy for "Theatre," came into my office with the galleys of my latest play review in his hand. Wearing an expression of solemnity, he said, "I am obliged to inform you that Miss Gould has found a buried dangling modifier in one of your sentences." Miss Gould is our head copy editor and unquestionably knows as much about English grammar as anyone alive. Gerunds, predicate nominatives, and passive periphrastic conjugations are mother's milk to her, as they are not to me. Nevertheless, I boldly challenged her allegations. My prose was surely correct in every way. Botsford placed the galleys before me and indicated the offending sentence, which ran, "I am told that in her ninth decade this beautiful woman's only complaint in respect to her role is that she doesn't have enough work to do."

I glared blankly at the galleys. Humiliating enough to have buried a dangling modifier unawares; still more humiliating not to be able to disinter it. Botsford came to my rescue. "Miss Gould points out that as the sentence is written, the meaning is that the complaint is in its ninth decade and has, moreover, suddenly and unaccountably assumed the female gender." I said that in my opinion the sentence could only be made worse by being corrected—and it was plain that "The only complaint of this beautiful woman in her ninth decade . . ." would hang on the page as heavy as a sash-weight. "Quite so," said Botsford. "There are times when to be right is wrong, and this is one of them. The sentence stands."

# New Criticism

I'll start with New Criticism because modern literary study arguably begins with New Criticism, and because it is probably, even today, the most pervasive way of looking at literature. It emerged in the struggle to make literary criticism a respectable profession, which for many scholars meant making it more rigorous, more like the sciences—a goal embodied in Wellek and Warren's landmark *Theory of Literature*

(1949). Wellek's chapter on "The Mode of Existence of a Literary Work of Art" is crucial: "The work of art," Wellek asserts, is "an object of knowledge," "a system of norms of ideal concepts which are intersubjective" (p. 156). What Wellek means by this difficult formulation, at least in part, is that "a literary work of art is in exactly the same position as a system of language" (p. 152). Because the work has the same sort of stable and "objective" status as a language, existing in a "collective ideology," governed by enduring "norms," critical statements are not merely opinions of taste: "It will always be possible to determine which point of view grasps the subject most thoroughly and deeply," and therefore "all relativism is ultimately defeated" (p. 156). This assumption is important, because although New Critics in practice have not always ignored authors, genres, or historical contexts, the purpose of their analysis of particular works, their "close reading," has been finally to reveal how the formal elements of the literary work, often thought of as a poem, create and resolve tension and irony. Great works resolve profound tensions, and therefore New Criticism's "intrinsic" analysis, dealing with the work in isolation, is implicitly evaluative.

Common sense might suggest that the function of criticism is to reveal the meaning of a work, but New Criticism attends to *how* a work means, not *what,* for a simple reason: as Cleanth Brooks (1947) puts it, the meaning of a work is "a controlled experience which has to be *experienced,* not a logical process" (p. 190). The meaning cannot, in other words, be summed up in a proposition, but the system of norms that constructs a reader's experience can be analyzed. So, the New Critic focuses on "the poem itself" (rather than the author, the reader, the historical context), asking "What elements are in tension in this work?" and "What unity resolves this tension?"

In Gill's story, the most obvious tension might be seen as that between right and wrong (or editor versus writer, or the world versus *The New Yorker,* or grammar versus style, or confidence versus doubt, or something else). Whatever the basic tension is determined to be, it must somehow be resolved if the text is to succeed, and New Criticism is inevitably teleological: endings are crucial. Thus a New Critical reading of Gill's passage might well focus on the reconciliation at the end, when Botsford pronounces "right is wrong." The New Critic would then consider, "How does this idea fit into the system of the work's tensions, and how is the tension ordered and resolved?" The following paragraph briefly suggests the sort of discussion that might be produced in response:

In Gill's story of the dangling modifier, Botsford solves the conflict between Miss Gould's rules and Gill's taste with a paradox that unifies the work: sometimes "right is wrong." Miss Gould was right to spot the error, but Gill was right to have written the sentence as he did. The profound irony of this solution is reinforced by various paradoxical images: for example, the dolphin is "diving skyward," an action that in its simultaneously downward ("diving") and upward ("skyward") implications embodies the same logic as a wrong rightness. The "progress downward" of the writer, and even his "becoming seclusion" (appealing to others; unknown to others), conveys the same image. In larger terms, the writer's "unshakable confidence" that quickly becomes a "dumb uncertainty" suggests the reversal that informs the story's truth. In such an upside-down world we would expect to find the imagery of struggle and violence, and such is indicated by the "yawning pit" and the "army of gnats." Such tension is harmonized by Gill's brilliant conclusion: in writing, conducted properly, the demands of correctness and style are harmonized by the writer's poetic instincts, just as the story itself is resolved by the notion of a correct error.

## Structuralism

At first glance, structuralism might appear to be simply the enlargement of New Criticism's project. Instead of focusing on the formal elements that create the experience of a particular work, structuralism aspired to deal, as Terry Eagleton (1982) says, "with structures, and more particularly with examining the general laws by which they work" (p. 94). A structuralist, for example, would be interested in isolating the conventions that allow us to identify a text as a story. In the case of Gill's passage, although it is an excerpt, many readers will perceive it to be self-contained. Is it then a story, an entity in itself, or is it meaningful only as a fragment, a part of *Here at the New Yorker?* If we consider how we decide whether something is a story, we might well agree that a passage becomes a story when it fits our ideas of what a story is, when it satisfies certain "general laws" of discourse regarding a "story." Some readers will assert that this passage does have a beginning, a middle, and an end; harmony, complication and crisis, and resolution. It also has a hero (the writer, who appears to be Gill), a helper (Botsford), and a villain (Miss Gould), essential entities in Vladimir Propp's (1968) formal analysis of the properties of one kind of story, the folktale. We can identify these elements, which some readers would say are essential to a story, because we can relate this story to other ones and to a paradigm of stories. We can imagine (and perhaps even recall) other stories involving a confident neophyte who encounters destructive forces, descends into despair and near helplessness, and then finds an unexpected helper and vindication. Such structuralist analysis moves into the realm of archetypal criticism (as in Northrop Frye's work) when it seeks the universal patterns, the "archetypes" which are the foundation of the system of "literature," rather than isolating the structures and relationships within a particular system of discourse.

To produce a structuralist reading, then, exposing a text's conventions and operations, we must first identify the elements of the text—the genre, the agents, the episodes, the turning points, whatever. Structuralists are naturally attracted to charts and diagrams because these are helpful in reducing the complexity of a text to some understandable pattern, which can be compared to other patterns, or their transmutation, or absence. This concern with conventions rather than discrete works means that structuralism, unlike New Criticism, is not implicitly evaluative. *Gulliver's Travels* and "Gilligan's Island" are equally worthy of analysis, at least structurally: they may, in fact, illuminate one another, since textual conventions appear in the relationship of texts. If all the stories in our culture conventionally end with the hero disappearing into the forest with a pack of multicolored dogs, as Joseph Grimes (1975) reports is indeed the case in one African culture (p. xx), then we recognize such an event as a discrete element: the ending element. In the case of Gill's text, one convention of a literary work that we surely recognize as missing is a beginning operation: a title. Does this lack alone disqualify the text as a literary story? If so, could we then add a title (what would it be?) and make the text into a story? If so, who would be the author of this story that didn't exist until we titled it? (We might also consider the status of this story before it was extricated from Gill's book.)

Because students' experience of literature may be limited, it's often helpful to supply comparable texts or to ask students to invent a comparable text. Here is my attempt to think structurally about this excerpt and analyze its most significant features, followed by a sketch of another story based on the same underlying features:

> The structure of Gill's text involves the repetition of an underlying sequence. This sequence, which we see in the first two paragraphs, might be represented this way:
>
> 1. Unrealistic confidence ("unshakable confidence") + critical forces (editors, copy editors, and checkers)→unrealistic doubt ("dumb uncertainty").

The same underlying structure appears in the last two paragraphs, except this time a particular example of the pattern is presented:

2. Specific instance: unrealistic confidence ("boldly challenged her allegation") + a critical force (Miss Gould)→unrealistic doubt ("still more humiliating").

In the final paragraph the pattern is inverted, which is a common occurrence in the concluding element of a series:

3. Unrealistic doubt (helpless to "disinter it") + a helpful force (Botsford)→realistic confidence (Gill's opinion is confirmed when "The sentence stands").

The same pattern is exemplified in the following plot:

1. Dreaming of future glory as an artist, a student comes to study at the university and discovers that art professors systematically show students how incompetent they are.
2. The art student turns in a project, and one faculty member explains in public how the project is grossly wrong. The student did not realize that he had departed from the assignment.
3. The chairman of the department then responds to the faculty member's criticism, saying that the assignment was a foolish one, and the student has demonstrated admirable creativity in revising the professor's directions and producing a good project.

## Deconstruction

New Criticism, like Current-Traditional Rhetoric, is product-oriented. It is perhaps then not surprising that my New Critical reading of Gill's piece focuses on the centrality of error, one of C-T Rhetoric's fundamental concerns. At first glance, Gill's story may appear to deflate Error's terror, since being wrong turns out to be right. If we press this close reading, however, asking if the text might say something other than what it appears to say, we move into the realm of deconstruction. Composition students in particular might be sensitive to the way Botsford's paradox reverses itself, unravelling Gill's grammatical triumph and plunging "the writer" in the space following the passage into an even dumber and darker uncertainty. It's bad enough for the writer at *The New Yorker,* as well as the writer in freshman composition, if the rules of writing are so complex that not even three people in America "can set down a simple declarative sentence correctly," if an experienced and accomplished writer can commit a major blunder without knowing it and without being able to fix it when he does know it. But *it's even worse* if the rules obtain in one case and not in another, and the rules for determining such exceptions don't seem to exist but are rather invented and applied by whoever happens to be in charge. Basic writing students, mystified by the rules of Standard English, live in just such a nightmare, I suspect.

In fact, Botsford's vindication is deceptive, for he does not actually say that sometimes right is wrong and wrong is right. He only says that sometimes "right is wrong." Certainly wrong is also occasionally wrong, and perhaps it is *always* wrong. But Botsford's apparent reversal of the dismantling of authors at *The New Yorker* is finally ambiguous, since we never know if the writer is ever correct, no matter what he does: "The sentence stands" indeed, but it stands with its error intact, a monument to Gill's inability and the inevitable error of writing— the way language masters us.

I am, of course, just applying some basic deconstructive moves to Gill's text, which seems especially receptive, given its overt oppositions and emphasis on language. Despite the reluctance of some theorists to define deconstruction (an action that deconstruction, by definition, renders futile), useful and clear explanations are available. For example, Barbara Johnson (1980) says that deconstruction proceeds by "the careful teasing out of warring forces of signification within the text itself" (p. 5). Jonathan Culler (1982) says that "to deconstruct a discourse is to show how it undermines the philosophy it asserts, or the hierarchical oppositions on which it relies" (p. 86). This teasing out or undermining might be described as a three-step process: first, a deconstructive reading must note which member of an opposition in a text appears to be privileged or dominant (writers versus editors, error versus correctness, men versus women, etc.); second, the reading shows how this hierarchy can be reversed within the text, how the apparent hierarchy is arbitrary or illusory; finally, a deconstructive reading places both structures in question, making the text ultimately ambiguous. For students to deconstruct a text, they need to locate an opposition, determine which member is privileged, and then reverse and undermine that hierarchy. Such activity often makes central what appears to be marginal, thereby exposing "hidden" contradictions, and encourages creativity (students should appreciate the playfulness and punning of much post-structuralist criticism) and scrutiny (in order to deconstruct a work, one at least must read it carefully). These seem like especially worthwhile activities to me.

We might also think about deconstruction in terms of structuralism, as "post-structuralism." If structuralism shows how the conventions of a text work, deconstruction aims to show how they fail. In our time, the genres "fiction" and "nonfiction" have proved especially interesting. Gill's passage would appear to be nonfiction, since Gill really did work at *The New Yorker,* and his book obviously employs the operations of autobiography. But look at Miss Gould's uncannily apt name: she is a Miss Ghoul, having unearthed a "buried" dangling modifier, decomposing Gill's sentence; Botsford, perhaps played by Vincent Price, enters with "an expression of solemnity," carrying this mutilated modifier that the author finds himself unable to "disinter." Miss Gould may not drink human blood, but she does have some strange nutritional ideas if "gerunds, predicate nominatives, and passive paraphrastic conjugations are mother's milk to her." Fortunately, the editor, a gardener, or rather a Gardner, who has the final responsibility for nurturing, pruning, and harvesting the writer's sentences, knows how to deal with buried modifiers. Thus, although we initially may place this piece into the nonfiction category, deconstruction calls such placement into question. People in nonfiction usually don't have symbolic names—do they? Of course, there was that White House spokesperson named Larry Speakes. And then my allergist in Tuscaloosa, whose name, prophetically enough, was Dr. Shotts. And twenty other folks I've known with strangely symbolic names. Deconstruction typically leaves us in uncertainty, but with a richer understanding of the categories we have put in motion.

Although deconstructive critics may well deal with pervasive, basic issues, they may also choose some marginal element of the text and vigorously explore its oppositions, reversals, and ambiguities. In fact, for some critics deconstruction is simply a name for close reading with a vengeance. The deconstructive critic, for example, might well decide to concentrate on the arguably marginal assertion that because of the editors' merciless corrections, a piece "will be much improved." The New Critic, I think, would not be very likely to consider this assertion central, the key to the passage. Yet, proceeding from deconstructive assumptions, bringing the marginal to the center, here is what happened when I turned on this assertion:

> Gill's anecdote clearly sets the world's writers against the editors, and the latter control the game. The editors and their henchmen, the checkers and copy editors, get to say what is wrong. They get to dig the "yawning pit" in front of the helpless writer's desk; they determine the "tiny elect" who can write correctly; they make the scores and hundreds of "hen-tracks" on the writer's manuscript which serve as testimony to the incompetence of writers, the near-impossibility of writing, and the arbitrary power of the editor. To be sure, it is acknowledged that these editorial assaults upon the writer serve their purpose, for "Thanks to the hen-tracks and their consequences, the piece will

be much improved." But the cost is clearly terrible. Not only is the writer unable to write his own name with any confidence; he has become a "poor devil," outside "the elect." In delivering his writing over to the editors, conceding their dominance, the writer inevitably places his own identity, perhaps even his very soul, in jeopardy, as the expostulation "oh, Christ!" comes to be an invocation to the only power who can save the writer from the Devil and the editor's destructive forces.

In fact, this story of the errors of writing actually reveals that the kingdom of editors is based upon a lie: it simply is not true, despite the beleaguered writer's admission, under torture, that "the piece will be much improved" by editorial intervention. Miss Gould's enormous grammatical lore does not improve the piece at all; her effort nearly made it "worse." And Botsford's contribution involves simply leaving the piece as it was written— a strange method of improvement. This instance, in other words, suggests that the writer need not approach dissolution in order to compose his writing. At the same time, Gill can never become again like the gill-less dolphin of the first paragraph, confidently "diving skyward," for the dangling modifier remains, a part of the sea of language the author cannot leave. In the end, both writer and editor are defeated by their inability to control their language, as the status of the writer at *The New Yorker* becomes a paradigm for the alarming status of writing itself: deceptive, mute, and intractable, "The sentence stands," neither improved nor made worse.

## Psychological Criticism

In its most commonsensical form, a psychological approach to a text simply involves focusing attention on the motivations and relationships involved in the text's production and consumption. The mental processes of author, character, and/or reader may be involved in such consideration. This analysis probably cannot go very far without crossing over some ground that Freud has landscaped, and I usually attempt to give students at least a basic understanding of Freud and how his ideas might be applied to texts. Many students think they already understand Freud: he's the guy who thought of everything in terms of sex. Freud did think that sexuality pervaded human activity, but the sexual drive is always in conflict with opposing forces. Our drive toward pleasure does not ordinarily have free rein, but is of course suppressed, relegated to the unconscious, where it does not slumber peacefully away but rather asserts itself indirectly, in dreams, jokes, slips of the tongue. This repression, which allows us to function in society, becomes a problem when the unconscious begins to enlarge its domain, creating hysterical, obsessional, or phobic neuroses that express the desire in a covert way.

And when the power of the unconscious starts to take over reality, creating a delusion, we have a psychosis.

At the heart of Freud's theory is his most outrageous claim: that even infants are sexual beings. The most fundamental repression, according to Freud, the famous Oedipus complex, is the mechanism by which the boy represses his incestuous desire for his mother. This repression supposedly occurs because the boy fears castration by the father, who represents "the Law." His deferred and hidden desire then activates the unconscious, the "place" where repressed desires reside.

Even these few comments on Freudian analysis suggest some interesting angles on Gill's text. Of course, the text provides a good deal of material for psychological speculation without the Freudian apparatus. For example, students whose writing will be read and evaluated by their peers are intrigued by what the passage implies about the psychological effects of criticism. Some of my students feel that they too have been traumatized by "pencilled hen-tracks of inquiry, suggestion, and correction," and the passage provides a good opportunity to consider how such feelings arise and what purpose, if any, they serve. But a Freudian approach, most students quickly see, is a good deal more fun. Here is some indication of the sort of thing psychoanalytical moves might produce:

> Writers are brought into the world by editors, and Brendan Gill is thus in a sense the product of Gould and Botsford's union. Gardner Botsford imposes the grammatical law in a fatherly enough way, but his counterpart, Miss Gould, functions only as a kind of uncreating anti-mother: she is a "Miss," and her notion of "mother's milk" is truly indigestible—"gerunds, predicate nominatives, and passive periphrastic conjugations." She nurtures neither writing nor writer.
>
> But, at the same time, the well-being of the writers at *The New Yorker* depends on her approval because, like Gill, they have accepted the criterion of correctness as patriarchal law. Miss Gould imposes that law to the letter, undermining the writer's self-esteem until finally his very identity is threatened, plunging him into such "self-doubt" that his name is called into question. He may then become an orphan; his work may be abandoned. In fact, the source of the writer's neurotic breakdown seems to be the linking of self to writing. Although the many corrections are imprinted upon the paper, Gill shifts them to the writer and transforms them from "pencilled hen-tracks" into stings. It is not, as we might suppose, the particular work that may be attacked so much it dies, but rather *the writer* who may be "stung to death by an army of gnats." Gnats do not, of course, so far as I know anyway, have stingers; they bite. The displacement here, one might argue, is the result of the writer's sense of personal vulnerability,

making the threat more plausible since being bitten to death by
gnats sounds absurd, while being stung is more ominous.

## Feminist Criticism

I have only recently stopped being amazed at how easily and enthusiastically my students take to feminist criticism. Part of its appeal, I
suppose, is its simplicity, at least on the surface: to practice feminist
criticism, one need only read as a woman. Such a procedure quickly
turns out to have a profound effect on the reader and the text—an
effect that hardly can avoid being political. Whatever students' sexual
politics might be, feminist criticism unavoidably involves them in
significant, timely issues. I do not mean to say that feminist criticism
is invariably easy or simplistic: oftentimes, even for a woman, reading
*as a woman* is extremely difficult, requiring the reader to dismantle or
discard years of learned behavior. And, of course, I am leaping over
the difficult question of what it actually means to read "as a woman."
Can men really do it? Isn't it absurd to assume that there is only one
distinctly feminine way of reading? But these questions need not be
answered in order for students to attempt to undo their sexual assumptions, try out new ones, or simply sensitize themselves to the
sexual issues present in a work. Not all texts, of course, lend themselves
easily to feminist criticism, but it is difficult to find one that completely
resists a feminist stance. I have found that Gill's passage easily supports
a familiar feminist observation, but it also repays a more aggressive
and perhaps even outrageous (or outraged) approach. Both appear in
the following analysis:

> We know that not all the writers at *The New Yorker* were men,
> even some years ago during Brendan Gill's tenure. So, when Gill
> speaks of "some writer who has made a name for himself in the
> world," and about the editorial "machinery" that besets "him,"
> Gill is of course referring to writers in the generic sense. One
> may still assert today, although less confidently than in 1975, that
> "himself" and "him" in this passage include "herself" and "her."
> Such a claim, that one sexual marker includes its opposite, may
> seem absurd—as if "white" included "black," or "communist"
> included "democratic." But the motivations for such a claim are
> suggested even in this brief passage, for Gill's story not only
> contains this obvious pronominal bias, still accepted by some
> editors and writers; the story also conveys more subtle messages
> about sexuality and sexual roles.
>
> For example, Miss Gould functions as a familiar stereotype:
> the finicky spinster, a Miss Thistlebottom, who has devoted her
> life to "English grammar" and its enforcement. She is a copy

editor, subservient to the male editor and writer, and her lack of imagination and taste testify to the wisdom of this power structure. This division of labor—male-creative, female-menial—is subtly reinforced by the reference to the "hen-tracks" that cover the writer's galleys, thus further associating petty correction with the feminine. But these "*hen*-tracks" (they could not be rooster tracks) are more than an aggravating correction; they even come to threaten the writer's very identity. In attempting to produce "his copy," the writer is in a sense attempting to reproduce himself. The "glory of creation" is his literary procreation, and thus Miss Gould's effort to remove a particular sentence is a symbolic threat to cut off some more essential part of the writer. It is, after all, a "dangling modifier" that she has located; and this dangling structure is in danger of being fed to the "yawning pit," symbolic of the feminine editing and its excising dangers.

Because Gill's initial image for the writer starting out at the magazine, the dolphin in the sea, derives some of its power from the well-established association of the ocean and the womb, the image of the yawning pit—not to mention the poisonous "mother's milk"—becomes more arresting. Even the error itself is subtly connected to the feminine, for the problem with the sentence is that part of it has "assumed the female gender." That part, of course, in the context of nagging copy editors who chop up one's prose, can only be a "complaint," which is allowed to retain its female gender. The nonagenarian's complaint itself seems strange: in the mode of feminine busybodies like Miss Gould, she laments not having "enough work to do." Miss Gould, similarly over-zealous, has herself done more work than is reasonable, and Botsford's pronouncement that "The sentence stands" returns her to her place, negating her feminine fussiness.

## Conclusion

One might want to point out, I suppose, that in offering this rehearsal of critical "approaches," I am assuming that plurality is better than unity, that the relative is better than the absolute (or even a quest for the absolute). And, given what I think we know about language and knowing, it seems silly to me to assume otherwise: as Jane Tompkins (1988) says, articulating a current commonplace, we are not "freestanding autonomous entities, but beings that are culturally constituted by interpretive frameworks or interpretive strategies that our culture makes available to us" (p. 734). In other words, the texts we read—when we look at books, at our world, at ourselves—are likewise constituted by these frameworks or strategies. Obviously, if this "reading" of meaning is correct, plurality offers us a richer universe, allowing us to take greater advantage of the strategies our culture makes available—

strategies that do not approach a text, but rather make it what we perceive. Our students therefore should learn how to inhabit the theories mentioned here—and a good many others.

To be sure, such plurality is not always comfortable. Furthermore, if we should agree that the more strategies students can deploy (or be deployed by), the more power and insight they can potentially wield, then must we also agree that there are no limits? Are all readings welcome, the more the merrier? My initial impulse is to say, "Yes, we can learn from *any* reading, from any set of interpretive assumptions. Come one, come all." We can see how readings that seem severely inattentive might offer useful insights: for example, in his essay on "How Readers Make Meaning," Robert Crosman (1982) reveals how one student's reading completely missed the significance of the hair on the pillow at the end of "A Rose for Emily," and yet this reading, comparing Emily to the student's grandmother, profoundly enlarged Crosman's understanding of Faulkner's story. We can even imagine how ludicrous errors might stimulate our thinking: my student who thought *The Hamlet* was by Shakespeare did lead me to ask (mostly in an attempt to ease his embarrassment) about Shakespeare's influence on Faulkner—perhaps *The Hamlet* in some sense *is* by Shakespeare, or is shaped by *Hamlet*. But we must admit that most readings in violation of shared interpretive strategies will usually be seen as inferior, if not wrong, and that finding insight in such violations often seems an act of kindness, a salvage operation.

I can also imagine theoretical possibilities that would not be welcome in my critical home, should they ever appear: Nazi criticism, racist criticism, electroshock criticism, for example. In other words, if we are not freestanding autonomous entities, we are also not entirely helpless, simply the products of the interpretive operations we inherit, "a mere cultural precipitate," as Morse Peckham puts it (1979, p. xviii). I would like to think we can resist; we can change; we can grow; we can, perhaps, in some sense, even get better. We can, that is, attempt to evaluate ways of making meaning, and their particular applications— and if we are very clever and very lucky, we may even modify interpretive frameworks, or possibly even invent new ones.

But only if we have some awareness that such frameworks exist.

### References

Brooks, Cleanth. 1947. *The Well-Wrought Urn*. New York: Harcourt Brace.
Crosman, Robert. 1982. "How Readers Make Meaning." *College Literature* 9: 207–15.

Culler, Jonathan. 1982. *On Deconstruction: Theory and Criticism after Structuralism*. Ithaca: Cornell University Press.

Eagleton, Terry. 1982. *Literary Theory: An Introduction*. Minneapolis: University of Minnesota Press.

Frye, Northrop. 1951. *Fables of Identity*. New York: Harcourt Brace.

Gill, Brendan. 1975. *Here at the New Yorker*. New York: Random House.

Grimes, Joseph. 1975. *The Thread of Discourse*. Paris: Mouton.

Johnson, Barbara. 1980. *The Critical Difference: Essays in the Contemporary Rhetoric of Reading*. Baltimore: Johns Hopkins University Press.

Peckham, Morse. 1979. *Explanation and Power: The Control of Human Behavior*. New York: Seabury.

Propp, Vladimir. 1968. *The Morphology of the Folktale*. Austin: University of Texas Press.

Tompkins, Jane. 1988. "A Short Course in Post-Structuralism." *College English* 50: 733–47.

Wellek, Rene, and Austin Warren. 1977 [1949]. *Theory of Literature*. New York: Harcourt Brace.

# 8 Contrarieties of Emotion; or, Five Days with *Pride and Prejudice*

Walker Gibson

Walker Gibson is Emeritus Professor of English at the University of Massachusetts–Amherst, where he has taught since 1967. Before this, he taught at Amherst College and New York University. He has published two volumes of poetry and two writing textbooks, and has edited a number of anthologies. His book *Tough, Sweet, and Stuffy: An Essay on Modern American Prose Styles* was selected for the Scholar's Library by the Modern Language Association.

In addition to his writing and teaching, Professor Gibson has been a force in the National Council of Teachers of English. He helped initiate the Council's Committee on Public Doublespeak; he has served as a member of the College Section Committee, of the Commission on the English Curriculum, and of the Executive Committee of CCCC. In 1973 he was elected president of the Council, and in 1988 he was given the Council's Distinguished Service Award.

Professor Gibson's essay is an elaboration and application of a remark he made to one of us shortly after the first Institute: that he had been reading the post-structuralists, and found this "new" territory rather familiar ground, given his training and work in the field of rhetoric.

*We can now appreciate how beautifully the ironies of the dialogue function in the curve of the main dramatic sequence.*

—R. A. Brower

I find myself (though technically retired) teaching *Pride and Prejudice* to a large group of undergraduates whose main interests are quite other than literature.

On the first day I write on the blackboard the familiar opening sentence: "It is a truth universally acknowledged that a single man in possession of a good fortune must be in want of a wife." That is a famous sentence, I tell the students. A lot of people—readers, critics, scholars—have remarked on that sentence over the years. Why do you suppose it has aroused such interest and attention? Read the first fifty pages, then go back to that opening sentence and write me a short paragraph explaining why you think it might be noteworthy.

The answers I receive, at the second class meeting, are probably predictable, but sobering nonetheless to an elderly Janeite. Here are two examples:

> The sentence shows that no matter how wealthy a young single man is, it doesn't mean anything and he is not truly happy until he has a wife to share it with. A man with no matter how grand a fortune is not complete and satisfied until he marries.

> It is generally safe to say, every man desires a woman for companionship, just as every woman desires a man. The relationship between man and woman has always been famous throughout all time periods.

There's some reader-response for you. No doubt *Pride and Prejudice* can be read, has been read, entirely as soap opera, as conventional romance. After all, girl meets boy, girl refuses boy, girl gets boy at last. But no, cries the elderly Janeite, it's not a soap opera. What to do?

We begin by looking at some clear and simple instances, early in the novel, where something is said and something else is meant. Jane Bennet falls ill at Bingley's home, and "his sisters declared that they were miserable. They solaced their wretchedness, however, by duets after supper." *Were* they miserable? Evidently not. Then why does the narrator say they were?

That's a tough question, which we'll put off for now. But we can say immediately that that sort of double-talk isn't likely in a conventional romance, while it is pervasive in the opening chapters of this novel. And now if we return to that very first sentence—"It is a truth universally acknowledged . . ."—a new look might be in order. *Is* it a truth universally acknowledged? Well, no. Some rich bachelors may be looking for wives, others not. Only to the Mrs. Bennets of the world, eager to dispose of marriageable daughters, is this "truth" acknowledged.

So there is this business of saying something and meaning something else. What do we call that? Students want to call it sarcasm, and I have to pull rank and insist on irony instead. There's something hostile about sarcasm, I say; let's call this irony and then it can include sarcasm as well as other less threatening examples of this device.

And do you use irony in your daily lives? Of course you do. Bring in next time an example of an ironical expression you have encountered in campus talk over the weekend.

And at our next meeting—this is the third day now—we share local ironies, dozens of them. A favorite involves the word *great*:

How was lunch at the dining commons today?
Oh, great.

How was that hour test you took this morning?
Great.

It may be that among the young that word is used more often ironically than otherwise.

And then we go irony-hunting through the early chapters of the book, which is great fun and easy to do. "Mr. Darcy is all politeness," says Elizabeth Bennet, and to the fool Sir William Lucas, standing there, she means just what she says. But we know, and we know she knows, that Darcy is by no means all politeness. As for Darcy himself, also standing there, how does he take this remark? Is he confused? Unnerved? Fascinated? We can distinguish at least three meanings for Elizabeth's words, and that without getting at all fancy.

Fourth day. Recall your remarks about men and women, love and marriage, when discussing the opening sentence last week. Now that you've completed reading most of the book, what do you think it is saying about love and marriage? Is it primarily *about* love and marriage? If it isn't about love and marriage, what is it about?

I am far from proud of this exercise. It so overtly invites the student to take a different tack that anyone who's ever *been* a student will recognize right away what she or he is supposed to do. (Though some don't, to be sure.) I'm moving them with a bulldozer. Still, many of them do move, and I receive some promising responses, particularly those that resort to the book's title:

> To the casual reader it may appear this novel is a romance, with its long drawn-out plot and eventual triumph of love over circumstance. However, to the discerning reader . . . Elizabeth becomes a universal hero by overcoming her own pride and prejudice.

> The most visible thing the book seems to be about is people's views of others and how they form their views. Elizabeth learns how incorrect she is . . .

> I do not think this book is about love and marriage, it is more focused on reality and the fact that superficial first impressions are not always the way things are.

Elizabeth Bennet is a wonderful person, as we all know; no wonder she is reputed to be her creator's favorite heroine. She is witty, strong-minded, affectionate, understanding—and about Wickham and Darcy she is *dead wrong*. And because she is so strong a character, her wrongness is magnified by her intensity and vehemence. Darcy, she tells him to his face, is "the last man in the world whom I could ever be prevailed on to marry." As one of my students put it, she "had an uncommon ability to back her judgments, which only served to further blind her from the truth." And so her conversion, her reeducation, is an especially agonizing process.

Fifth day—they've finished the book now—and we spend some time looking at those passages where Elizabeth is slowly and painfully changing her assumptions. There is some interesting language here. For example, in one chapter, just after she has received Darcy's long letter of explanation, Elizabeth is still dominated by "a strong prejudice against everything he might say." Yet she feels "a contrariety of emotion." "Her feelings as she read were scarcely to be defined." Yes, for the act of changing assumptions defies definition. It is a "mortifying perusal." "How differently did everything now appear." " 'How despicably have I acted,' she cried. 'I, who have prided myself on my discernment. . . . How humiliating is this discovery!' " The experience is overwhelming and exhausting. "After wandering along the lane for two hours, giving way to every variety of thought, reconsidering events, determining probabilities, and reconciling herself as well as she could, to a change so sudden and so important, fatigue, and a recollection of her long absence, made her at length return home." Though the book at this point is scarcely beyond the midpoint, it is only a matter of time before this change, "so sudden and so important," brings the plot to its happy conclusion.

Well then. We've noticed two things in our talk about this book. One has been a particular device of language—we've called it irony—in which something is said that demands another interpretation. We reread the statement in various ways, from various points of view. (It is *not* a truth universally acknowledged. . . .) As Wayne Booth (1974) has memorably told us, our understanding of irony begins with denial: no, that can't be true as stated; something else must be meant.

The other thing we've been noticing has been Elizabeth's moving conversion, her "mortifying perusal" of her assumptions and her eventual progress to a *re*view of her values. Her prejudice overcome at last, and Darcy's pride somewhat less convincingly overcome, the cheerful ending is inevitable.

And now (for it's on to something else next week), can I suggest to my class that these two observations of ours may have something in common? I cannot ask them to make much of this; I can't make much of it myself. But let's suppose (I say to them) you wanted to write a novel in which a main point is the conversion of a strong-minded person from deep error to enlightened truth, a novel in which the reinterpretation of evidence would be crucial. If you wanted to write such a novel, isn't it possible that you might (perhaps unconsciously) seize on *irony* as a way to demonstrate, on a small scale, the very process your entire novel is demonstrating in the large? The process is that of destroying one formulation in order to arrive at another. That is what happens with irony and that is what happens to Elizabeth Bennet.

One of the principal tenets of post-structuralism is the "irreconcilable difference between word and object, . . . an uncloseable distance between self and other," to quote a writer in this collection (Myra Jehlen). There is, of course, nothing new in that warning. It might be wholesome for us all to be reminded that something like twenty-five centuries ago, the pre-Socratic philosopher Gorgias had this to say: "That with which we communicate is speech, and speech is not the same thing as the things which exist, the perceptibles; so that we communicate not the things which exist, but only speech" (Freeman 1966, p. 361). And a modern critic (G. B. Kerford), summarizing the contribution of Gorgias and the Sophistic movement, writes as follows:

> What did emerge was a realisation that the relationship between speech and what is the case is far from simple. While it is likely that fifth-century thinkers all were prepared to accept that there is and must always be a relationship between the two, there was a growing understanding that what is very often involved is not simply a presentation in words of what is the case, but rather a representation involving a considerable degree of reorganization in the process. It is this awakening of what has often been called rhetorical self-consciousness that is a feature both of contemporary literature and of theoretic discussion in the fifth century. (1981, p. 78)

*Pride and Prejudice* is perhaps not the first book one might choose to demonstrate the outreaches of post-structuralist theory. Jane Austen, we assume, seldom doubted "the things which exist," and her ironies are "stable" ones, pointing us toward realities and values we are invited to share and believe. Nevertheless this is a book whose author is a master of "rhetorical self-consciousness." Casting about in the mystery of experience for a way of expressing a change of heart ("scarcely to be defined"), she arrives at irony to represent in miniature the perils of taking language at face value. Elizabeth's "reading" of Darcy and Wickham early in the novel is like my students' reading of the opening sentence: she believed what she saw, what she was told. As we appreciate in detail that often playful change of heart that irony demands, we appreciate all the more Elizabeth's overwhelming "mortifying perusal." It seems to be one of those cases, deliberate or not, where a device of language was chosen that miraculously reflects larger purposes. And one of those larger purposes is a warning that any post-structuralist could applaud: watch out for language, for seeing is not believing.

Indeed, if we live in a world where we recognize anew the disparity between word and thing, then irony may be one of our better ploys for coping with that knowledge. Through irony we convey to our listener something like this: I know you know that I know that I'm only using words as I talk to you, and you know I'm aware of their limitation. Nevertheless, as I *play* with those words and force redefinitions of them, we share at least a bit of fellow-feeling and comradeship in our predicament, and I look forward to your playful reply.

## References

Booth, Wayne C. 1974. *A Rhetoric of Irony.* Chicago: University of Chicago Press.

Brower, Reuben Arthur. 1951. *The Fields of Light,* 175. New York: Oxford University Press.

Gorgias. Quoted in Kathleen Freeman. 1966. *The Pre-Socratic Philosophers.* Cambridge: Harvard University Press.

Kerford, G. B. 1981. *The Sophistic Movement.* New York: Cambridge University Press.

# 9 Feminism, Deconstruction, and the Universal: A Case Study on *Walden*

Irene C. Goldman

Irene Goldman is an assistant professor of English in her fourth year of teaching at Ball State University, in Muncie, Indiana. Ball State is a large state university (18,000 students) which has evolved from a teachers college. Her regular teaching load is three sections each semester, composed generally of an undergraduate survey of American literature, a graduate/undergraduate course titled "Women in Literature," and a graduate seminar in American literature, most recently in Twain, James, and Wharton. She was a participant in both the 1987 and 1988 Summer Institutes.

Dr. Goldman is firmly committed to the university's Women's Studies program, and for this program organizes a lecture series and a "women's week" of activities for, by, and about women. About the teaching of literature, she writes, "I believe in teaching reading and thinking skills, particularly insofar as those skills allow the student to uncover the hidden assumptions in a text. I also believe in increasing the variety of texts taught regularly so that a fair proportion of works by women, by non-whites, and by non-Christian writers are taught."

Feminism, because of its overt political stance, remains a highly controversial position for one to espouse in the academy, both as literary critic and as teacher. A feminist critic takes for granted that the structures of gender and sexual difference have been enormously influential in all areas of human existence and that we cannot understand history, politics, or culture—and that means literature—until we acknowledge this influence. A feminist teacher recognizes that students come to the classroom already formed by those structures, and that part of the teacher's task is to unmask gender-based structures and to support students in the process of change and growth that will inevitably begin with that unmasking. Consequently, acknowledged subjectivity and overt attention to politics become key elements of feminist literary criticism.

These elements are also, interestingly, key parts of some of the contemporary critical theories discussed in this volume. Like reader-response theory, feminist criticism is personal and reader-centered; it insists that reader and text are inseparable and that perception *is* interpretation. Like deconstruction, it is radical and disruptive, and it insists that we recognize the political content of all uses of language. This essay will argue, then, that a feminist literary critic and teacher can combine strategies from these contemporary critical techniques to teach traditional texts in a way that will refuse to reinforce their inherent gender biases.

Reading as a woman, says Judith Fetterley (1978), is a different experience from reading as a man. Most male texts require of their readers complicity in viewing the world in their terms, particularly in viewing women in their terms. Hence, Fetterley argues, the female reader is put in the peculiar position of being unable to locate herself in the text. Fetterley's best illustration of this is her analysis of Washington Irving's "Rip Van Winkle" (which should be read in its entirety), wherein she raises the question that, if a woman reader cannot imagine herself as Rip because he is so clearly male, and she cannot be Dame Van Winkle, who is not a person but a scapegoat—the enemy, the other—where, as a woman reader, is she to stand in relation to the text? And, worse still, if escaping work, responsibility, and political upheaval (remember, Rip sleeps through the Revolutionary War), all of which are symbolized as a shrewish wife—if this is the American Dream, what, she asks, are the results of it for you, a woman? Who is left raising the children, carrying on civilization, even while being blamed for its evils? The answer to either question can only be disastrous to a woman's psyche, particularly to young women like our students, just emerging into their sexuality and facing decisions and pressures about love and marriage. As a reader, a woman is forced either to identify against her very self—to agree with the narrator's view of women, perhaps even to deny the existence of women as sentient beings—or to be accused by the literary establishment of willfully misreading the text.

Such is the central insight of Fetterley's book *The Resisting Reader,* which demonstrates persuasively the ground that the feminist critic shares with the reader-response theorist. If meaning is made, as the latter argues, in the dynamic interaction between reader and text, then the gender dynamics between female reader and male text will be an important element of the process.

And what about deconstruction? If one of the results of post-structuralist criticism is to collapse the differentiations among reader, method, text, and interpretation, it seems logical that a feminist stance will have implications for a deconstructive reading as well. Barbara Johnson (1985) tells us,

> Deconstruction has sometimes been seen as a terroristic belief in meaninglessness. . . . It is commonly opposed to humanism, which is then an imperialistic belief in meaningfulness. Another way to distinguish between the two is to say that deconstruction is a reading strategy that carefully follows both the meanings and the suspensions and displacements of meaning in a text, while humanism is a strategy to stop reading when the text stops saying what it ought to have said. (p. 140)

Another way of expressing the difference is that while New Critical, humanistic reading seeks to find the interpretation that is most unifying, that can incorporate the most of the language in the book, deconstruction focuses on the points at which unity becomes impossible, on the concepts that must be left out in order to give the appearance of unity, the places where meaning is most noticeably unstable. This is a perfect strategy for the feminist critic, who will argue that one point at which supposedly unified and universal meanings of texts almost always unravel is the assumption that what is true for "man" is also true for woman. The feminist critic is in a position to notice certain kinds of absences, gestures of exclusion, false assumptions of inclusiveness, that a non-feminist critic might miss. These are the very points that the teacher will want to highlight for students in order to unmask the truth that many texts we have called universal are in fact male-gendered and arise from and support structures that subjugate women.

To illustrate how these theories might be made into reading/teaching strategies, let us examine a familiar text, taught in nearly every introductory American literature class, Thoreau's *Walden.* Great claims are made for *Walden,* some by Thoreau himself. The written word, Thoreau tells us (and Stanley Cavell, among others, argues that he is making a case for his own writing here), is "at once more intimate with us and more universal than any other work of art" (p. 93). *Universal*—"including or covering all . . . collectively. . . without limit or exception" (*Webster's* 1984). The claim of universality that Thoreau here makes for books—and, by implication, for his own—is the same one teachers make in choosing *Walden* again and again as one of the great works of American literature that must be studied by all students. (Do you know of an anthology of American literature that does not include it, or a survey course that does not teach it?)

In fact, Thoreau makes even larger claims for the authority and importance of books and their authors:

> Books are the treasured wealth of the world and the fit inheritance
> of generations and nations. Books, the oldest and the best, stand
> naturally and rightfully on the shelves of every cottage. They
> have no cause of their own to plead, but while they enlighten and
> sustain the reader his common sense will not refuse them. Their
> authors are a natural and irresistible aristocracy in every society,
> and, more than kings or emperors, exert an influence on mankind.
> (p. 93)

Teachers and scholars of *Walden* seem to agree that the book is
worth studying by all students of literature, not just as a representative
American text but as some sort of guide to living. Stanley Cavell
assumes this throughout *The Senses of Walden* (1972) as he asks how
"we," that is, readers of *Walden,* are to "keep faith with" or "abide"
Thoreau's words. Townsend Scudder, in his foreword to the Modern
Library edition, tells us Thoreau was "a moral philosopher" with "a
passion for wise and honorable living" (p. xiv). Thoreau was a transcendentalist, he says, and transcendentalists

> represented God on earth; they were His agents because they were
> trying to live in His image and they believed that men might yet
> found Heaven on earth by looking into their own hearts for the
> rules of life and by following the direction of their finest instincts.
>     Thoreau was the most enduring of the lot because he had the
> most intimate knowledge and understanding of nature.... (p.
> xiv–xvi)

A rather strong claim for the universal value of the text. Lauriat Lane,
too, gives it the authority of a religious text. In his volume *Approaches
to Walden* (1964) he says, "*Walden* is a religious book, even for many
readers a kind of scripture, a sacred writing" (p. 5). One of the essays
he includes in the section of the book on the "uses" of *Walden* is
Kenneth Burke's "Literature as Equipment for Living," which argues
that people read "for promise, admonition, solace, vengeance, fore-
telling, instruction, charting, all for the direct bearing that such acts
have upon matters of welfare" (p. 102). By implication, this is a way
to use *Walden*. And in case we miss the point, Lane also includes
several long verses from the Gospel according to Saint Matthew.

All of this points to the conclusion that we—all of us—read *Walden*
as Thoreau instructs us to read it, that is, as a manual of how and
why to live the spiritual and physical life of an individual, to search
for the truth of what we are.

But does this "we" include women as well as men?[1] What will a
feminist reader do when endeavoring to deconstruct such a text? The
deconstructivist will tell us that no truth is whole or universal, and
that there is always already within any notion an excluded other without

which the first could not exist. A feminist critic will tell you that Thoreau's text on what it is to be "man" excludes women and yet depends on the idea of woman for meaning. The feminist/deconstructivist reader, then, will concentrate not exclusively on the universal truths of *Walden,* as a humanist critic might, but on the places where meaning shifts and contradicts itself insofar as gender is concerned.

We know, of course, that *Walden* is famous for its contradictions, exaggerations, and reversals. At least two of America's leading deconstructivists have put their minds to the task of teasing out its meanings and blocks to meaning. Walter Benn Michaels (1977) noticed twelve years ago that Thoreau's contradictions had been explained away by means of several different strategies: first James Russell Lowell cited them as characteristic of Thoreau's personality, then formalist critics turned a vice into a virtue and praised them as beautiful paradoxes that work to illuminate a literary, if not a logical, truth. In 1972 Stanley Cavell appealed to the spirituality of the reader, who, by means of revelation, brings the contradictions into a "visionary union" (Michaels, pp. 145–46). Michaels himself concludes, as any good deconstructivist would, that the dilemma of reading *Walden* is ultimately unresolvable, for the text both authorizes and repudiates the reading strategies it proposes. Barbara Johnson (1987), in a more recent inquiry into the difficulties and obscurities of *Walden,* concludes, "The perverse complexity of *Walden*'s rhetoric is intimately related to the fact that it is never possible to be sure what the rhetorical status of any given image is" (p. 55). In other words, the literal is figurative is literal, and so on ad infinitum. I offer yet a different way of reading *Walden,* one that will help students to understand that what Thoreau says about the nature and purpose of "man" is in fact meant to be about just that: man. Not woman, but man.

### Deconstructivist Theory and *Walden*

One of the first attributes of a text that the deconstructivist critic notices is ambiguous words, and one of the first groups of words that feminists find ambiguous is *man, mankind,* and *he.* They are words that Thoreau uses constantly; in fact, it would not be unreasonable to say that the main thrust of *Walden* is to assert what man should be. Early on in the first chapter he tells us,

> Talk of a divinity in man! Look at the teamster on the highway, wending to market by day or night; does any divinity stir within him? His highest duty to fodder and water his horses! What is

his destiny to him compared with the shipping interests? Does not he drive for Squire Make-a-stir? How godlike, how immortal, is he? See how he cowers and sneaks, how vaguely all the day he fears, not being immortal nor divine, but the slave and prisoner of his own opinion of himself, a fame won by his own deeds. Public opinion is a weak tyrant compared with our own private opinion. What a man thinks of himself, that it is which determines, or rather indicates, his fate. Self-emancipation even in the West Indies provinces of the fancy and imagination. —What Wilberforce is there to bring that about? Think, also, of the ladies of the land weaving toilet cushions against the last day, not to betray too green an interest in their fates! As if you could kill time without injuring eternity. (p. 7)

His next paragraph begins with the now-famous statement, "The mass of men lead lives of quiet desperation."

What are we to make of the concept of man as Thoreau uses it here and throughout the book? The humanist critic—and probably most teachers—would argue that *man* is meant as a universal term here to include both men and women. But several clues in the text argue against that claim. How then can we "de-fine," that is, limit the meaning of, *man*? If, as deconstructivists argue, terms define themselves against each other in a system of meanings, against what other terms does Thoreau set *man*?

There are several ways in which Thoreau defines *man* by opposition, two of which show up in the passage above: man/God and man/beast. A third opposition is man/Nature (it may help here to recall Emerson's famous definition in "Nature" of Nature as all that is NOT ME). All of these, as all oppositions, are hierarchical: God is privileged over man, and man is privileged over beast. The problematic one is man/Nature; while Thoreau seems to privilege Nature over man, I will argue that in fact he privileges man over Nature. In all of these oppositions, the assumption is that *man* means humankind, that is, man and woman. But I will also argue that Thoreau means *only* man, for when he wishes to include women, he does so separately. It is particularly important that we guide our women students in this understanding so that they are not forced into identifying unwittingly against themselves.

Let us go back to the passage. When Thoreau accuses the common teamster of not having divinity within him, or not being sufficiently godlike, he sets up the man/God opposition, for if man should be *like* God, he cannot therefore *be* God. Yet it is also this spark of divinity within man that separates him from the beasts. It gives him his ability to think about himself and to strive for mastery over beast, both the beast within and without. Therefore, man is also that which is not beast. Indeed, our teamster fodders and waters his horse, proving himself caretaker of beast rather than beast himself. So far, man is not God and not beast, but somewhere in between, a classical-enough definition.

But the definition is complicated by Thoreau's assertion that man has failed in both of these identifications. If he fails at being godlike, which is the trait that makes him man in the man/beast system, but rather cowers and sneaks and allows himself to be enslaved, then he is not only not man, but also not *not* man, that is, not beast. But if he is not beast, then he must have some divinity within him, precisely what Thoreau argues he has not. Consequently, he is not God, and not *not* God. So, in two definitional systems in which Thoreau asks us to consider the meaning of man, he actually erases the possibility of a stable meaning for the concept "man" by denying that man is either one term or the other in the binary oppositions.

The next discovery involves the hierarchy man/woman, a hierarchy that teachers of *Walden* ignore when they assume universal appeal for the text. It is a common assumption, and here a dictionary is instructive. In Webster's *Collegiate,* the first definition of man is "a human being; *esp*: an adult male human." The meaning is fuzzy—when does *man* mean human, and when does it mean adult male human? Since no critic, and few teachers, that I have encountered addresses the problem explicitly, we see that the assumption must be that when Thoreau says *man,* he is using the universal *man,* and is therefore including women. That he is not can be demonstrated in several ways.

Thoreau tells us in the second paragraph of the book whom it is he addresses:

> Perhaps these pages are more particularly addressed to poor students. As for the rest of my readers, they will accept such portions as apply to them. I trust that none will stretch the seams in putting on the coat, for it may do good service to him whom it fits. (p. 4)

At that time, of course, very few students were women; although Oberlin opened its doors to women in the 1830s, not until the Morrill Act funded higher education during the Civil War did other schools begin to admit women. Vassar College, the first fully accredited women's college, opened for business in 1865 (Woloch 1984).

Further, the examples Thoreau uses of people—either exemplary or not—are almost invariably men. Men are the teamsters, the ones with shipping interests; men are the ones who have to get a living (not true, of course, but it seems true in Thoreau); men are the ones who stand to inherit and who have the freedom to make the choices that Thoreau later either praises or condemns them for making. All the objects of his admonitions are portrayed in exclusively male terms; women would indeed stretch the seams of the metaphorical coat he offers his readers on the first page.

Further, when Thoreau wishes to include women, he does so specifically. When, for instance, he argues that most of what we think ourselves busy with is easily let go in an emergency, he says that when a fire bell rings "there is hardly a man on his farm . . . nor a boy, nor a woman, I might almost say, but would forsake all and follow that sound" (p. 84). And if we look back at our original passage, we notice that, toward the end, he adjures us to "Think, also, of the ladies of the land" doing what they do best, sewing toilet cushions. The "also" gives it away: if we were thinking of all humanity when he was discussing divinity and likeness to God, we are here corrected; we should have been thinking only of the men. A final example (though not the only other one I could cite) comes when, in the Conclusion, Thoreau admonishes his readers to be "the Lewis and Clark and Frobisher of your own streams and oceans" (p. 286). "Are these the problems which most concern mankind? Is Franklin the only man who is lost, that his wife should be so earnest to find him?" (p. 286). Only mankind of the male sex have wives—if we women were thinking ourselves included in that group of lost men who should explore our own streams and oceans, we are again abruptly corrected. Hence we have quite a gap for women readers, who are thus left out of all of Thoreau's remarks about the nature of the world, of man, of culture, and of how one should conduct one's life.

Let us move on to the other opposition I spoke of after man/God and man/beast: man/Nature. This is the most telling of all, for here is where Thoreau's argument relies on the idea of woman even as it excludes women themselves. Thoreau, like Emerson and many others before him, always speaks of Nature as a "she." While this is an ancient conception, it is also particularly appropriate for the New England transcendentalist when we consider that, if Nature is all that is not me, and if the "me" is male, then Nature must be female.[2] And nature is conceived metaphorically as female to mankind's male, make no mistake. One morning Thoreau awakens to "dawning Nature, in whom all creatures live, looking in at my broad windows with serene and satisfied face, and no question on *her* lips" (p. 253). Of course only in woman can creatures live, either as fetus or as lover. Mother or lover, Nature greets her man serenely and with satisfaction. She is something to be observed, too, he tells us later; she is not afraid to "exhibit herself" to "hunters, fishermen, woodchoppers, and others" (p. 189) who spend their lives in her fields and woods. Woman as object of the male gaze. I am reminded here of Thoreau's words from an earlier book, *A Week on the Concord and Merrimack*: "Thus, by one bait or another, Nature allures inhabitants into her recesses" (p. 315). Clearly Nature is female to mankind's male, and therefore woman is excluded from this conception of mankind.

At first the reader might think that Thoreau privileges Nature over man. Indeed, Michaels argues this when he says, "Thus, through most of *Walden* . . . the human and the natural are conceived as standing in implicit opposition to each other. Nature has a kind of literal authority precisely because she is not one of man's institutions. She serves as the location of values which are real insofar as they are not human creations. She is exemplary" (1977, p. 138). He cites by way of proof Thoreau's exhortation "If we would restore mankind . . . let us first be as simple and as well as Nature ourselves." We are told to spend at least one day living as "deliberately as Nature," and there are various other places where Nature is set out as a model for man to emulate.

But truth will out, and there is a darker side to Nature, a side which man must overcome if he is to be a Christian, to have that spark of divinity that sets him above the beasts. "If you would avoid unclean-ness," Thoreau tells us, "work earnestly, though it be at cleaning a stable. Nature is hard to overcome, but she must be overcome. What avails it that you are Christian, if you are not purer than the heathen, if you deny yourself no more, if you are not more religious?" (pp. 198–99). He is speaking, of course, of chastity and sensuality. Not surprisingly, when it comes to Nature as sexually female, then she must be overcome. These passions seem to be a part of Nature that, in contrast to the rest of Nature, rests within man, rather than man within it. And so the binary opposition breaks down here, too. Nature is both all that is not me and something within me. (An interesting sidelight that the feminist critic will note is how the man's sexual desire for a woman is imagined in terms of an alien, specifically female, nature that resides within him. Thus the male psyche subtly blames woman for his desire for her.)

Reading the text this way, the deconstructivist critic demonstrates that although the existence of real women is all but completely repressed in Thoreau's text on man, nevertheless a controlling metaphor of the text depends on defining man in specifically gendered terms against a female Nature, which he must ultimately overcome. Thus the concept of female is essential to Thoreau's meaning. This leaves the feminist/deconstructivist with a dilemma: while the feminist critic can argue that *Walden* is not, as so many scholars assume, universal, for it excludes women, the deconstructivist critic is left with the reinscription of the idea of woman into the text. Real women and their real lives may have slipped Thoreau's mind, but the text could not exist without the notion of female, that is, something opposite in sex to man against which he can define his existence.

## Reader-Response Theory and *Walden*

I promised early in this essay to include reader-response theory, and here is where it becomes appropriate for the feminist teacher whose task it is to guide students through difficult texts. If the experience of women is absent from a text, if woman is not included in Thoreau's discussion of what it is to be human, what is the woman reader to do? If *man* and *mankind* are always male, then she cannot, as her male peers can, be one of the students learning at Thoreau's feet. For instance, Thoreau complains that "The man who independently plucked the fruits when he was hungry is become a farmer; and he who stood under a tree for shelter, a housekeeper. . . . We have built for this world a family mansion, and for the next a family tomb. The best works of art are the expression of man's struggle to free himself from this condition" (p. 33). Here it is again, as in "Rip Van Winkle" and in so much of American literature—the family and home as symbol of that which keeps man from being independent, an artist, human. This is extremely painful to young readers, especially those just emerging into adulthood and making decisions about marriage and family. The young woman is forced into a position of blaming herself for entrapping her man, and the young man is encouraged to believe that she is. The woman is also excluded from the possibility of being an artist herself; in fact, any student who wants a family is told that (s)he must struggle against that desire in order to create art.

We can thus see some points at which readers of both genders can be subtly swayed by the text. But the woman reader especially has no place to locate herself in Thoreau's text. She must, therefore, as Judith Fetterley tells us, resist it even as she reads. She must assert herself at every exclusion; at every moment in the text where her experience is denied or denigrated she must talk back to the text or lose her status as a human being. It is a very difficult and painful task to perform, more so if done within the sponsorship of a literary establishment that requires her to suspend her disbelief willingly or else to be accused of willfully misunderstanding the text.

Here is where the feminist teacher must guide and support the student in a resisting reading of the text. Instead of requiring her to suspend disbelief, to go along with the text and therefore to say that it is a universal truth that all artists are men and that all good artists must break away from the ever-entrapping female, the teacher encourages her to counter it with her own intuitive truths. The wise reader knows that there was never a golden age in which people needed no shelter but a tree, no food but fruit—always there were babies to feed and shelter and protect, always there were families. In resisting the text this way, the feminist reader unmasks it as a document profoundly affected by structures of gender, a text that often espouses a somewhat narrow, incomplete—rather than universal—truth about human life.

This does not mean that we should stop teaching *Walden*. Much of what Thoreau says seems to have enduring value for men (and, after all, nearly half our student population is men), and much has value for all people. Further, of course, we greatly admire Thoreau's rhetorical skill. The point is to make overt those presently hidden assumptions that denigrate or exclude women. All of us have been brought up in a social system profoundly affected by gender roles that privilege men over women, and all of our cultural artifacts, if read attentively, will reveal the effects of that system. Thoreau is not alone here. Further, deconstructivists tell us, language depends on a system of meaning that is both culturally determined and unstable. All texts, like all thoughts and all people, are limited. To say that *Walden*'s truths are not entire and perfect and universal is to accuse Thoreau of nothing more than being human, to notice that his language functions in the way of all language and that his attitudes are formed by the prevailing structures of his culture. And reader-response criticism tells us that all evaluations are based on subjective opinion; there is no such thing as an unbiased, objective reading of a text. Why, then, should women be forced to read as men (blacks as white, poor as rich) or else to be told that to object to Thoreau on grounds of gender, race, or class is to misread the text? Let us not, as Barbara Johnson says humanistic critics do, stop reading when the text stops saying what it ought to have said. Let us seek the fullest, most accurate reading of a text that we can. In that way we will serve our students by revealing how structures of gender, race, and class influence our lives and our culture, and thereby start them on their journeys of growth and change.

### Notes

1. It seems evident to me that Thoreau's "we" also does not include non-white men or men not of genteel birth. The text can, I am sure, be

deconstructed on lines of race and class as well, though that will not be my effort here.

2. I recognize that this is a simplification of Emerson's statement, which claims that even one's body—and hence one's sex—is Nature, rather than me. But a feminist deconstructive reading of Emerson would, I suspect, quickly tease out the inconsistencies of such a claim.

## References

Cavell, Stanley. 1972. *The Senses of Walden.* New York: Viking.

Fetterley, Judith. 1978. *The Resisting Reader: A Feminist Approach to American Fiction.* Bloomington: Indiana University Press.

Johnson, Barbara. 1987. "A Hound, a Bay Horse, and a Turtle Dove: Obscurity in *Walden.*" In *A World of Difference.* Baltimore: Johns Hopkins University Press.

————. 1985. "Teaching Deconstructively." In *Writing and Reading Differently,* edited by G. Douglas Atkins and Michael L. Johnson, 140–48. Lawrence: University Press of Kansas.

Lane, Lauriat, Jr., ed. 1964. *Approaches to Walden.* San Francisco: Wadsworth.

Michaels, Walter Benn. 1977. "*Walden*'s False Bottoms." In *Glyph 1,* 132–39. Baltimore: Johns Hopkins University Press.

Thoreau, Henry David. 1950 [1854]. *Walden.* In *Walden and Other Writings.* New York: Modern Library.

————. 1950 [1849]. *A Week on the Concord and Merrimack Rivers.* In *Walden and Other Writings.* New York: Modern Library.

*Webster's Ninth New Collegiate Dictionary.* 1984. Springfield, Mass.: Merriam-Webster, Inc.

Woloch, Nancy. 1984. *Women and the American Experience.* New York: Alfred A. Knopf.

# 10 "Professor, Why Are You Wasting Our Time?": Teaching Jacobs's *Incidents in the Life of a Slave Girl*

Warren Rosenberg

Warren Rosenberg has been teaching English since 1970 at a variety of levels and schools—both full- and part-time, in high schools, community colleges, and four-year institutions. He is now an associate professor at Wabash College in Crawfordsville, Indiana, a small (800 students) liberal arts college for men. Wabash is a pre-professional institution with a student-teacher ratio of 11:1 and therefore a strong emphasis on teaching and one-to-one contact. Historical coverage remains at the core of its English department offerings. Professor Rosenberg teaches American literature to 1900, composition, ethnic literature, black literature, literature and film, and women's studies.

Like many of us, Professor Rosenberg "realized that [his] pedagogy was operating years behind [his] current scholarly and theoretical interests, and that non-canonical as well as canonical works need to be taught using the full range of contemporary critical approaches." Professor Rosenberg's essay evolved from ideas in conflict, conflict drawn from his research, his classes, and the Summer Institutes.

One of five members of the English faculty (all male), Professor Rosenberg has "compensated for the absence of women in the classroom by choosing texts by and about women and encouraging students to read them with empathy and a high level of gender consciousness." He is now "working in the classroom and in [his] scholarly writing to focus feminist critical analysis on 'male' texts and ways of knowing."

> *I see clearly, now, not only certain ways in which theory can help us solve curricular and pedagogical problems; I see also how teaching can help theory pose and elaborate those problems. I see that teaching and theory are always implicated in one another.*
>
> —Robert Scholes, *Textual Power*

I, like many of my colleagues, have been struggling for a number of years to reconcile my evolving scholarly interest in the issue of canon formation and expansion and my immediate practical need to teach a survey course in American literature to 1900. I must choose certain texts and exclude others within a departmental context that labels mine one of six "core" courses, four of which all English majors must take and be examined on in a written and oral senior comprehensive exam. The course is also seen by advisors as a useful introductory literature course for freshmen and sophomores, and students themselves see it as "safe," for most of them have had what looks like a very similar course in high school. In fact, the course as I taught it for years was virtually identical in form and content to the one taught in most American high schools, although I prided myself on teaching the works with greater sophistication—by virtue, no doubt, of my doctorate in the field. All the familiar names were there in the expected chronological order and under the standard period rubrics—the Puritans (Winthrop, Bradstreet, Taylor, Edwards), the Colonials (Franklin, de Crevecoeur, Jefferson, Paine), the Transcendentalists (Emerson, Thoreau), the Romantics (Poe, Hawthorne, Melville), and the Realists (Whitman, Dickinson, James, Twain, Crane). Since the books which had formed my view of American literature—Matthiessen's *American Renaissance,* Feidelson's *Symbolism and American Literature,* Chase's *The American Novel and Its Tradition*—logically supported (because they actually created) this canon, the imperatives to keep the syllabus as it had been handed to me were formidable.

Then I began to read those critics Frederick Crews has recently labeled "The New Americanists": Judith Fetterley, Annette Kolodny, Sacvan Bercovitch, Nina Baym, Jane Tompkins, Henry Louis Gates, Jr., Werner Sollors, and Paul Lauter, among others, who excited me with the possibility of opening what had seemed to be a closed literary world. By initially deciding to teach Harriet Jacobs's *Incidents in the Life of a Slave Girl* (1861) and Kate Chopin's *The Awakening* (1899), admittedly only two new writers out of twenty, I felt the exhilaration of making the same break for freedom that, as I had been pointing out for years to my students, was a major theme in American literature. But like Hester and Dimmesdale when they finally got out into the forest, or Huck on Jackson's Island, or Christopher Newman in Paris, freedom felt very good for a while but then rapidly turned into something less appealing. There were shadows in the forest, and unforeseen snags in the apparently open river.

A major snag for my students, a generally well-prepared all-male group primarily from Indiana, has been Jacobs's book, especially the way I first introduced it in 1984. Chopin's novel was a departure from the rest of the syllabus as well—the only novel written by a woman, with a plot that revolves around women's lives and issues (child rearing, social interaction, romance), and a style that can seem lyrically excessive at times. But the book is also familiar enough in style and content to be accessible to twentieth-century readers. It has a crafted plot with a dramatic conclusion, familiar character types, traditional symbols; it is, in short, what everyone recognizes as literature. Jacobs's book, on the other hand, a hybrid of slave narrative and "sentimental" novel, apparently inconsistent in style and structure, the work of a nonprofessional, created a mini–student rebellion. Reactions ranged from polite condescension to outright hostility. One extremely bright student spoke for others, I am sure, when he asked me in class, "Professor, why are you wasting our time?" With my back against the blackboard literally and figuratively, I asked myself whether, in fact, I was.

After that first unsettling experience I briefly considered dropping *Incidents* from the course, but I have kept it and its presence has forced me to modify how I teach. As a result of my struggles to teach this book effectively, I now realize that the current desire to introduce non-canonical texts into our still predominantly canonical courses must be accompanied by a revisioning of our theory and pedagogy. Teaching Jacobs's book has both instigated and helped in this revisioning process by leading me and my students to a deeper questioning of what constitutes literature in general and "American" literature in particular.

I first read of Jacobs's book in Paul Lauter's (1983) *Reconstructing American Literature: Courses, Syllabi, Issues*. This extremely useful collection proved that at least in selected classrooms instructors were already opening up the canon. As Lauter notes in his excellent introduction, traditional survey courses were "simply not truthful, nor professionally current. The pictures they present to students of the American literary imagination or of American life and thought are woefully incomplete and inaccurate" (p. xii). My positive response to this view was instinctive, but my training had blinded me to its broader theoretical implications. After all, "integration" had been the social rallying cry of my upbringing in the fifties and sixties. Yet my academic literary training was grounded in the implicit elitism which stood behind "New Critical Formalism," a graduate school label that had no real "critical" determinacy for me until much later. If the power of a theory is attested to by its invisibility, New Critical Formalism was very powerful indeed. Otherwise I would have attended more carefully to Lauter's warnings that "while formalist *explication de texte* was effective both as a classroom tactic and for exploring a great many powerful texts, it provided no useful basis for approaching that great body of literature that placed a premium on simplicity, transparency, and emotional directness—from American Indian chants and spirituals to Langston Hughes and Gwendolyn Brooks, from *Uncle Tom's Cabin* to

*Daughter of Earth*" (p. xviii). Although now I believe that these texts will bear more formalist analysis than Lauter allows, they cannot be approached in that way alone.

In 1984 I learned this lesson the hard way by merely putting *Incidents* into my syllabus between Melville's "Benito Cereno" and Whitman's poetry and waiting to see what would happen. Obviously I foresaw the students making connections between Melville's story about a slave uprising and Jacobs's about slave resistance, and I hoped that they would carry Jacobs's theme of the struggle for freedom into their reading of Whitman. Otherwise, feeling apprehensive about the student reception to the slave narrative as literature, I intended to teach the book as I would any other fictional text, even though in the first line of her preface Jacobs writes, "Reader, be assured this narrative is no fiction" (p. 1). To protect her own identity and the identities of those who helped her escape, Jacobs does create names for all of the "characters" in her story, and calls herself Linda Brent in the text. And in many ways she does become a character, both narrator of and actor in her own life story. I chose to stress the larger fiction-like aspects of the book—the dramatic conflict between Dr. Flint, the evil master, and Linda, the attractive mulatta; her seven-year confinement in a tiny crawlspace from which she could see her children but not reveal herself to them; her eventual escape. I was so eager for the class to read the book as an exciting novel that I even shortened the text, assigning only through chapter XXX, "Northward Bound," cutting the final forty pages set in the North because I saw that section as anticlimactic. Only in subsequent semesters did I realize how important the ending is for Jacobs's purposes. Because of the Fugitive Slave Law, Linda Brent was not really free when she crossed the Mason-Dixon line, and Jacobs wanted her Northern readers to suffer over her frequent hairbreadth escapes when she was already living in New York and working for an influential family (Mary and Nathaniel Parker Willis). Only when her employer buys her and gives her her freedom, related in the last chapter, does Brent with bitter sarcasm bring her narrative to an end: "A human being *sold* in the free city of New York! The bill of sale is on record, and future generations will learn from it that women were articles of traffic in New York, late in the nineteenth century of the Christian religion" (p. 200).

In retrospect, my anxiety over the text's generic acceptability seems odd, given that the first third of the standard survey course is studded with works students would not generally define as literature: Puritan sermons and diary entries, Franklin's *Autobiography,* letters from Jefferson and Madison, Emerson's essays. But I did not make a case for *Incidents* on the grounds that our definition of literature should be broadened. I did not make any case at all, because my experience with the canonical works had made me lazy about the need for such justification. Of course we had talked somewhat about the literariness of a sermon, letter, or essay, about the historical and cultural reasons these modes seemed to predominate, but the power of the authors' names established legitimacy. Reading Franklin may not have provided as many literary pleasures as reading Hawthorne, but the students believed it was an equally important use of their time. This sense of inherent legitimacy covered stylistic "problems" as well, and might account for their willingness to accept Cooper's stilted diction but not Jacobs's.

But who was Harriet Jacobs (Linda Brent)? This turned out to be a critical question, when the terms *author* and *authority* were seen as one. If she had been a slave, then could she have written her book? How much help did she get from professional author Lydia Maria Child? Despite Child's introduction, which argues that her revisions were "trifling," and despite an appendix with two letters corroborating Jacobs's authorship, when I first taught the text students tended to doubt that Jacobs could have written her own book. In this, they were in line with historian John W. Blassingame (1976), who in his influential *Slave Testimony: Two Centuries of Letters, Speeches, Interviews and Autobiographies* also doubts her authorship. I was not then familiar with Jean Fagin Yellin's (1981) discovery of a cache of Jacobs's letters which match her book stylistically and thus "authenticate" her having written it, nor was Yellin's new edition of *Incidents,* which includes an excellent introduction, notes, and supporting documents, available. Even if Jacobs had written her own book, some of my students still argued, is it worth our time to read the work of an unknown writer? Who are we leaving out? Following the densely structured and linguistically assured "Benito Cereno" in the syllabus, Jacobs's book looked simplistic, episodic, uneven, unstructured; presented without any explanatory defense, she didn't have a chance against the major canonical writers. Students wondered why she broke up her narrative with chapters VII, IX, XII, and XIII on slave life, Nat Turner's rebellion, and slavery and the church—embedded and apparently momentum-killing tracts. By cutting the text, I was also sending them the message that, unlike *The Scarlet Letter,* this narrative did not have overall structural coherence. Many students also winced at the language Jacobs used to describe one of the most compelling incidents in the book, her decision to enter into a sexual relationship with a prominent white neighbor rather than submit to the advances of her master:

> With all these thoughts revolving in my mind, and seeing no
> other way of escaping the doom I so much dreaded, I made a
> headlong plunge. Pity me, and pardon me, O virtuous reader!
> You never knew what it is to be a slave; to be entirely unprotected
> by law or custom; to have the laws reduce you to the condition
> of a chattel, entirely subject to the will of another. You never
> exhausted your ingenuity in avoiding the snares, and eluding the
> power of a hated tyrant; you never shuddered at the sound of his
> footsteps, and trembled within hearing of his voice. (p. 55)

My male students—would women respond differently?—had difficulty with the "O virtuous reader" apostrophe, the "snares," and the
general shuddering and trembling, concluding that this was a nineteenth-
century Harlequin romance, not a "legitimate" work of literature. I do
recall that first year trying to create some context for this style by
referring to the popular American woman writers—Stowe, Sedgwick,
Warner, Cummins—whom Hawthorne condemned so roundly as that
"damn'd mob of scribbling women" (Freibart and White, p. 356). Of
course, these unfamiliar names meant nothing to my students, and I
knew them only slightly better at that time through Nina Baym's (1978)
*Woman's Fiction: A Guide to Novels by and about Women in America
1820–1870*. The question of whether popular female writers could
produce anything of value never came up, but the issue of whether a
slave narrative was literature at all was raised. The book is so relentlessly
propagandistic; Jacobs so frequently breaks into the narrative to address
the reader directly and plead for an end to slavery that the effect of
her story seems deliberately undercut. Aren't morals in literature to be
more subtly delivered? We moved on to Whitman with a universal
sense of relief.

Although many interesting questions were raised and much often-
heated discussion was generated, I did not want to duplicate this
experience in future semesters. Both Jacobs and I were on the defensive,
and the great majority of students that first semester were justifiably
not convinced she should be taught at all in a literature class. The
resistance I met to introducing the text led me to examine the existing
canon more critically, and I learned in practice then what Gerald Graff
(1986) and others have been arguing currently: that "all teachers of
literature operate on theories, whether they choose to examine these
theories or not" (p. 41). Consequently, I sought, for the first time in
my teaching, theoretical justification for what I was doing. Because the
revisionist critics I had been reading theorized differently about American literature, I was able to see that there *was* a theory or, at least, a
less consciously formulated ideology, behind the canon I had been
teaching. This realization necessarily changed my classroom approach,

for knowing that there are conflicting theories about what constitutes American literature, I could not justify keeping my students from knowing about, nor from participating in, the exciting critical debate. To help them, I would have to familiarize myself with as much contemporary critical theory—feminist, new historical, structural or intertextual, and deconstructive—as time and patience would allow— and somehow revise my survey course, assuming that for the time being survey courses will continue to hold their powerful positions, in a more theoretically self-conscious way.

Inspired by the kind of critical questioning of the canon feminist critics have been engaged in in recent years, I now begin my survey course by encouraging students to question the syllabus I distribute. After listing on the board all of the writers they are familiar with, I ask them what these writers have in common. When we have agreed that they are primarily white Protestant males from the Northeast (most students need to be told precisely where, and are often amazed that Hawthorne lived a literal stone's throw from Emerson and was a friend of Melville), we have begun a critique that will ultimately pave the way for Jacobs.

We discuss how canons are created, as well as the extreme recentness of the American canon itself, and consider in detail Nina Baym's (1985) "Melodramas of Beset Manhood: How Theories of American Fiction Exclude Women Authors." Initially, I summarized Baym's arguments for the class. I had always been uncomfortable about giving critical essays to introductory-level classes, and only occasionally did so in advanced classes. More recently, however, I have distributed the essay itself and asked for a one-page précis and response. I was pleased with how well the students understood the essay and with how their reading it enhanced class discussion, and I saw that my previous reluctance was based on the self-serving formalist concept that theory was a distraction to the "real" work of close textual analysis. And although I believe the emphasis on primary texts should be maintained, especially in introductory courses, allowing students to read critical essays gives them a greater sense of empowerment and consequently of commitment to the course as a whole as they come to understand why certain texts are being assigned and others not.

### The American (Male) Myth of Freedom

Baym's essay is particularly useful to me because I have structured my survey around the question "What is American about American literature?" and she clearly shows me how my own answer to that question has been shaped by critics of the forties and fifties, who, according to Baym, "used sophisticated New Critical close-reading techniques to identify a myth of America which had nothing to do with the classical fictionist's task of chronicling probable people in recognizable social situations" (p. 71). Baym describes this myth as positing an "essential" American who seeks a romantic other place where *he* (the figure is generally male) can be alone away from the destructiveness of society (often represented by women) and "inscribe, unhindered, his own destiny and his own nature" (p. 71). In addition, this desire for escape is almost always embodied in a text that itself formally rebels against societal norms. Clearly such a definition of Americanness and American literature would fit most of the major canonical figures and exclude almost all of the writing by women and minorities in the nineteenth century, which tended to be more conventional in subject and form. Thus, Baym illustrates how white male critics have universalized their particular value system through their control, until only recently, of the scholarly and academic world.

Interestingly, Jacobs's book also embodies this American myth of freedom. Linda obviously seeks to escape from slavery. We might even see her as a solitary figure resisting society as Natty, Thoreau, and Bartleby do, separating herself in a crawlspace for seven years to maintain her individuality. But to force her text into this narrow, essentially masculine view of the "American" myth would be to ignore the reality the canonical figures often seek to repress. For Linda Brent is totally connected to her milieu by family ties, by the Fugitive Slave Law, and by slavery itself. There really is no escape and, in fact, Brent does not want to escape from the oppressive "feminized" home the canonical figures ostensibly flee. A home is the very thing she wants. Even after she is legally free, in the next-to-last paragraph of her novel, Brent says, "The dream of my life is not yet realized. I do not sit with my children in a home of my own. I still long for a hearthstone of my own, however humble" (p. 201). Brent's dreams and concerns are clearly not the same as those of the male canonical figures. At least, they are not the dreams these figures foreground. (For example, despite Huck's protests for wanting to light out for the Territory, there is his frequently noted desire for a real home.)

We can see dramatically how much the canon has been based on a particular male perspective and not on a universal perspective if we note the anthologizing of the *Narrative of the Life of Frederick Douglass* (1845) and its apparent thematic compatibility with the standard authors. (Jacobs had no doubt read Douglass in her years working in abolitionist offices in Rochester, New York.) When I ask my students to compare excerpts from Douglass with Jacobs's book, however, they note the dramatic difference between the slave experiences of males and females. Particularly in the chapters on Douglass's battle with Covey, the Negro breaker, they see the male emphasis on physical resistance and dominance when the "fighting madness" comes on Douglass. As he concludes, "I was a changed being after that fight. I was nothing before; I was a man now. It inspired me with a renewed determination to be a free man" (p. 968). Linda Brent, on the other hand, can only physically resist Dr. Flint's sexual advances up to a point and then she must use intellectual and social stratagems. Unlike Douglass, who is often shifted about and has no firm connection to any one place, Brent, her parents, and her grandparents are an integral part of one town for almost their entire lives. Brent's grandmother is a freed slave who has considerable standing in the community. When she can, Brent uses Flint's concern for his public image and desire for continuing good relations with those around him to keep him from raping her. Ultimately, though, she relies on her wits and circumstances to keep him at bay. Once, after escaping him and finding a hiding place, she sees Flint pass in the street and reflects, "Anxious as I was, I felt a gleam of satisfaction when I saw him. Thus far I had outwitted him, and I triumphed over it. Who can blame slaves for being cunning? They are constantly compelled to resort to it. It is the only weapon of the weak and oppressed against the strength of their tyrants" (pp. 100–101). Obviously, Douglass did not have to worry about sexual violation, and he even seems detached from his whippings. Terrible as they no doubt were, his mater-of-fact descriptions ("I remained with Mr. Covey one year, and during the first six months there I was whipped, either with sticks or a cowhide whip, every week" [p. 962]), give the impression that his essential self remained unviolated. And, significantly, he did not have to worry about children, Brent's most profound "link to life."

Her children are the focus of Brent's life. Although she sometimes seems to be illustrating Edna Pointellier's dictum that she would give her life but not her self for her children, Brent does put their freedom first. Her escape into hiding was part of a stratagem to keep them from being sent to the plantation. The link to her children makes certain scenes in the book—like Brent's having to watch silently from her hideaway as her son is brutally attacked by a dog—emotionally powerful. In discussing this theme, students can make connections to Hester Prynne in *The Scarlet Letter* and to Edna in *The Awakening*. Children limit the freedom of these women with positive and negative effects, just as Brent's do. In fact, the complexity of the mother-child relationship which underlies the positive view of the nineteenth-century home establishes a useful corrective to the valorization of the unencumbered male. Where is Emerson's family in his essays? Does Thoreau really care about anyone but himself? Should we condemn Dimmesdale as much for his failings as a father as we do for his hypocrisy as a minister? Since teaching Jacobs I have even suggested to students that Melville's "Bartleby" can be read as a critique of this male myth as the lawyer tries to reconcile his parental feelings for Bartleby with the demands of his office life. Bartleby had made the office into his home, but this confuses the simple and rigid distinctions between the male and female spheres that the lawyer feels compelled to maintain. When the lawyer finally realizes the problem and invites Bartleby to his real home, it is too late.

By contradicting and by revealing contradictions within the prevailing myth of American literature, Jacobs's book emphasizes that all books mythologize real life and do so for particular purposes and for distinct audiences. Whether we value any given text, then, depends as much on whether we feel it speaks to us (or to our internalized myth) as it does on any intrinsic value the text may have. Such a realization naturally forces us outside the works themselves because we can no longer assume the universal validity of the theory that had shaped this particular form of the canon. Once outside the works, we find ourselves almost inevitably examining the historical, social, and cultural milieu which had produced the suddenly more complex literary world we have rediscovered.

## Applying a New-Historical Approach

With students predisposed from the first day to see canon formation as a human, sociohistorical process and not as divinely ordered fiat, we can, as a first step, engage each text in the survey from the perspective of how it aligns with the myth outlined by Baym or how it emerges from an alternate reality with differing values. This sets the stage for a "new-historical" approach to texts that will tend, sometimes disturbingly for the students, to equalize each's importance. The approach is "new" historical in that we can no more assume a stable, unexamined historical context than we can assume a stable canon. Although attempting to place a literary text within its sociohistorical milieu is itself a revolt from New Critical Formalism, if one does not also question the historical theory one employs, a new myopia will obtain. As Cathy N. Davidson (1986) argues in her important new-historicist reading of early American fiction, *Revolution and the Word: The Rise of the Novel in America,*

All history is choice, discourse that begins with the very questions the historian chooses to ask (or not ask) of his or her own version of the past. Fiction cannot be simply "fit into historical context," as if context were some platonic pigeonhole and all that is dark or obscure in the fiction is illuminated when the text is finally slipped into the right slot. If we argue that history provides the context, then who or what, we must also ask, provides the history? . . . The relationship [between fiction and history] runs two ways, which is to say that the connections between the history of story and the story of history are multiple and complex. (p. 82)

To appreciate Jacobs's *Incidents,* students need to know more than what the Mason-Dixon line and the Fugitive Slave Law of 1850 were, facts they can get from the text itself. Davidson's use of the term *discourse* is central here because it implies a vital relationship between the writer and her world that can only be understood through an historically grounded questioning of audience, purpose, and reception.

For students to ask these questions, they do need to learn some literary history that will certainly challenge some of their most deeply held prejudices. As Jane Tompkins (1985) argues, extending Baym's position in her important essay "Sentimental Power: *Uncle Tom's Cabin* and the Politics of Literary History," "twentieth-century critics have taught generations of students to equate popularity with debasement, emotionality with ineffectiveness, religiosity with fakery, domesticity with triviality, and all of these, implicitly, with womanly inferiority" (p. 82). Because Jacobs clearly intended her book to be read, in part, as a "sentimental" novel, the embodiment of a critically debased tradition, Tompkins's resurrection of the genre can help students appreciate how a nineteenth-century reader would have responded. Here we can see the merging of the new-historical approach with a structural or intertextual analysis. The novel-like chapter headings, the direct appeals to the reader, the tearful separations from family, the references to God and religion, the emphasis on details of home life, all of which are found in *Incidents* as well as in *Uncle Tom's Cabin,* can be seen not as flaws but as necessary elements in an immensely popular genre, one that Tompkins believes was ultimately designed to wrest power from men.

Although the anthology I have used most recently, *The Harper American Literature* (1987), does not have any excerpts from popular women's novels (and unfortunately I have found it too expensive for students to order Lucy Freibert and Barbara White's anthology *Hidden Hands* [1985], a collection of excerpts from these works), I do assign a chapter from *Uncle Tom's Cabin* to illustrate its stylistic and structural similarity to Jacobs's book. I also hand out a question sheet before students begin reading, one which encourages them to consider intended audience and authorial purpose, thus violating two formalist fallacies that had for years kept me from asking similar questions of canonical texts. Initial questions include the following: "How is reading Jacobs different from reading Hawthorne and Melville? In what ways is it similar?" "Although she writes that the book is a true narrative, in what ways does she manipulate the story to make it seem like a novel? Why might she do this?" "What is her purpose in writing the book?" "What is her intended audience? How do you know?" Such questions tend to place the book within its time, allowing students to begin to see that like Paine and Jefferson in the revolutionary period, Jacobs was writing to make things happen in the real world, not to create "high" art that would transcend that world. Her book was aimed primarily at a Northern white middle-class female audience who could be moved enough to support abolition and the war effort which was just beginning the year her book was published. Should these practical intentions make her work any less valuable as literature? Now, understanding the historical context, the class can at least discuss this question more equitably.

Continuing our new-historical/intertextual reading, we can evaluate *Incidents in the Life of a Slave Girl,* despite its strong resemblance to nineteenth-century women's fiction, as primarily a slave narrative, although a uniquely female version as our comparison to Douglass's narrative illustrated. Like the popular novels, in Tompkins's view of them at least, the slave narratives were written to move the emotions, effect moral change, and ultimately alter the existing social structure. In the same way that students need to be introduced to popular fiction of the period, they need to learn of the great popularity and importance of the hundreds of slave narratives being written at the same time. This genre, Theodore Parker believed, was the only "wholly indigenous and original" American literature (Davis and Gates 1985, p. xxi). And certainly most literary histories ignore the importance of the slave narrative to the development of literary realism. Here is history from the bottom up—not the voice of the Harvard-educated elite, or of a white Quaker poet imagining himself into the body of a slave woman (marvelous and earthy as Whitman can be), but the experience of slavery from the pen of a slave. After the question of authorship has been dealt with, this is the aspect of Jacobs's book that requires no sales job. The incidents themselves are gripping, although gripping in a different way from those Douglass relates in his *Narrative.*

As they compare Douglass and Jacobs, students also see how the pieces share some stylistic and structural elements, although without reading all of both texts or other texts they will miss some parallels. (I hope to include all of Douglass's narrative in future classes.) Once the "I was born . . ." openings, the early awareness of being slaves, the struggle for literacy, the mental and physical suffering, and the ultimate escape north are noted or pointed out, students can note structural similarities to earlier texts—Puritan diaries, Franklin's *Autobiography,* Mary Rowlandson's captivity narrative—and to future works like Richard Wright's *Black Boy,* Ellison's *Invisible Man,* and Walker's *The Color Purple.* Such intertextual awareness tends to increase the literary interest we have in a work that can be seen as part of a larger tradition or traditions.[1]

Although our attempts in class to find a comfortable generic category for Jacobs's book frequently lead us back to the uniqueness of the text, I am not expecting students to find some special status or "greatness" in the book to make it worthy of inclusion in the canon. Yet all of our new contextualizing and theorizing have not made the issue of value disappear. Rather, the issue has been recast. New Critical Formalism asks us to find some *inherent* value in the richness and complexity of a work's language, in its structural coherence, or in the way it modifies existing literary forms. Studying Jacobs shows us that such formal conventions cannot be evaluated in isolation from the social context that gives them meaning. So, for example, the apparent structural incongruities that bother readers—the interpolated chapters on apparently extraneous matters—might be seen not as flaws in what should be a seamless text, but as acts of aesthetic intention which have meaning and value that remain to be discovered. Valerie Smith's introduction to the Schomburg Library edition of *Incidents in the Life of a Slave Girl* attempts just such a deconstructive reading. Smith believes that Jacobs found neither the woman's novel nor the slave narrative sufficient for her needs: "By manipulating linguistic spaces—verbal equivalents analogous to the garret in which she hides for several years and from which she orchestrates her freedom—she interrogates the two genres and points out their inadequacy to her story" (p. xxxiii). Such a reading allows us to understand and value Jacobs's larger structural designs as well as her manipulation of the specific language she employs. We can see her use of melodramatic diction, personal revelation, dispassionate reportorial description, jeremiad-like appeals to the reader as, to use Kathleen Diffley's (1988) terms, intricate "formal tactics" employed because "the less favored the voice, the more resourceful it must be to make itself heard" (p. 7). Although Diffley's neo-formalist approach, her belief that "any maneuver in how a story gets told is worth attention, especially once we realize that language as a system is not completely self-referential" (p. 8), helps us better understand and value Jacobs's text, it applies to all literature. We, therefore, need not abandon all close textual analysis to appreciate non-canonical works.

My American literature survey students now generally tell me in class and in response papers that they see Jacobs's text as appropriate and even necessary to the course. More important, as I introduce more non-canonical texts, including anthologized and unanthologized Native American materials and more works by women, the sense of an hegemonic canon in whose shadow we are constantly working begins to dissipate. But perhaps because I am still rooted in an earlier mind-set, and no doubt because I see it as my professorial role, I continue to struggle with the shape of the course and wonder about its coherence. I am concerned by Peter Carafiol's (1988) recent assertion in *College English* that the canon breakers I have been following are pursuing a romantic impossibility by attempting to include *everything* as a reaction against historical exclusion. He sees their desire to open the canon as incompatible with their aim of writing a "coherent, integrated story about our literary past. . . . Americanists cannot have it both ways. Coherence means exclusivity, diversity means disorder" (p. 611).[2] At present in my survey course I have decided to tolerate a certain degree of incoherence of content in order to embrace a coherence of pedagogical goals and strategies. In their end-of-term paper assignments and on essay exams, I ask students to consider canonical and non-canonical texts together so they are in effect making coherence for themselves. But what primarily holds the class together is a kind of dialogic pedagogy operating each day and outlined to a large extent above. Wayne Booth (1986), in a *Critical Inquiry* essay, "Pluralism in the Classroom," argues that any time one introduces at least two distinct modes of inquiry in the class a sense of humility results that is a "prerequisite of all further learning." The point of the literature class is not to discover a single right reading (or right text, I would add), but to discover what "any one reading really amounts to. That discovery takes place within the dialogue of the classroom itself, and it suggests a final sense of pluralism in the classroom: the honoring of the plurality of human centers that any classroom holds" (p. 479). This pluralistic mode of learning can result from including diverse voices like Jacobs's in the literature class, and it stands, to my mind, as the ultimate rationale for their inclusion.

Yet, as I noted at the outset, external institutional and societal pressures to maintain the survey course and its traditional content persist. In a recent meeting, my small department reaffirmed the centrality of the core survey course to our curriculum. When we tried to agree on a comprehensive question for senior exams, however, we found the task virtually impossible; we had assumed a common ground that seems not to exist. Nationally, events like the resistance at Stanford to the inclusion of minority literature in their all-college humanities course and the formation of the ultra-conservative National Association of Scholars promise to keep feminists and other academic liberals struggling, at least for the immediate future. But in my classroom at least, retreat is neither desirable nor possible. Teaching Jacobs's *Incidents in the Life of a Slave Girl* has had a transforming effect. To conclude where I began, with an image from Robert Scholes, Jacobs has forced me and many of my students outside the "unquestioning march" of the traditional canon. And "to step outside the line of march," Scholes writes, "to scrutinize the device and see it as strange for the first time— defamiliarized, as the formalists put it—is to become, perforce, a theoretician" (p. 11). I strongly sense as I read my colleagues' work and hear and speak with them at conferences that now many are stepping outside the march together, which in the next decade should make transforming our teaching of literary studies a less isolating pursuit.

## Notes

1. See the essays by Olney, Stepto, and Baker in Davis and Gates (1985) on generic classification of slave narratives and their relationship to the American tradition. The place of the woman's slave narrative in the black female narrative tradition is explored in, among other places, Barbara Christian's *Black Women Novelists: The Development of a Tradition, 1892–1976* (Westport, Conn.: Greenwood Press, 1980), Mary Helen Washington's *Invented Lives: Narratives of Black Women, 1860–1960* (Garden City, N.Y.: Doubleday, 1987), and Hazel Carby's *Reconstructing Womanhood: The Emergence of the Afro-American Woman Novelist* (New York: Oxford University Press, 1987).
2. Although Carafiol's provocative and sometimes intemperate essay effectively describes the anxiety associated with canon revision, his either/or reduction of the struggle strikes me as escapist, especially at this time. His critique of the concept of "American" literature itself seems theoretically correct and logical given the terms of his argument, but to abandon the label entirely would be to ignore two hundred years of cultural history. I still find considering what is American about American literature a useful hermeneutical tool.

## References

Baym, Nina. 1985. "Melodramas of Beset Manhood: How Theories of American Literature Exclude Women Authors." In *The New Feminist*

*Criticism: Essays on Women, Literature, and Theory,* edited by Elaine Showalter, 63–80. New York: Pantheon.

———. 1978. *Woman's Fiction: A Guide to Novels by and about Women in America 1820–1870.* Ithaca: Cornell University Press.

Bercovitch, Sacvan, ed. 1986. *Reconstructing American Literature.* Cambridge: Harvard University Press.

Blassingame, John W. 1976. *Slave Testimony: Two Centuries of Letters, Speeches, Interviews and Autobiographies.* Baton Rouge: Louisiana State University Press.

Booth, Wayne. 1986. "Pluralism in the Classroom." *Critical Inquiry* 12, no. 3: 468–79.

Carafiol, Peter. 1988. "The Constraints of History: Revision and Revolution in American Literary Studies." *College English* 50, no. 6: 605–22.

Chase, Richard. 1957. *The American Novel and Its Tradition.* New York: Doubleday.

Crews, Frederick. 1988. "Whose American Renaissance?" *The New York Review of Books* 35, no. 16: 68–81.

Davidson, Cathy. 1986. *Revolution and the Word: The Rise of the Novel in America.* New York: Oxford University Press.

Davis, Charles, and Henry Louis Gates, Jr. 1985. *The Slave's Narrative.* New York: Oxford University Press.

Diffley, Kathleen. 1988. "Reconstructing the American Canon: E Pluribus Unum?" *The Journal of the Midwest Modern Language Association* 21, no. 2: 1–13.

Douglass, Frederick. 1987 [1854]. "The Life and Times of Frederick Douglass." In *The Harper American Literature,* edited by Donald McQuade. New York: Harper and Row.

Feidelson, Charles, Jr. 1953. *Symbolism and American Literature.* Chicago: University of Chicago Press.

Fetterley, Judith. 1978. *The Resisting Reader.* Bloomington: Indiana University Press.

Freibert, Lucy M., and Barbara A. White. 1985. *Hidden Hands: An Anthology of American Women Writers, 1790–1870.* New Brunswick: Rutgers University Press.

Graff, Gerald. 1986. *"Taking Cover in Coverage."* In *Profession 86,* 41–45. New York: Modern Language Association.

Hawthorne, Nathaniel. Letter to William Tincknor. 19 January 1855. In Freibert and White, 356.

Jacobs, Harriet. 1987. *Incidents in the Life of a Slave Girl, Written by Herself,* edited by Jean Fagan Yellin. Cambridge: Harvard University Press.

Kolodny, Annette. 1984. *The Land before Her: Fantasy and Experience of the American Frontiers, 1630–1860.* Chapel Hill: University of North Carolina Press.

———. 1975. *The Lay of the Land: Metaphor as Experience and History in American Life and Letters.* Chapel Hill: University of North Carolina Press.

Lauter, Paul. 1983. *Reconstructing American Literature: Courses, Syllabi, Issues.* New York: The Feminist Press.

McQuade, Donald, ed. 1987. *The Harper American Literature.* New York: Harper and Row.

Matthiessen, F. O. 1941. *American Renaissance.* New York: Oxford University Press.

Scholes, Robert. 1985. *Textual Power.* New Haven: Yale University Press.

Smith, Valerie. 1988. Introduction. Harriet Jacobs's *Incidents in the Life of a Slave Girl,* xxvii–xl. New York: Oxford University Press.

Sollors, Werner. 1986. *Beyond Ethnicity: Consent and Descent in American Culture.* New York: Oxford University Press.

Tompkins, Jane. 1985. "Sentimental Power: *Uncle Tom's Cabin* and the Politics of Literary History." In *The New Feminist Criticism,* edited by Elaine Showalter, 81–104. New York: Pantheon.

Yellin, Jean Fagin. 1981. "Written by Herself: Harriet Jacobs's Slave Narrative." *American Literature* 53 (Nov.): 479–86.

# 11 Delivering on the Promise of Liberal Education

Joel Wingard

Joel Wingard is an associate professor of English at Moravian College, in Bethlehem, Pennsylvania, where he has been on the faculty for eight years. He has taught also at Louisiana State University and at Doane College, in Crete, Nebraska. At Moravian, Professor Wingard teaches each semester a section of freshman writing and a section of the introductory literature course he describes in his essay. In addition, he teaches courses in twentieth-century British literature and in newswriting. He advises the student newspaper, directs interns in journalism, and advises English/journalism majors.

Moravian College is a coeducational independent liberal arts college associated with the Moravian Church in America. The sixth oldest college in America, it traces its ancestry to Moravia (now part of Czechoslovakia) and the educational vision of John Amos Comenius. The college's 1,200 students come chiefly from Pennsylvania and northern New Jersey.

In more than a decade of teaching at liberal arts colleges, I have taught many introductory literature courses, courses required as part of that set intended to broaden students' intellectual and cultural horizons and liberalize or make free their thinking. Such literature courses also exist to acquaint students with the major works of the canonized writers in one literary tradition or another—American, British, Western—or in one or more of the usual genres—fiction, poetry, drama. For instance, the catalog of Moravian College says, "The liberal education program is designed to provide a student with a frame of reference for formal studies, to assist in the integration of course work, and *to enhance the qualities of judgment and freedom of mind that distinguish a liberally educated person*" (emphasis mine). The catalog goes on to say that the liberal education program requires students to take a literature course because "through the study of literature [students gain] knowledge of the imaginative uses of language with which the creative writer expresses humanity's noblest thoughts and deepest emotions" (pp. 23, 25). Being trained as a literary historian and formalist critic myself, and sharing

149

those orientations tacitly with my English department colleagues, I have always assumed a formalist model of reading in these courses. I have further assumed that close reading (the analysis of a text's formal features and subsequent interpretation to discover meaning) exercises students' critical thinking skills. I have equated the exercise of critical thinking skills with intellectual liberalization, and I know I have not been in the least bit peculiar in that thinking.

At the same time, I have always felt some degree of dissatisfaction with these courses. As required introductory courses, they draw students with different backgrounds and with different motivations. Some are nascent English majors who have a grounding in the canon and in the New Critical methods that their high school teachers have been taught and in turn teach. They are eager to read and discuss literature. Most are not nascent English majors, however, and this large group often becomes lost or disinterested, feeling that there is a "correct" knowledge of literature that is the province of English majors and teachers. After midterm, active participation and real involvement in the class has shrunk to the handful of English majors and perhaps a few other hardy types. Attendance declines, and the experience—for both students and teacher—becomes a dreary one of making it through the term to the final. In the process, most students' critical thinking skills are stifled, not exercised, as their learning goals shift from liberalization to limitation: they want to know only the "correct" answers so they can get passing grades on their papers and the final exam. Recognizing this, I had always focused blame on students and on myself: students for not being willing or able to exercise their critical thinking skills; myself for tiring of trying to lead the unwilling or unable and consequently falling back on inculcating "correct" analyses and interpretations. I had never, however, seen a problem in the critical assumptions and model for reading implicit in my approach to these courses.

## A Different Method

Since participating in the 1987 NCTE Summer Institute on recent critical theory, I have twice taught an introductory literature course called "The Experience of Literature," in which I put some of those critical approaches to use, finding reader-response and cultural criticism ideally suited to this kind of course in a liberal arts college environment. In this course, students have maintained their motivation to learn in a liberalizing way throughout the term and have often performed in ways that demonstrate their liberalization. What had heretofore been the goal, seldom met, has become the *method,* whereby the goal is met *as* it is practiced. Students of all majors, not just English, find they can be successful as readers and writers in terms other than arriving at "correct" (i.e., teacher-sanctioned) analyses and interpretations. Their intimidation in the face of literature is reduced as their empowerment as readers is realized. Their writing has a chance to be much more genuine, meaningful to themselves and satisfying to read—not just a wooden and usually unsuccessful academic exercise. And literature has a real chance to do what I and liberal educators in general have always supposed it to do: liberate students' minds.

In the preface to his book *The Meaning of a Liberal Education* (1926), Everett Dean Martin, then-director of Cooper Union, avers that liberal education

> is a spiritual revaluation of human life. Its task is to *reorient* the individual, to enable him to take a richer and more significant view of his experiences, to place him above and not within the system of his beliefs and ideals. . . . [A] liberal education [is] the kind of education which sets the mind free from the servitude of the crowd and from vulgar self-interests. (p. viii)

My syllabus for English 109, "The Experience of Literature," tells students that the course will

> introduce you to the three major genres of literature—fiction, poetry, drama—and to the acts of reading and responding to literature. . . . [I]t aims to improve your reading skills, to make you more aware of what is involved in reading a text, to strengthen your written expression and to exercise your intellect.

I will proceed by taking up those aims one at a time. First, however, I will provide a little background as to how I came to make the claims I have made so far.

I will not testify to a sudden conversion in a flash of insight. Indeed the origins of whatever conversion I have undergone are lost in the mists of time three or four years back. Intellectual curiosity, or the dissatisfaction with my literature classes that I mentioned above, led me to read more or less randomly in contemporary literary theory. I started with a collection of essays called *Writing and Reading Differently: Deconstruction and the Teaching of Composition and Literature* (Atkins and Johnson 1985). Reading this in isolation, with no immediate colleagues who were conversant in any of this theory, I let it incubate. At the same time, it shook me up enough (or, in post-structuralist terms, *solicited* me) to sharpen my sense of dissatisfaction with my literature courses. In the spring of 1987, I drew the assignment to teach

English 109 in the fall term. I had an eye out for an anthology and a mind open to a new approach to take in a new (for me) course. The timing was right for the first NCTE Summer Institute, whose topics were post-structuralism and reader-response and cultural criticism. I was receptive, and my school was financially supportive. Some years earlier, I had chaired a session at the Pennsylvania Council of Teachers of English annual meeting in which Gary Waller and Kathleen Mc-Cormick described the cultural studies curriculum in the English Department at Carnegie-Mellon University. Knowing I would be attending the Summer Institute, and remembering the interest I had felt in what Waller and McCormick were talking about, I ordered their anthology, *The Lexington Introduction to Literature* (Waller, Mc-Cormick, and Fowler 1987), for my course. At the same time I obtained another book by Waller and McCormick (with Linda Flower), *Reading Texts: Reading, Responding, Writing* (1987). Though not an anthology, this is a textbook for a literature class which I have used as a teacher's manual to the Waller, McCormick, and Fowler book. (I have subsequently assigned it as a textbook in a January Term 1989 class in "Reading a Novel.")

   *The Lexington Introduction to Literature* (which I will hereafter refer to as *LIL*) is one of the first introductory literature anthologies to be constructed substantially along the lines of contemporary critical theory.[1] Its "Preface for Teachers" says that the book "pioneers a fundamental shift in the way we teach introductory literature courses and reflects some of the most useful insights, concepts and tools of recent theory and criticism" (p. v). In both *LIL* and *Reading Texts,* McCormick and Waller try to locate themselves between the poles of subjectivity and objectivity that they define in reader-response criticism. They use cultural criticism to do this. When, in their prefaces, they describe their theoretical approach, they are at pains to say how cultural criticism provides a corrective to the emphasis on subjectivity in some reader-response critics. Cultural criticism, they say in *Reading Texts,* studies "both readers and texts . . . within the complex cultural dynamics of their time" so that they are not "regarded as isolated, purely subjective entities" (p. vi). The important chapter in *Reading Texts* on "Reading to Write Response Statements" (which I have drawn upon heavily for my English 109 class to supplement similar discussion in *LIL*) elaborates a theoretical position framed by McCormick in a 1985 article in *College English.* In this article she describes shortcomings in the reader-response approaches of David Bleich and Norman Holland on the one hand and Elizabeth Flynn and Bruce Petersen on the other. She acknowledges Bleich's and Holland's contributions to "shifting classroom emphasis from texts to readers," but argues that they "stop short of explaining how readers are influenced . . . by language and society" and that for Bleich and Holland "the role of the reader seems primarily to be a passive one, simply to react to a text rather than to analyze factors influencing those reactions" (p. 836). She acknowledges Flynn's and Petersen's "reader-oriented pedagogy," but complains that they employ it "to maintain the notion that understanding 'the text itself' is the ultimate goal of a literature course" (p. 837). The position McCormick argues—and on which the discussion of response statement assignments in *Reading Texts* is built—goes beyond Bleich and Holland, Flynn and Petersen to see response statements as

> more than records of subjective reactions, [as] ways of integrating more traditional historical and philosophical material as well as more contemporary issues of literary theory into the classroom without sacrificing the spontaneity of students' initial responses and without reifying the text or the reader. (p. 837)

Building on these ideas and the understanding I developed from the Summer Institute, I stress reading as an activity by having my students write frequent response statements to selections they read. Basic to the response statement as constructed by Waller, McCormick, and Fowler is a heuristic (p. 15) that asks students the following: What was the initial effect of the text on you? How do you account for that effect, in terms of features of the text and qualities of yourself as a reader? What does your response tell you about yourself or your society? *Features of the text* are literary conventions or anything else a reader notices and responds to in reading. *Qualities of the reader* are divided according to repertoires of knowledge: general and literary. The general repertoire includes all values the reader brings to the reading situation; the literary repertoire includes previous experiences with and expectations about reading literature (*LIL,* pp. 13–15).

Students typically write three hundred to five hundred words in response to these basic questions or to more specific ones provided for individual texts. The key here is that these are not "themes about literature" wherein students attempt or pretend to make "objective" interpretive or analytical statements about a text—the traditional kind of writing in the literature class.[2] Response statements focus on the activity and process of reading, which includes the reader-as-subject as well as the text-as-object, focusing on the interaction between the two. For example, in about the fourth week of the term, my students read Ronald Sukenick's story "The Birds." I ask them to respond to the unconventional nature of the story, to describe how they do or do not make sense of it and to refer to assumptions from their general or literary repertoires that clash with the unconventional strategies of the text. One student responded as follows:

> Because of its unconventional nature, I was barely able to make sense of "The Birds" at all. In fact, had I not been reading this story for a class, I would have completely disregarded it and not followed it through to its conclusion. I hesitate to even term the ending of this story a conclusion because there is nothing to conclude. From the beginning, I felt like I was reading the writing of someone who had a bad hit of acid and only later went back to try and make sense of it.
>
> Basically, the meaning I extracted from "The Birds" was that the author could somehow compare the people of the world and their situations to the flight and characteristics of birds, all the while coming up with governmental anarchy in the end. This whole technique was very difficult for me to deal with. The story neglects everything that I have been taught about writing or that I am used to reading. . . .
>
> The very structure of the story was alien to me and contributed to my negative reactions. Also, there was no plot per se and the beginning was so unclear that there was nothing to grasp onto in hopes of creating some meaning from the story. This definitely goes against my general assumptions of short stories. . . . (York)

Once a few preliminaries are out of the way, students write a response statement for nearly every class meeting (I collect them a few hours in advance of the class meeting so that I can read them and respond—graded or not—before class discussion). This may sound like a chore; usually close to thirty students are enrolled in my section of English 109. But it is not a chore; it is a joy to read these responses. Students tend to be relaxed and natural in their writing, speaking in authentic voices—as was my student writing on "The Birds"—instead of in an academic voice that is not yet theirs. Reader-response teaches them that uncertainty in reading is not necessarily a defect, so they are free to be uncertain. These reader-centered assignments allow students to see that their responses to literature matter—whether or not they are English majors, whether or not they have in the past been rewarded by their English teachers for their insightful readings. Response statements tend to make all students insightful readers, because they do not limit insight to statements about the text. Neither the teacher nor the English major is established as a master reader. So students, with their own authority, become involved and maintain their involvement throughout the semester. On the cover page of a formal paper in my "Experience of Literature" class, one student creatively rewrote the title of the course as "new experiences in literature." I took that as both a compliment and a sign of the success of this course. In my January Term course, "Reading a Novel," a student who had also taken my "Experience of Literature" class (where we did *not* read a novel) volunteered this statement in her reading journal:

> In class last semester, we were learning how to make a "close," "strong," "complete" reading and I like the way I read much more now. This way even if I am faced with an unconventional text that I do not understand I can react with frustration and allow myself to try to think of the things about myself that are holding me back from comprehending. Possibly I did not understand the text because I do not think in that pattern or I have never experienced that situation. I realized from the readings we did in class a lot about me as a reader. (Sauter)

## Extending Response Statements

Response statements in my course also form the bases of formal papers students write and which, by English Department mandate, are essential graded elements in all introductory-level literature courses at Moravian. Students in my "Experience of Literature" class write three formal papers: one on their reading of a short story, one on their reading of a poem, and one on the effect of library research on their *re*reading of a short story, poem, or play. The paper assignments tell students to pick a text for which they have already written a response statement. They are asked to reread the text as well as their initial written response. Following Waller and McCormick in *Reading Texts* (p. 93), I tell students,

> A formal paper should differ from a response statement *only* in its greater coherence, more formal organization, greater detail and persuasiveness, *not* in its methods of approaching the text. The theories and assumptions that underlie your response statements apply equally to your more formal papers.

> The writing goals and reading strategies for response statements are equally important for writing a formal paper. In other words, in writing your formal paper, you do not have to determine *what* the meaning of a text is. Rather, you can pursue the goal of analyzing *how* meaning is constructed through the interaction of text and reader.

> You may choose to write on such issues as: a) the ways in which your reading strategies intersect with the text's strategies; b) how your assumptions about literature influence you to read a text in a certain way; c) how some aspect of your general repertoire clashes or harmonizes with the text's; d) how the text opens up

multiple interpretive options; or e) you may develop a strong
reading of the text.

The formal paper thus extends and deepens the student's first response
to the text; she or he is writing about *reading* the text, not about the
text as an object. The "critical apparatus" the student needs has already
been taught and learned *in the process* of approaching literature in a
reader-centered way, instead of being applied from the outside when
the writing occasion calls for it. Some of the terminology may be new,
but the method taps into what students already know, so they really
have less content to learn, and the departmentally required writing
assignments fit more naturally into the flow of reading and writing in
the course.

The third paper in our mandated sequence is a research paper—
that old bugaboo to students and teachers alike. Reader-response and
cultural criticism expand the possibilities for success here, too. Instead
of asking students to find published critical analyses or interpretations
that support hypotheses they have developed out of reading a text
(which is what happens in the *ideal* student research paper), I ask them
to broaden their repertoires with respect to an author's biography,
canon, genre, or cultural situatedness. Library research produces this
broadening. The purpose of their research paper is to see how their
rereading of a text is affected by having broadened their repertoire.
Recall the response statement to "The Birds" from which I quoted
earlier. The student who wrote that chose to do her research paper on
her reading of that text. Here are some excerpts, with the student's
citations omitted:

> Because of its very unconventional nature, my initial response
> to "The Birds" was a negative one. The very structure of the
> story neglected everything that I had been taught about writing
> or that I had been accustomed to reading. There was no plot per
> se and the beginning was so unclear that I found myself with
> nothing to grasp onto in hopes of creating some meaning from
> the fragmented text. This definitely presented a problem for me
> in that any conventional reading strategies or assumptions I had
> been using were not effective in this case. Obviously, it was
> necessary for me to discover a way in which I could broaden my
> perspective as a reader in order to deal more effectively with the
> text. The method I used to do this was through research. By
> researching the thoughts and strategies of the author I was able
> to reread the story and approach the text with unrestricted
> expectations.
>
> One of the main reasons for my negative reaction to the story
> was the form in which it is written. I expect a piece of fiction to

have certain conventions related to characterization, description, and plot. I considered fiction not as an art form, but simply as another way of conveying information. Through my research of the author I realized that writing is just as much a form of art as music or painting. After all, they are all forms of composition. The art of fiction lies in opening the reader to experience beyond language or, as Sukenick declares, ". . . to get people unstuck from a formulated kind of response and open them up to another."

Consequently, I decided to approach my rereading of the text as a form of composition—an ongoing interchange between the page and the mind of both the reader and the author. As Sukenick says, "It seems all the more important that you should get rid of old forms and allow new forms to grow out of your own experience." This is precisely what I attempted to do when devising a new reading strategy by leaving the formal conventions of plot, character, and language structure behind. What I discovered was an artful collage not only of language, but also of characters— characters that I did not even perceive in my initial reading. . . .

Actually, the form of the text is the more interesting element of this composition. Sukenick even admits that what he is trying to do is "call attention to the text itself so that it becomes . . . a kind of object that returns the reader to his own imagination." When concentrating on the form of the text, I was able to make some sense of it by reading it as a collage of words. The text is actually a linking of separate fragments that are not altogether separate once one realizes that it is a combination of several different forms of writing and improvisation. . . .

Through my research of the author I learned a great deal about my own reading strategies. Even though I have acknowledged before that reading is a learned process and that the reader contributes to the meaning of the text, I also realize that I did not even give the text a fighting chance in my initial reading. I totally disregarded the text and its author as something totally out of the ordinary and in doing so, I restricted my expectations to the traditional. . . . I have always thought that one of the most important things about fiction is its honesty and now I realize that it may be the breaking down of language that releases that honesty. (York)

Is it not plain that this student has learned something valuable, and that the learning is integral to the process? That she has learned not just the procedures of library research merely for the purposes of serving limited academic ends, but something about herself, how she reads, what she thinks about fiction as art? Is not her growth evident in what she says and how she says it? Granted, I would prefer that she recognize how she is privileging the author as a source of truth about the text. But in my experience there is more life in this paper than there is in the typical traditional literary research paper.

## Benefits and Implications of the Approach

Reader-response and cultural criticism offer another benefit that may seem antithetical to the introductory literature teacher's assumed goal of fostering literary appreciation (where "appreciation" is taken to mean "fondness for"). Response statements encourage students to see negative responses as worthy of expression, and cultural criticism provides a mechanism by which a student's negative reaction to a text may become a learning experience. A negative response may work better than a positive response, because positive responses often happen with texts that seem to be "easy" to read or that lend themselves to consoling readings. When that happens, students may have more difficulty analyzing the cultural causes of their response than when they have a more strongly negative initial response. For instance, in a recent assignment to develop a more formal paper out of an initial response statement to a poem, some students chose to write on Frost's "The Road Not Taken," an easy text for most of my homogeneously white middle-class students. The poem confirms the American cultural belief in freedom of choice and in choosing independently, even nonconformingly. That is, students who come to the poem with these values already in their general repertoires tend to see the poem in these terms, and they may therefore have difficulty stepping back from their perspective to recognize that their reading *is* culturally determined. The poem consoles them because it gives back what they put into it. Other students in the same class, bringing the same acquired values to reading Gwendolyn Brooks's "We Real Cool" tend to have a strongly negative initial reaction to what they perceive as the anti-social attitude expressed by the voice in that poem. But instead of having students turned off to a reading they don't like, reader-response and cultural criticism give them something to do with that negative response by inviting an examination of what produces it—what combination of features of the text and aspects of their value systems.

A reader-response and cultural criticism approach also has implications for which texts are read and studied. The emphasis on the students' literary repertoires tends to heighten their awareness of what they have read before, and the continual reference to factors in the students' cultural repertoire tends to broaden their understanding of *reading* to include texts from other media. Students who would not usually excel in the literature class, yet are readers of their own culture, may feel validated by the freedom they are given to bring into academic consideration texts from their own canons. *LIL* anthologizes verses by Bob Dylan, Paul Simon, and Laurie Anderson, for instance, as well as ones by Shakespeare, Sidney, and Dickinson. For his formal paper on reading a poem, one student—a sophomore accounting major, a passing student but not one who would normally be seen as distinguishing himself in the literature classroom—developed his response statement to Bruce Springsteen's "Darkness at the Edge of Town." The paper was excellent, one of the three or four best in the class, in large part because the assignment did *not* ask him to analyze or interpret the text, to discover a meaning "in" the text and argue that it was objectively "there." Instead he was permitted, even encouraged, to bring in his avidity for Springsteen's lyrics, his identification with a person who carries a secret around inside him (as the speaker in the text seems to do), and his ability to picture the situation the speaker seems to describe. This student also showed me that he was making intellectual connections of his own by raising the point that this text had a performative dimension, that listening to a recording of Springsteen and his band singing "Darkness at the Edge of Town" affected his reading of the printed verse. (He even handed in a cassette recording of the performance with the final draft of his paper!) I saw this student coming alive intellectually, claiming a strong sense of ownership of his idea. He learned through his own successful efforts that he was an important agent in the reading transaction, and he went on to read, and read well, traditional canonical texts such as *Hamlet* and *Rosencrantz and Guildenstern Are Dead* and to write well about them.[3]

In another case, another student, also not fitting the usual paradigm for academic success in a literature course, was encouraged by this approach to develop a strong reading of Frost's "Stopping by Woods on a Snowy Evening." He read the speaker in the poem as Santa Claus, pausing on his annual rounds. His paper acknowledged the effects the holiday season was having on his reading, and it explained how he saw the figure of Santa Claus in Frost's poem. This was a plausible reading, although surely not a traditional one. In a course with the traditional interpretive model of reading, this student's paper would likely have failed; certainly "Stopping by Woods on a Snowy Evening" is not "about" Santa Claus making his Christmas Eve rounds. Or, if the instructor had read a first draft of the paper with this student's thesis, the student would have been discouraged from arguing such a personal reading. But that is not what happened. Instead, this student had a successful reading and writing experience and produced a paper that I enjoyed reading. The measure of his success, for me, was that he was able to recognize and articulate what was involved in his reading of the poem. He saw that he had a strong initial response to the text and that, at first, he could not account entirely for why that was so. He saw that something was drawing him back to the poem again and again; that he was able to summarize the "surface argument," what the poem seemed to be saying, as well as identify a gap in his reading— *who* the speaker is who stops by the woods; that he filled this gap with something from his cultural repertoire: the notion of Santa Claus or, more properly, *his* notion of a Santa Claus who is both duty-bound and an aesthetic dreamer. He showed me that he had *learned* not just about the text but about himself, who both reads "Stopping by Woods" and has his reading written by his relationship to his culture. Finally, his reading was useful to me in that it opened up a way of seeing that particular text.

I am convinced that these two students and the others I have referred to became stronger readers through this course—stronger than they would have been without it, stronger than they would have been with a course that used a New Critical or traditional literary-historical model of approaching literature. One element of that strength is especially evident in the cases of the last two students mentioned: a greater respect for themselves as readers and thinkers and writers—and to the extent that those selves affect what we usually call *them*selves, as people, too. I think this self-respect is healthy in another way: it tends to increase respect for others' ideas as well. With discussions in this course illustrating varying readings (in terms of both styles and results), students learn both to value and to challenge their own readings. With the chance to compare their readings with others comes the chance to understand and explain themselves, along with the tempering influence exerted by others bringing *their* understandings and explanations into the conversation. They learn that there is no *one* correct reading, that there are many valid readings.

Yet such a relativistic tendency has not, in my experience, led to solipsism or defensive postures in which readings are merely asserted and not explained. Having students recognize the extent to which their culture determines their responses is liberating. In seeing themselves as culturally influenced in certain ways (for example, in terms of gender, race, social and economic class—even college major), students also gain some perspective on what they are *not* and acknowledge that being otherwise constituted would make them read otherwise. The self-reflection this realization prompts is another emancipation, or a step toward it, because many students—my students, at least—have not given much critical thought to themselves in relation to their culture; they take themselves for granted. And younger college students seem to be at an age or developmental stage (or perhaps it is merely a cultural situation!) where they are ready for and interested in this kind of analysis, both for what they have to learn about themselves and for the sake of learning itself. I find students typically saying that the discussions, the sharing of responses, and the response statements "open their eyes" to other people's ideas and to the factors that produce those ideas. I read "minds" for "eyes" in that metaphor.

I have tried to explain how a reader-response/cultural criticism approach makes this particular course ideally suited to a liberal arts education. By way of concluding, let me make the claim as boldly as I make it to my students. In my syllabus I say this:

> If you give [this course, with its approach] a chance, it should make you a stronger student all the way around, because it will heighten your consciousness of your role in making meaning of experience, any experience, and because it will improve your critical powers. In the largest sense, those are some of the best things you can learn from a liberal education.

I strongly believe what I say here. The approach I use constantly asks students to look into the cultural and ideological factors that determine what they are as readers and in turn how they produce meanings in interaction with literary texts. It is but a short step from there, with the theoretical groundwork already laid, to the realization that the world is full of texts, is a text itself, whose meaning(s) is/are produced in large part by the perspectives a "reader" brings to the reading experience. This understanding is essential to a liberal education: to its methods as well as its purposes. Going all the way back to Bishop John Amos Comenius, the "father of modern education," whom Moravian College in particular claims as its philosophical guiding spirit, we find that a liberal education is supposed to open up, not close down, the student to the world and the world to the student. It is supposed to introduce, not conclude; to show, not to tell; to lead, not to force. Eschewing the teacher-as-master-reader and the expert-lecturing-to-novices models, and adopting instead a self-analytical and self-discovery model, the reader-response/cultural criticism approach in the introductory literature course may contribute to the student's liberalization. To those of us who believe in and try to practice the aims of liberal learning, that is strong endorsement indeed.

## Notes

1. Another book, *Literature: Options for Reading and Writing,* edited by Donald Daiker et al. (Harper and Row, 1985 [2nd ed., 1988]) draws on

reader-response theory in its recommendations to students to keep a response journal. An anthology edited by Martha McGowan, *Literature: Experience and Meaning* (Harcourt Brace Jovanovich, 1988), also draws, to a lesser extent, on reader-response theory, and a 1989 book edited by Thomas McLaughlin, *Literature: The Power of Language* (Harcourt Brace Jovanovich) does the same in a more thoroughgoing way.

2. For instance, in an introductory British literature survey I have taught at Moravian, I used to give a writing assignment that asked for "an objective statement communicating your understanding of some aspect of the text, as opposed to a subjective response expressing yourself encountering the text for the first time . . . [an] understanding based on either analysis or interpretation or both." The assignment told students "the situation is an academic one, concerned with objective knowledge and empirical data" and that their papers would be evaluated in terms of "the carefulness and clarity of [their] observations and . . . thinking, the intellectual convincingness of [their] understanding, and the formal correctness of [their] writing." As a heuristic device for specific topics, I included with the assignment a detailed outline of literary elements that presumably could be analyzed objectively and from which analysis an interpretation could be built. The elements were the conventional ones—plot, character, tone, symbol, point of view, language—and the assumption implied throughout the assignment was that since these were features *of* the text, an interpretation based on observing them would be objectively derived *from* the text. Similarly, a recent introductory literature anthology—*Interpreting Literature,* edited by K. L. Knickerbocker et al. (Holt, Rinehart and Winston, 7th ed., 1985) includes more than a dozen pages of critical apparatus to be applied to writing a paper about poetry and offers as purpose options these two: explication and analysis. I take these to be typical and traditional paper assignments in the literature class.

3. In the course of routine reporting to me about my students' Writing Center visits, David Taylor, Writing Center director, observed that the students in my "Experience of Literature" class "tend to have a much stronger sense of ownership of their ideas and writing, and are usually much more active in their tutorials as they continue to try to work out their own meanings of . . . texts. Literature isn't something that is dead for them; it has clearly become something that has affected them on a personal level" (memo to the author, Nov. 17, 1988). Taylor's interest in the sense of growth and empowerment of student writers is manifest in his article "Peer Tutoring's Hidden World: The Emotional and Social Issues" in *Writing Lab Newsletter* 13 (January 1989): 1–4.

## References

Atkins, C. Douglas, and Barbara Johnson, eds. 1985. *Writing and Reading Differently: Deconstruction and the Teaching of Composition and Literature.* Lawrence, Kansas: University Press of Kansas.

McCormick, Kathleen. 1985. "Theory in the Reader: Bleich, Holland, and Beyond." *College English* 47: 836–50.

McCormick, Kathleen, and Gary Waller, with Linda Flower. 1987. *Reading Texts: Reading, Responding, Writing.* Lexington, Mass.: D.C. Heath.

Martin, Everett Dean. 1926. *The Meaning of a Liberal Education.* New York: Norton.

*Moravian College Catalog.* 1987. Bethlehem, Pa.: Moravian College.

Sauter, Tina. "Journal." Unpublished manuscript, written for English 109 at Moravian College, January 1989.

Waller, Gary, Kathleen McCormick, and Lois Josephs Fowler, eds. 1987. *The Lexington Introduction to Literature.* Lexington, Mass.: D.C. Heath.

Wingard, Joel. 1987. "Syllabus for English 109: The Experience of Literature." Bethlehem, Pa.: Moravian College.

York, Lisa. Response statement and formal paper, "The Birds." Written for English 109 at Moravian College, Fall 1989.

# 12 Teaching Literature in the Post-Structuralist Era: A Classroom Teacher's Agenda

Lloyd N. Dendinger

Lloyd Dendinger is professor of English at the University of South Alabama, a twenty-five-year-old institution that draws its student population—some 10,000 undergraduate and graduate students—largely from its home city of Mobile and from southern Alabama, southeastern Mississippi, and southwestern Florida. His publications include articles on the works of Robert Frost in the *Southern Review* and *American Quarterly,* and on the work of Stephen Crane in *Studies in Short Fiction.*

Of his teaching Professor Dendinger writes, "I think of myself first and foremost as a classroom teacher. I teach American literature at all levels: a sophomore survey course, advanced undergraduate courses, and graduate seminars in the American Romantics and Modern Poetry. Once each year I teach a section of freshman composition." Professor Dendinger's institution sponsored his participation in the first Summer Institute, and he, in turn, taped the sessions so that he could present them to his colleagues at the University of South Alabama. Thus the conversation that started at Myrtle Beach has continued within his English department and in his college classroom.

In addition to his teaching, Professor Dendinger is active in community outreach programs. He lectures and does dramatic readings in the schools and at community functions.

To start with the underlying question: how does someone like me respond to the vigorous intellectual crosscurrents of the contemporary literary scene, particularly as those crosscurrents threaten the viability of the canon by and in which I was trained and have taught throughout my career? First, a few words about "like me" and "respond": I am a tenured professor of English at a relatively young state university. I am white, male, middle-aged, and of northern European extraction. My Ph.D. is from Louisiana State University, my dissertation on Robert Frost. Although not a disciple of the New Critics, I recognize that the principal set of critical theories influencing my teaching strategies and objectives derives from their work.

That I "respond" to that underlying question implies an audience. My secondary audience is made up, imaginatively, theoretically, of all of my professional colleagues who are interested in the teaching of the English language and its literature. However, what I undertake to write here has something of the character of a dramatic monologue, intended to provide a rational articulation of my most fundamental professional responsibilities to myself. I am, then, my own primary audience, for I have a basic professional responsibility to understand both what is going on in my field and how that understanding affects my teaching.

I mean to explore that understanding and its effects in a three-part discussion that will begin with "canon," turn next to "pedagogy," and finally to my own individual "teaching agenda." I can clear the deck by summarizing my three proposals.

What I propose to do about the canon is to go on teaching traditional American writers, mostly male, mostly of northern European stock, against the backdrop of current challenges to that canon posed by deconstructionist, reader-response, and, most particularly, feminist and black critics.

What I propose to do methodologically is to continue in the classroom with a New Critical orientation made manifest by the close reading of texts against the backdrop of the ideological challenges of contemporary criticism to that approach, particularly against propositions such as that of Harold Bloom (1979) that there is no "the Paradise Lost" (p. 8).

Which is to say that I propose holding a steady, traditional course that will, as it always has at its best, remain open to dissenting voices and actively encourage the expression of dissent in its quest to realize more fully what it means to be human.

## Canon

The most exciting thesis in the ongoing discussions about canon formation is the political one, the one which raises questions about the basis of authority in a pluralistic, democratic society. Immediately behind considerations of what I teach are questions about why I teach that text and not another and questions about who decides which texts should be taught. I find such questions highly compatible with the classroom agenda I draw from the traditional nineteenth- and early twentieth-century American canon and will develop the theme of that compatibility in the final section of this paper. Here, I want simply to say that teaching the traditional canon does not preclude my active participation as a classroom teacher in the contemporary debates about canon.

These debates constitute the backdrop against which I will continue to teach the most traditional American authors. My students are introduced to the major outlines of the ongoing discussions about canon formation before we turn to the texts of Emerson, Thoreau, Hawthorne, Whitman, Dickinson, and Twain, among others, in my nineteenth-century classes, and Frost, Pound, Williams, Stevens, Faulkner, Hemingway, Steinbeck, Porter, O'Connor, and Welty, among others, in my twentieth-century classes.

I ask my students to consider that these and other select texts once constituted the canon of American literary studies and that now the very notion of canonical texts is being seriously challenged and to some extent replaced by other approaches to the study of literature. What was once described as the mainstream is now widely thought to be more properly considered one of the tributaries to that mainstream. The overwhelming question is why we should be embarking upon this tributary rather than one of the several others we might take. I have a three-part answer.

## 1. The Historical Arguments

There are two principal sets of historical arguments for continuing close study of the pantheon of white, largely male (I do teach most of the traditional women writers, with particular interest and emphasis on Emily Dickinson), European, and, to a large extent, New England American writers of the nineteenth and early twentieth centuries. First, the very fact of the contemporary challenges to their centrality requires that we know them, their texts, their biographies, and their milieus. If we should ever decide neatly and finally that the course of history responsible for their preeminence was a total disaster, even then it would be better that we know them well than that we rewrite history. From our vantage point, they were largely both sexist and racist, but surely there can be little understanding of liberation without an understanding of bondage. As we consider turning away from a canonical orientation, we need to know as much as we can about those texts which are considered canonical.

The second historical argument is that the white male European authors constitute one of the tributaries to the mainstream of American literature and therefore should be taught. However limited their perspectives, however political their rise to eminence, taken together as "canon" they constitute, nevertheless, a major commentary on the

American historical experience. There is, it seems to me, a real danger that we will do precisely what we accuse those who hold to the canonical perspective of doing, which is to rewrite history, making exclusions which will reflect not a new universalism but rather the provincialism of our time. Such exclusiveness on our part is more likely to be the result of benign neglect than of hard-line political exclusion. That is, no one is likely to propose that we stop teaching Emerson because of his views. But what we are experiencing already is the filling up of what might be considered a new canon with not only a fuller representation of minorities but with increasing emphasis on contemporary writers. We need badly to understand how limited and privileged our view of history has always been. But as we move to broaden and deepen that understanding, we must be careful, as we expand and redefine the canon, to hold on to what we have as well, lest we find from some future revisionist perspective that what we accomplished in the late twentieth century was the substitution of one canon for another.

## 2. The Logistical Argument

A skeptical though friendly colleague recently cautioned me about my "proposals," which open me, he said, "to the charge that what I am doing is justifying existing practice, and that what we want is not to be figures in the backdrop but figures center stage." That is (if I understand the argument), all of us, the "we" of "what we want," belong center stage. To which I answer, "Yes, of course." But to philosophically affirm democratic pluralism does not provide a classroom agenda. That affirmation tends rather to frustrate any particular agenda by the richness of its cultural diversity and abundant detail.

Black literary history needs to be "told." The black aesthetic and critical perspectives need to be explored and made available. Women writers need to be recognized, read, and taught. The feminist critical perspective needs to be explored, developed, and made available. The Native American cultural history and aesthetic need to be told. The Hispanic story needs to be told. I was delighted recently to read Marilyn Butler's (1987) "Revising the Canon," wherein she predicts that "within another generation, if wealth and prestige within the American university system continue to shift to California, we are surely destined to see another revision. If this one puts down genuine local roots, it might reflect the interests and backgrounds of California's Hispanic and Chinese" (p. 1349). Surely Oriental cultural contributions need to be identified, explored, understood, and taught. Emerson, Whitman, and Twain need to be read and taught. All of these needs exist. And the greatest need of all is the evolution of a culture in which we have gone beyond the need to think in these terms because of the assimilation of all of the parts into the democratic whole.

With these fine affirmations made, I must turn to the more mundane matter of my reading list for next quarter. Surely, I will want black writers on that list. And women writers. And Hispanic. And Native American. And Oriental. And our newest citizens: Cambodian, Vietnamese, and Iranian-American writers. And Cooper, Emerson, Whitman, Melville, Twain, Hawthorne, Jewett, James, O'Connor, Porter, Chopin, Welty, Frost, Sexton, Wharton, Faulkner, and oh, well, I have the complete list in my files somewhere. Center stage is going to be a little crowded, to say nothing of my ten-week quarter. I hear the voice of my colleague in friendly protestation: "Now you are being ridiculous. This is simply absurd." Precisely. None of us can accommodate everyone anywhere, but most particularly not in the classroom. We must each of us carve out a piece of the canon newly defined, an agenda, and teach it against the backdrop of the cultural diversity of a pluralistic, democratic society.

### 3. The Race/Gender Argument

I cannot take on the democratic agenda in the classroom, simply because it is logistically impossible to do so. Also, I am given pause in my exploration of agendas outside the one I am most professionally confident about because some of the people who should know are questioning my white male capacities for such exploration. I am most tentative and frankly uneasy about this line of argument. But what is someone like me to say to the following account of the feminist agenda?

> A major theme in feminist theory on both sides of the Atlantic for the past decade has been the demand that women writers be, in Claudine Herrmann's phrase, "voleuses de langue," thieves of language, female Prometheuses. Though the language we speak and write has been an encoding of male privilege, what Adrienne Rich calls an "oppressor's language" inadequate to describe or express women's experience, a "law of the Father" transforms the daughter to "the invisible woman in the asylum corridor" or "the silent woman" without access to authoritative expression, we must also have it in our power to "seize speech" and make it say what we mean. More: there is a desire to make female speech prevail, to penetrate male discourse, to cause the ear of man to listen. (Ostriker 1986, pp. 210–11)

I am admonished here, am I not, at the very least to be silent and to listen. That may be very good advice, and I am listening. But how am I to "teach" in that wholly passive, silent mode? And what is someone like me to say to Houston Baker's (1976) question: "What if Black creativity is the result of a context—a web of meanings—different in kind and degree from that of white commentators" (p. 53)? Am I not again being relegated to a passive, silent role which disqualifies me from the classroom, except perhaps as a beginning student, where the black agenda is being pursued? My problem here is that I am more inclined to agree than to disagree with both Ostriker and Baker. We really don't know with any finality just what psychological and hence rhetorical configurations are imposed by sex and race. I acknowledge my need to listen to women and to blacks about the distinctiveness and dimensions of their human experiences. However, isn't the compelling corollary to that proposition that perhaps I, as a white male, have something to tell women and blacks about the white male's experience on the North American frontier in the eighteenth and nineteenth centuries? I need to listen to blacks and women. Perhaps blacks and women need to listen to me on the subject of the European male's fascination with and mythic celebration of the American wilderness.

The basic problem of canon is precisely the basic challenge of democracy. It is the challenge of the motto "E Pluribus Unum." How can we be one people while at the same time not only tolerating, not even only respecting, but affirming and celebrating our differences? The process goes on. We are doing it, meeting the challenge, in the democratic society at large. We are affirming the ideal whole while contending with the parts—in the classroom, the courtroom, and the workplace—against the backdrop of that ideal affirmation.

## Pedagogy

The substantive challenges to the traditional canon are primarily political in nature, coming from women and our national minorities demanding their right to be heard. The philosophical challenges to our traditional understanding of "text" and "textuality" complement the political ones by shifting the focus of our attention from canonical texts to "discourse." If we agree with Harold Bloom that there is no "the Paradise Lost," we might be more readily agreeable to expanding the canon beyond those limits where it can continue to accommodate Milton's epic. (This is not Professor Bloom's argument.) That is, the political demands to add more texts threaten the privileged items of the canon by providing less and less time, space, and energy for them—

in textbooks, classrooms, and discussions—a threat that might in time result in exclusion by benign neglect. The philosophical refocusing of attention from texts to discourse complements that tendency by its implicit disparagement of canonical texts as texts. If the privileged texts of the traditional canon lose their New Critical autonomy, they are more easily "moved over" to make room for other texts.

The essential irony of deconstructionist attacks upon texts is that they all take place *in* texts. We cannot introduce students to the contemporary challenges to textuality without critical texts in hand. That is obvious enough, but it needs to be pushed back another step: we cannot introduce students to challenges to literary texts without first making literary texts accessible to them. In short, I consider myself a teacher of reading and my primary responsibility the "passing on" of texts to my students. In my advanced and graduate classes, I introduce names and terms from contemporary criticism and take every opportunity throughout the semester to return in the context of our consideration of *The Scarlet Letter* or *Huckleberry Finn* to such references. But that is backdrop, not foreground. I continue in my classes with the New Critical orientation in the close reading of texts, concerned with matters of syntax, diction, imagery, and metaphor. That is, my concern is with a close reading of texts designed to transform the texts from the page to the minds of readers.

In my classroom methodology, my principal point of engagement with contemporary criticism is with the challenge to the authority which the New Critics assigned to texts. Long before I knew the term *reader-response criticism,* I had begun developing my own approach to teaching reading as something other than the rote assimilation of authoritarian interpretations of literary texts. At some stage, we must teach the reader to read for meaning independent of our meanings (though the two may, more or less, coincide). That is, of course, easier said than done, since our meanings are as closely attached as the skin on our backs. My attempts to resolve this critical pedagogical problem have been to create what I (and others, of course) call a "community of readers."

The community-of-readers approach is a pedagogical, that is, a practical, approach that will not resolve ontological and epistemological questions about absolute meaning or truth. It provides a practical middle ground between the New Critical autonomous text and its solipsistic antithesis wherein the text means whatever a reader wants it to mean. And most importantly, it provides a means of building reader confidence by making it possible for an individual reader to stand outside the "community" of any group—classroom, critical, philosophical—as a one-person nucleus of a potential new community. That is, we work toward shared meaning with the understanding that the meaning arrived at is relative, not absolute, and that any one of us may break new ground with a reading not in agreement with that of the classroom or the larger community.

The principal challenge of this approach comes in the handling of the unavoidable tension between my "authority" in the classroom and the freedom imposed upon my students by my insistence that they find their own meaning for the text. The tension is unavoidable because my authority is also unavoidable. I reject as untenable the proposition that I am "just another reader" among readers. I am an experienced reader. I do carry "readings" of texts with me into the classroom. Those readings reflect value judgments, my biases, my "agenda." Nor can I escape from the institutional authority invested in me by the traditions of the classroom, most particularly my contractual agreement with the institution to evaluate and grade my students.

But my authority has deeper roots than that. I have read "these" books; my students have not. I do not have dogma for them, but I do have experiences and values. I believe that the sharing of those experiences and the expression of those values are not only compatible with but essential to the teaching of the humanities in a democratic society. And the essential corollary to that proposition is that I must also "teach" students to find their own meanings, and that I must evaluate them on the clarity and originality of their thinking and on the rhetorical effectiveness of their articulation of their views.

### Agenda: The Idea of America

*Agenda* as I have been using it throughout this essay has a very particular meaning for me. It is close to *theme* or *thesis,* but not a synonym for either, being more individual or personal. I have various classroom agendas, depending upon the class level and subject matter. I have a writing agenda which runs through all of my classes with decreasing importance as I move from freshman composition to my graduate literature classes. I have a reading agenda which is also a part of all of my classes with varying degrees of concentration depending upon need. The writing agenda is not wholly my own. I am still highly dependent upon others when it comes to teaching composition, especially at the freshman level. The reading agenda is my own, which is not to say I know all there is to know about it. But I am confident in a very personal way about my professional reading objectives for my students and how most effectively to achieve them.

Milton says in the *Areopagitica* that he hates a "pupil teacher" (p. 440). I take him to mean by that someone who teaches without a personal agenda. I am, myself, most a pupil teacher in the freshman composition classroom. But I am not a pupil teacher in my literature classes. I have found a thesis "through" the professional channels of graduate study and years of classroom experience which I have made my own and which I now "profess." I affirm with enthusiasm the agendas of our national minorities, of blacks, women, Hispanics, Native Americans, Orientals, Indonesians, of all of us to be fully and equitably represented in a truly national canon. But these individually are not my agenda. Most importantly, I believe that my affirmation and excitement about them derives largely from the fact that my agenda— drawn from the traditional American literary canon, beginning with, most particularly, Emerson—prefigures the attitudes toward the intrinsic worth of the individual human being fundamental to the current expansion of the canon.

In upper-level and graduate courses, the intrinsic worth of the individual as celebrated in the frontier culture of nineteenth-century America is the basic thesis of my classroom agenda. It finds its most explicit expression in Emerson, Thoreau, Whitman, and Twain. In 1985, the year of the centennial celebration of the publication of *Huckleberry Finn,* I delivered a paper in which I speculated about the novel's "place" in the American literary canon for the second hundred years of its history. How are we to go on making it meaningful, I wondered, as the dynamics of the American historical experience continues, through the assimilation of the peoples of the world, to give us an audience of ever-changing, ever-widening cultural diversity? To particularize my meditations, I tried to imagine teaching the novel as a national classic to some of our newest citizen-students, say those in Dade County, or newly arrived from Cambodia. This attempt involved a three-part deliberation.

## 1. The Adventures of Huckleberry Finn

A primary meaning of *Huckleberry Finn* is that we are more likely to be moral creatures on a raft on the Mississippi River than we are anywhere else in the world. I over-particularize for emphasis. Restated more broadly, it is the romantic/transcendentalist proposition that a person is innately good, and that there is a natural self, naturally good, that can best be made manifest (tapped, discovered, or rediscovered) in a natural environment. This proposition sends Huck running at the end of the novel from a corrupt and corrupting society. It is that never-to-be-ended flight from civilization into the wilderness that will be the most difficult of the novel's themes to make meaningful for my Cambodian American, and my Latin and African American, and even for my European American students in 1990, when the current migratory waves have subsided.

The romantic/transcendental theme which affirms the moral superiority of the natural man is complemented in *The Adventures of Huckleberry Finn,* as it is pervasively through nineteenth-century American literature, by the celebration of individuality, with all the political implications of that celebration. I am more optimistic about the continuing vitality of this "half" of the book's meaning. It has occurred to me, particularly with regard to our recent immigrants from Cambodia and Vietnam, that the escape by water would provide a point of vicarious entry into the novel, given their most recent experiences. That is, they might readily identify with the flight by water from social injustice and political oppression. The difficult matter to explain, given that analogy, would be why Huck lights out for the territory after he and Jim have been freed.

The secondary, complementary meaning of Huck Finn is that, given the moral superiority of the natural being, the ideal of human behavior will always be in opposition to social norms and established moral values. Huck tried to pray, but since it did not work for him he gave it up, making manifest his quintessentially "new American" character, as we do ourselves, so long as we continue to applaud his honesty while ignoring the discarded tradition as relatively unimportant.

The historic background for Twain's celebrating the individual, and his honesty in rejecting the religious traditions embodied in prayer, comes into focus through consideration of Emerson's 1832 resignation from the Unitarian Church over the subject of the Communion Sacrament. His sermon on that occasion, "The Lord's Supper," and his poem "The Problem" spell out clearly the conflict between his sense of "truth-as-perceived" and that presented by tradition. In both the sermon and the poem, his rejection of tradition is set, it seems to me, in a notably tolerant attitude. In the poem he tells us,

> I like a church; I like a cowl;
> I love a prophet of the soul;
> And on my heart monastic aisles
> Fall like sweet strains, or pensive smiles:
> Yet not for all his faith can see
> Would I that cowled churchman be. (p. 347)

In the sermon he says, perhaps a little defensively, "I am not so foolish as to declaim against form. Forms are as essential as bodies;

but to exalt particular forms, *to adhere to one form a moment after it is outgrown, is unreasonable* [italics mine], and alien to the spirit of Christ" (p. 99). I believe that Emerson's resignation from the church in 1832 is one of the most symbolic acts in the context of the nineteenth-century development of a distinctive American character. I have always been particularly grateful to him for the tolerance of his rejections of, most fundamentally, dogma—a tolerance embodied for me in one of the most inspirational passages in American literature:

> I have no hostility to this institution. I am only stating my want of sympathy with it. Neither should I ever have obtruded this opinion upon people, had I not been called by my office to administer it. That is the end of my opposition, that I am not interested in it. I am content that it stands to the end of the world, if it please men and please Heaven, and I shall rejoice in all the good it produces. (p. 101)

Huck is not opposed to prayer; it simply does not work for him. His rejection and tolerance in the sphere of religion are paralleled by his aesthetics as he tries to view Emmeline Grangerford's art sympathetically. Others see something of beauty in her art and so he tries also to be moved positively by her paintings, coming only reluctantly finally to admit that, try as he may, they always give him the fantods. One could cite various other parallels to such tolerant rejection, but the central point is made, of course, in Huck's treatment of Jim, whom he tries earnestly but unsuccessfully to see as a subhuman slave rather than as a man and as a friend.

The conflict between experience and tradition is a central theme not only in Emerson and Twain, but overtly and dramatically in Thoreau and Whitman, and significantly—though less apparently—in Hawthorne and Dickinson. Thoreau would sign off from society. Whitman celebrates the "scent of his armpits [as] aroma finer than prayer" and counts his "head more than all the sects and creeds"(p. 42). The forest scene in *The Scarlet Letter* poses essentially the same moral dilemma as does the conclusion of *Huckleberry Finn,* the significant difference being precisely where in the narratives each dilemma occurs. Hawthorne poses it early enough to effect a resolution in the final scaffold scene. Twain's positioning prevents resolution, and so Huck goes on running. That is, Hawthorne has not moved as far as has Twain in freeing himself from tradition. That does not make him less American or even less important to our understanding of the cultural dynamics of the period. It does, however, blur the distinctiveness of the character of Dimmesdale in contrast to that of Huck as representative of the evolving culture, as representative of that new national entity, the American.

## 2. The New Dogma

In *Culture and Anarchy,* Matthew Arnold argues that great human achievement comes from those "who either belong to Establishments or have been trained in them" (p. 1121). I understand him to mean by that, say, that Milton's achievement depended upon Genesis in particular and upon the fifteen hundred years or so of tradition based upon that text which provided not only the material for his epic but the cultural mythos necessary for its creation. Much the same thing could be said for Chaucer, in particular, and on the continent very clearly so for Dante. All of which is obvious enough, it seems to me, but it is useful nevertheless when one considers that the American literary artists of the nineteenth century had no "establishment" in the sense that English and continental writers had. Ignoring the indigenous culture, they saw themselves as having no past. The nineteenth-century American "institute of letters" undertook as its central historic mission the deliberate, calculated rejection of such tradition. Emerson's "American Scholar Address" is the manifesto of that mission. "Song of Myself" and *The Adventures of Huckleberry Finn* are its two major artistic achievements. The primary meaning of the novel, the moral superiority of the natural being, and the celebration of individuality even when that individuality conflicts with established norms of behavior, give rise to an implicit third meaning, which is, in Emerson's words, that "Each age must write its own books" (p. 51). To try to convey that theme, the novel's implicit theme, in a book is to involve oneself in, in at least the general sense of the word, paradox. The dogma of our new American—as he is represented by Emerson, by Thoreau and Whitman as personae, and Huck Finn—is that there can be no dogma. The "book" which teaches that each age must write its own books demands, if we are to take it seriously, that we discard it "generationally." How then are we ever in such a cultural milieu to establish a "classic" literature? Twenty-five years, a quarter of a century at the outside, should be all we can ask for in longevity from "American" books. Oh, we'll keep some indefinitely on back shelves as records of the past, as period pieces. But we can't expect an American essay, novel, or poem, the "American Scholar Address," *Huckleberry Finn,* "Song of Myself" to last—yet we find ourselves in the second century of all three.

A crucial step in the evolution of my classroom agenda came for me with the realization that this apparent paradox, i.e., the rejection of books (of tradition) by means of books, embodies the paradoxical genius of the very "idea" of America.

## 3. The Idea of America

I am uncertain about the continuing vitality of *Huckleberry Finn*'s romantic/transcendental theme, that of the moral superiority of the natural being. I am a little more confident, however, that we will go on affirming the novel's central place and vitality (in contrast, I mean, to a period piece, read and known primarily by specialists) because of its complementary theme, its celebration of the individual in conflict with social norms of behavior and established moral values. To do this we must explain to our newest citizens why, after the successful trip by water to freedom, Huck finds it necessary to go on running. That is, we must address the seeming paradox that is the idea of America.

The idea of an American character is affirmed by a series of historic and psychological denials. It begins with the political denials of the American Revolution and comes down in recent history to Martin Luther King's denial, not of his race, but of the proposition that race has anything to do with the dignity and rights of an American citizen. Though it is too early to see with clarity, we are currently witnessing something very like the civil rights movement of the fifties and sixties in the heightening of the national consciousness about sexual identity, which is giving rise more explicitly than ever before to the denial that such identity has anything to do with an individual's dignity and freedom. Huck's implicit denial of Tom's influence, of Pap's and Miss Watson's authority, and of the social mores which demand that he turn Jim in, all come together in his flight to the wilderness.

As we enter the second century of *Huckleberry Finn*'s history, I see three possible categories for its continuing place in our national life. The first is serious enough in some ways, but I will not here concern myself much with it. That is, the novel has already been trivialized in the marketplace to sell bubble gum and soap powder, and that use will surely continue. In that category, Huck and Jim become cartoon characters, and their flight down the river, sicklied over with a filmy cast of nostalgia, becomes cute and stupid.

The two other categories are both those of classic national literature. One is the classic that has been pushed off the front shelf of contemporary vitality and interest but preserved by specialists as a valuable period piece. The other is, of course, the status that, in spite of attacks and criticism, the novel has largely enjoyed for a hundred years now. The difference between these two kinds of classic, it occurs to me, might be clarified by returning once more to the river to consider two possible symbolic configurations of the passage to freedom which it represents.

In the context of nineteenth-century romantic/transcendentalist concerns, the river runs contrary to the historic, progressive direction of modern America. That is, freedom exists in running away from modern, urban, industrialized society into the wilderness. Thus, at the end of the novel, Huck must keep running. If that is the best we can do (and that is not bad) in explaining the flight to my bright Cambodian student perplexed by the novel's conclusion, then I think the novel is destined to move to the back shelf as period-piece classic: an important and marvelous book, but one growing cold with the passing years and attracting fewer and fewer serious readers.

The alternative is that though Twain literally "meant" to have Huck flee to the wilderness, in the energy of his creative imagination he transcends that meaning with one in which the importance of the river transcends that of Huck. The river does not flow away from his history but rather flows through the heartland of the nation as a timeless symbol of the idea of America. And that idea is that there is a fundamental self which is free and dignified and equal in worth to all other such selves. Our distinctive national history might, it seems to me, be seen as a process by which that primarily transcendentalist concept has been converted into a social/political ideal. The river that still runs through, not away from, America is the symbol of that selfhood, of that American definition of individuality. It promises me a place where I can free myself of all other identities—religious, racial, sexual, corporate, and even familial—to stand and to declare myself in terms of what I am truly moved by and what just gives me the plain fantods. In my closing rhapsody, I do not want to forget what I know, which is that it often takes an awful lot of anguish and even tragedy to reach the river. IBM, Xerox, AT&T, the Democratic Party, the Republican Party, feminists, black aestheticians, Marxists, the KKK, the Moral Majority, etc. are all breathing down my neck, and in very specific instances are ready to come down hard on me for daring to declare my independence of them. The river is sometimes reached only after blood has been shed or lives have been drained and wasted in endless hours in the courtroom. But the belief in the possibility of such independence and such freedom is still our most distinguishing national idea, the idea of America.

*The Adventures of Huckleberry Finn* is a commercially successful novel written by a middle-aged white male of northern European extraction, whose success as an author, by the time he had written the novel, made him a member of the literary and economic establishment. Nevertheless, to read it with an understanding of the dynamics of the relationship between Huck and Jim is to widen and deepen one's appreciation of what it means to be human. It is a story in the first place about a boy and a man on a raft on the Mississippi River. The story does not include in a significant manner women, nor Hispanics, nor Native Americans. But it is, nevertheless, a book about all people—a book about all of us. In its deepest significance it is not about men or women, or about boys, or whites or blacks. It is a book about an idea—the idea of the supreme worth of the individual regardless of race, gender, creed, or social or economic class. It is about the idea of America. In this great nineteenth-century novel of democracy, Mark Twain shows us the idea. In the great nineteenth-century American poem of democracy, Walt Whitman tells us what it is explicitly:

> I celebrate myself, and sing myself,
> And what I assume you shall assume
> For every atom belonging to me, as good belongs to you.

## References

Arnold, Matthew. 1938. *Culture and Anarchy. English Prose of the Victorian Era,* edited by Charles Frederick Harrold and William D. Templeman. New York: Oxford University Press.

Baker, Houston, Jr. 1976. "On the Criticism of Black American Literature: One View of the Black Aesthetic." In *Reading Black: Essays in the Criticism of African, Caribbean, and Black American Literature,* edited by Houston Baker, Jr. A Cornell University Monograph. Ithaca, N.Y.: Cornell University.

Bloom, Harold. 1979. "The Breaking of Form." In *Deconstruction and Criticism.* New York: The Seabury Press.

Butler, Marilyn. 1987. "Revising the Canon." *Times Literary Supplement* (Dec. 4–10): 1349, 1359–60.

Emerson, Ralph Waldo. 1950. *Selected Prose and Poetry,* edited with an introduction by R. L. Cook. New York: Rinehart and Co.

Milton, John. 1959. *Areopagitica.* In *Major British Writers,* edited by G. B. Harrison, et al. Vol. I. New York: Harcourt, Brace and World, Inc.

Ostriker, Alicia Suskin. 1986. *Stealing the Language: The Emergence of Women's Poetry in America.* Boston: Beacon Press.

Whitman, Walt. 1959. *Complete Poetry and Selected Prose,* edited by James E. Miller, Jr. Boston: Houghton Mifflin.

# 13 Dispatching "Porphyria's Lover"

Joseph Dupras

Joseph Dupras is an associate professor at the University of Alaska–Fairbanks, where he has taught for eleven years. He teaches a wide variety of courses, including graduate seminars in British literature of the Victorian and Romantic periods and undergraduate courses in literary criticism, nineteenth-century British literature, and writing. He has served as acting head of his department and director of undergraduate studies, and has been a judge in the NCTE Achievement Awards in Writing program. A participant in the 1987 Summer Institute, he is now at work on a number of projects, among which is what he terms a "reader, glossary, and instructional aid for the classroom use of current interpretive theories and practices."

Professor Dupras has published frequently on the works of Robert Browning and the Brontës. Recently, he was cited in Lisa Birnbach's *College Book* as one of the three best teachers at his university. His students, he tells us, know him as "Dr. Doom."

After a recent honors "lit. & comp." class on Robert Browning's "Porphyria's Lover," one student's remark ("You've ruined the poem for me!") and another's question ("Do you like this poem?") suggested that, despite my intention—to increase their appreciation for a literary classic—I had not achieved the ends I had hoped for. Perhaps because the students were willing to accept the teacher's intellectual mastery and aesthetic taste, they had not experienced the "textasy" I had hoped for, but had been spectators at a pedagogical "texticide." I had been unable to resist strangling "Porphyria's Lover" to make it serve my professional self-image; and having done so, I could not convince my audience that I was still in heaven and all was right in the classroom. Nevertheless, my arrogance had helped a few of these young readers see that the role of teacher-as-interpreter might conflict with another aim of teaching: to bring students to the pleasures of literature. They made me stay after class to learn this lesson.

My approach to "Porphyria's Lover" had become stale and disengaged because I felt that my competence with formalist techniques made my status as master reader secure. Teaching a text as "perfectly pure and good" (l. 37), making sense of it, allowed me to control the classroom. The students knew who was in charge. Such a teacher-centered approach, however, made it less likely that students would be active readers. When a master reader forcefully determines its "meaning," a text dies.

But the reading of literature need not conclude so (un)wisely. The students' innate urge to reread might have survived if I had "produc[ed] a perforated, elliptical, drifting, skidding discourse" instead of a fixed, authoritative interpretation (Barthes 1986, p. 177). An enigmatic text—and all texts are in some degree enigmatic—calls for an inconclusive reading, which protects both text and literature class from the effects of professorial authority. Even if I have to feign confusion, my students gain interpretive resiliency, which makes them more involved with the text—dialogic partners in the critical enterprise. If "Porphyria's Lover" were either too accommodating or too vagrant, it would not produce an active reader—one who wishes, according to Wolfgang Iser, to avoid the extreme reactions of "boredom and overstrain" (1974, p. 275), which halt reading altogether. Although "Porphyria's Lover" is one of Browning's most accessible works because of its grotesque sensationalism and relatively simple style, the poem has a will that defies interpretive strangulation.

The students who disliked the way I had dispatched the text preferred to have it on their own terms. My unwillingness to relinquish "Porphyria's Lover" diminished the poem, yet its status as a "classic" made me reluctant to open it to multiple interpretation. The fact that I had paid a high academic price to own the poem was not my students' concern. In their minds my strength as a specialist in Browning's poetry weakened me as a teacher; hubris and selfishness had slipped into the classroom behind a cloud of scholarly authority. We were, together, performing a self-reflective, hermeneutic version of "Porphyria's Lover."

With better planning I might have focused the class's attention on several ways that the poem prescribes such a performance. The manner in which Porphyria and her lover deal with each other and understand their situation mirrors what may happen in the teaching of literature, particularly as the teacher gains in experience and age. Students being introduced to literary analysis need to understand meaning to be the product not only of one reading but also of a sequence of multiple (mis)readings. Teaching becomes less coercive when discussions of "Porphyria's Lover" reflect the exercise of power both inside and outside the text. Instead of the helplessness and anger my students experienced in relating to the poem and to my reading, they might have enthusiastically shared the lover's tensions between knowledge and uncertainty while "liv[ing], from the inside, in a certain identity with the work and the work alone" (Poulet 1972, p. 62). Such an interpretive communion does not prevent a strangulation like that depicted in "Porphyria's Lover," but the text's, and reader's, "deaths" would be comparably inconclusive. The poem's design, its "utmost will" (l. 53) to be read, matches an interpreter's aim to enter the perpetually recreative aesthetic life. Only a diminished capacity for reading, a failure of will, my students were telling me, could truly put an end to "Porphyria's Lover."

One way to lead students beyond dead-end explication and the resultant death of the text is to highlight the interpretive process itself, showing that confidence and frustration collaborate in critical reading. By proposing that "Porphyria's Lover" allegorizes reading, an instructor can present texticidal interpretation as the easy way out—a side-stepping of what may seem to be unnecessary complication, methodological baggage. Initially, students who are beginning to learn about the importance of literature and how to read it think that teachers make complicated what is really simple and easy. Close analysis is not, students tell us, fair to the author or to the text: such analysis takes advantage of a defenseless text, an absent author. They see critics, frustrated that literature has the first word, needing themselves to have the final word to establish their own authority and worth.

Changing such students' attitudes toward the function of criticism, when "of reading as a noble intellectual exercise they know little or nothing" (Thoreau 1971 [1854], p. 104), involves indicating that a poem as easily read as "Porphyria's Lover" nonetheless resists the interpreter's arrogance and power. Browning's text encourages readers to see themselves as soulmates of his ideal poets, the "Makers-see" (*Sordello* 3.928). But it also disappoints, not because of artistic inadequacies but because of its indeterminacies, which impel an instructor to consider other critical methods instead of claiming to have finished the reading(s).

English professors will always teach reluctant students. If reluctance manifests itself as silence, the teacher can encourage students to articulate whatever they have mastered, regardless of apparent (in)significance, by imagining aloud what they might say. Causing them to put words in their own mouths may prime them to articulate, and then revise, their reading. If reluctance is the result of the need to own the poem absolutely, the instructor can demonstrate that interpretive disagreements are what decide literariness—that the classics of literature tend to be wanton and are never really owned by anyone. Disputes (even anticipated ones) over interpretive rights thus supplant the need for absolute certitude, both embracing and dispatching contraries, so that the educational process can go forward.

Yet another way of bringing indeterminacy into the classroom is to have students read the poem aloud. If I read the poem aloud at the beginning of a class, I own it vocally. But if I let students read it too, or, perhaps better, first, I illustrate the potential multiplicity of meaning. Students who impersonate Porphyria's lover sound themselves as well as re-sound figures of speech (their own and the text's). If a blind-mouthed pupil reads, the poem may seem to suffer—but wise students will prepare the text for reading. Oral reading also underscores the diversity of our skills as readers and listeners. Interpretation is a necessarily intrusive voice, without which "Porphyria's Lover" is dumb. Simon Petch miscalculates the importance of readers' being able to "*see* rhyme and verse-form as well as hear intonation and rhythm, . . . formal devices [that] often function as comments on what is being said" (1984–85, p. 38). But just because the lover's "voice reads its meaning into hers [Porphyria's]," we who use our eyes and ears are not deterred from "imposing [our] own voice[s] on Browning's poem" (p. 42). A mature reader's voice differs from the lover's, whose puerility is not only more conspicuous but also louder when "Porphyria's Lover" is something to talk over, literally and figuratively.

The quality of this oral performance depends upon the reader's ability to read ahead—to preview the poem's structure. The lover's impatience becomes more pronounced when a reader's voice stresses the anaphoric and conjunctive *and*'s in the first twenty-five lines so that they counterpoint the iambs; the insistent repetition conveys the watchful protagonist's disturbed emotions. A student bent on "recitation" may contrive for the lover an otherwise unavailable voice and thereby raise the volume of "Porphyria's Lover," which "exists most potently as an interplay of voices" (Petch, p. 42). Moreover, alert to accentual punctuation, an oral reader can modulate the lover's confident intentions by lengthening the pauses in the discourse. For instance, an intervening comma at the climactic moment of strangulation, "Three times her little throat around, / And strangled her" (ll. 40–41), complicates the event; it no longer seems quite so inevitable or horrible, but rather accidental, wistful, or playful. Porphyria's immunity, caught in the reassuring chiasmus—"No pain felt she; / I am quite sure she felt no pain" (ll. 41–42)—tranquilizes the lover but also sharpens his disappointment. These equivocations, less evident in a silent reading, emerge when a reader voices the lines. As Roland Barthes says, "In the text, only the reader speaks" (1974, p. 151). From this we hope students learn that when a reader speaks, not only the text listens, and that when the instructor "has not said a word" (l. 60), their mixed anxiety and enthusiasm are precisely what a literary performance demands.

The situation depicted in "Porphyria's Lover" is analogous to the situation an interpreter faces in determining the "meaning" of a text. Always intertextual—always originating from a rich literary and experiential world—a text (like Porphyria) glides into the life of an attentive reader who wants to dominate it by inferring its "utmost will" and who expects the poem's vitality to depend on interpretive intervention. Moreover, the reader often seeks a sign that some higher consciousness (usually the creative author) monitors the process of mastery and revival. Just as Porphyria's and the lover's actions filter through the latter's wild imagination, so the poem occurs in a reader's mind, which tends toward similar eccentricity. Every one of our readings strangles "Porphyria's Lover" anew, as we forcefully consolidate its lines into "one long yellow string" (l. 39); but we also suppose that the text's virtual intelligibility flatters our self-images, thus satisfying a mutual "utmost will" to take in (that is, to involve, deceive, and consume) each other. Involved in a responsive reading, a text must remain somewhat mysterious, only "murmuring" (l. 21) to signify its deepest alliance with criticism. The loving reader frequently has to suffer the intellectual and emotional indignity of being treated as a sulking, selfish juvenile in whom the text's surprises prompt new maturity.

The process of critical reading, a rite of passage through *liaisons dangereuses* toward a coveted *jouissance,* gains some measure of control over a text, but for "Porphyria's Lover" or any work to survive, the text must continue to perplex—just as the world of the poem perplexes the narrator, who is unable to know whether his actions have God's concurrence, indifference, or condemnation. Without some such conception of literary analysis as perpetual, students are likely to consider the practice mystifying and the results arbitrary, or vice versa. But if the teacher makes a point of periodically noting aspects of texts that mark them as interpretable or that replicate interpretive procedures, critical inquiry as a varied, rehabilitating activity becomes possible.

Interpretations of "Porphyria's Lover" that extrapolate from its first five lines what will happen in the other fifty-five lines finish the poem's and the reader's work prematurely. However, if a reader studies the lover's emotional turmoil as carefully as the lover listens to the storm outside his cottage, Porphyria's murder is not so predictable. Our first sympathies ought to be with the lover (as a heartbroken listener to an outrageous storm). When we consider the lover more pathetic than psychotic, the poem appears less controllable and his actions less culpable. But because mastery preoccupies the typical critic, Porphyria must die to secure interpretation. Nevertheless, if Porphyria not only dies but also revives at the hands of her lover, at most only half the poem's action is credible as an instance of rough sex turned homicide. Fotheringham explains the whole episode as "a romance of passion . . . [taking] place only among the wild motions of a lover's brain" (1887, p. 152). How justifiable, then, is moral outrage if we take "only a madman's word that there *was* a crime and that it was committed in such a way" (Gridley 1972, p. 56)? However, an inability to differentiate actuality from hallucination, like the chronic problem of distinguishing between literal and figurative meaning, need not deter further reading. A class bent on testing interpretive strategies will not surrender just yet to aporia, if the instructor has other ways of making students throw up their hands when they reach an impasse. Has the course of critical reading ever run smoothly?

Perhaps a few students will welcome the chance to show that Porphyria remains thoroughly in charge of the situation, which only seems to portray psychopathic reprisal for her "struggling passion" (l. 23). The lover presumes to rewrite her character, yet he cannot withstand her allure. Even after her strangulation he fears her "utmost will," which keeps him guessing. He considers her eyelids "a shut bud that holds a bee," which he "warily oped" (ll. 43–44) because even "dead" she has the power to retaliate; however, Browning makes the duplicitous syntax (a simile that confuses manner and identity) suggest that the lover is that "shut bud" with Porphyria buzzing in his head. Closed of mind and chauvinistic, he cannot match her subtlety, which outstrips his rage for control in this "study in fetishistic pseudosex" (Crowell 1972, p. 80). Committed to a maddening love, the lover celebrates yet fears Porphyria's happy, painless death. His love of Porphyria keeps him possessed; and his desperate attempt to become a god fails: he is more hers than she is his. He both does and does not want to be the love of her "smiling rosy little head" (l. 52), in a travesty of that "moment, one and infinite" ("By the Fire-Side," l. 181), when Browning's better lovers, being most unselfish, find mutual fulfillment. Like a child, Porphyria's lover sees her hair as "yellow" (ll. 18, 20), not golden, flaxen, or blonde, as he would had he a more mature mind and vocabulary. As a (s)mothering femme fatale who must handle a callow lover, Porphyria knows best that, in bringing him up, her erotic mirth depends on their make-believe. If, by feigning a little death and resurrection, she can enhance her lover's self-image, so much the better in raising his enthusiasm for being her demon lover, the demanding subject of her "utmost will."

The poem's obliquities seem to have given Browning pause, too; perhaps he, as much as the speaker, "debated what to do" (l. 35) when Porphyria's sexual initiative challenges her slumped, short lover (she has to stoop for his cheek to rest on her bare shoulder) to prove his "love of her" is not entirely "in vain" (l. 29). Regardless of whether the lover's actions constitute murder or fantasy, a Victorian poet even a little squeamish about the prospect of fully representing a sexual encounter beyond line 35 must have seen Porphyria's death and revival as a suitable euphemism to keep his poem alive and, ironically, inoffensive. Today's students could conclude the episode more forthrightly, but their own discretion will usually prevent them from addressing eroticism directly. What they cannot say any better than Browning confirms that moral and aesthetic values still connect their generation with the Victorians; this also illustrates E. D. Hirsch's distinction between intrinsic "textual meaning in and for itself" and extrinsic "significance" (or relevance) as a guide in basic literary education (1967, p. 211). Furthermore, students who think that authors have ready answers to interpretive questions will find intriguing Browning's indecision about his poem's main character. The title, changed from "Porphyria" to one of two "Madhouse Cells" (with "Johannes Agricola") and finally to "Porphyria's Lover" (DeVane 1955, p. 125), ought to offer a class its first clue about the poem's primary focus, but from the outset Browning's erasures diversify reading. "Porphyria's Lover," like any text under revision, dispatches authority, first its author's and then its readers'; Browning "declined to play God" (Petch, p. 43), and readers inherit the troublesome task of properly disposing of the poem to grant its "darling one wish [to] be heard" (l. 57).

The relationship between Porphyria and her lover constitutes every reading activity, which whether for information or pleasure involves the reader's incompleteness, augmented and alleviated by the text. The ideal situation, then, is our being sufficiently satisfied by canny reactions to "Porphyria's Lover," but also feeling that its cleverness, and ours, is a safeguard against the possibility of a final reading. Just as Porphyria's indeterminacy confounds her inexperienced lover, the poem prevents us from exhausting its meaning(s) and stifling critical potential. Student readers mature when they develop a healthy mistrust of a confessional text and are prepared "to collaborate in the production of [the author's] work" (Sartre 1975, p. 40). "Porphyria's Lover" is, on one level, so easily understood that it can become unreadable—an academic exercise, with its students either victims or deferential lovers of the need for (un)critical closure. Whether Porphyria or her lover teaches the other a more enduring lesson is unclear from the text, but students of the poem's counterpoises learn that having the last word is the most mortal sin in literary scripture.

## References

Barthes, Roland. 1974. *S/Z*. Translated by Richard Miller. New York: Hill and Wang.
————. 1986. "To Learn and to Teach." In *The Rustle of Language*. Translated by Richard Howard, 176–78. New York: Hill and Wang.
Browning, Robert. 1981. *The Poems*. Edited by John Pettigrew. Vol. 1. New Haven: Yale University Press.
Crowell, Norton B. 1972. *A Reader's Guide to Robert Browning*. Albuquerque: University of New Mexico Press.
DeVane, William C. 1955. *A Browning Handbook*. 2nd ed. Englewood Cliffs, N.J.: Prentice.
Fotheringham, James. 1887. *Studies in the Poetry of Robert Browning*. London: Kegan Paul.
Gridley, Roy E. 1972. *Browning*. London: Routledge.
Hirsch, E. D., Jr. 1967. "Objective Interpretation." In *Validity in Interpretation*, 209–44. New Haven: Yale University Press.
Iser, Wolfgang. 1974. "The Reading Process: A Phenomenological Approach." In *The Implied Reader*, 274–94. Baltimore: Johns Hopkins University Press.
Petch, Simon. 1984–85. "Character and Voice in the Poetry of Browning." *Sydney Studies in English* 10: 33–50.
Poulet, Georges. 1972. "Criticism and the Experience of Interiority." In *The Structuralist Controversy: The Language of Criticism and the Sciences of Man,* edited by Richard Macksey and Eugenio Donato, 56–72. Baltimore: Johns Hopkins University Press.
Sartre, Jean-Paul. 1975. "Why Write?" In *What Is Literature?* Translated by Bernard Frechtman, 32–60. New York: Torchbook-Harper.
Thoreau, Henry D. 1971 [1854]. *Walden.* Edited by J. Lyndon Shanley. Princeton: Princeton University Press.

# 14 Reading "Life in the Iron-Mills" Contextually: A Key to Rebecca Harding Davis's Fiction

Jane Atteridge Rose

Jane Atteridge Rose is an assistant professor at Georgia College, in Milledgeville, Georgia—a senior comprehensive college within the state system. At this institution she carries a full load of courses that includes composition, American literature, modern fiction, and black literature. She also coaches the debate team. Although she does not teach women's literature, she sees herself as a feminist scholar, for feminist theory informs all her teaching. The essay included here combines topics from both Summer Institutes, for it "applies the contextual theories of Tompkins and the feminist theories of Gilbert and Gubar in a reading of practical criticism."

Prior to this year, Professor Rose taught for seven years at the University of Georgia, first as a teaching assistant and then as an instructor. While working on her Ph.D. in American literature at this large state university, she taught freshman and sophomore core courses in English, particularly computer-assisted composition.

Critical awareness, according to Professor Rose, "is nowhere more necessary than in small colleges with limited course offerings." She believes that "when there is not much latitude for text selection, a great deal can be accomplished by approaching standard texts with new awareness—by calling old assumptions into question." Professor Rose is currently writing a volume on Rebecca Harding Davis for the Twayne United States Authors Series.

In April of 1861, when the American political consciousness was shaken to its foundations by the attack on Fort Sumter, the American literary consciousness was shaken by the publication of Rebecca Harding Davis's "Life in the Iron-Mills" in the *Atlantic Monthly*. Davis's story still fascinates readers today. It finds its way into a variety of college courses: in history courses it is read as a treatment of American industrial conditions; in literature courses it is read as an example of early naturalistic realism; in women's studies courses it is read as the work of a female literary imagination; and in cultural studies courses it is read as a perspective on marginalized Americans.

Despite its presence in these various curricula, however, neither the work nor its author have found full acceptance in the literary community. This is true particularly of traditional literary historians, but also, to a certain extent, of feminist critics.

Traditionally, literary historians have noted Davis's precocious realism, comparing her to the later Emile Zola. They point with admiration to passages in "Iron-Mills" such as one in which the narrator says to the reader, "Hide your disgust, take no heed to your clean clothes, and come right down with me,—here, into the thickest of the fog and mud and foul effluvia." However, they have then dismissed her work as too flawed to warrant serious critical attention, noting that passages like the above conclude with the sentimental assertion that "there is a secret underlying sympathy between that story and this day with its impure fog and thwarted sunshine" (p. 13). *The Literary History of the United States* (1946) accurately represents this attitude, stating that "unfortunately the faults of melodrama and didacticism mar even the best" of Davis's realism (1:881).

Since Tillie Olsen's insightful biographical interpretation in the Feminist Press edition of "Iron-Mills" in 1972, Davis's story has also been studied as an imaginative reworking of the author's experience as a woman. Although "Iron-Mills" gained new life as a literary text with this recovery, it has continued to stimulate surprisingly little feminist scholarship. Critical inattention here suggests that viewed from a feminist perspective, as from a realistic one, Davis's work often disappoints. Perhaps feminists are put off by her development of male and female characters with conventional gender-specific attributes. She tends to cast males in the role of heroic self-realization and to assign females to sacrificial redemptive roles, as she does in "Iron-Mills" with Hugh Wolfe, the alienated artist, and his pitifully deformed cousin, Deborah Wolfe. Or perhaps Davis's tendency to focus on men in male situations casts her as a male manqué in the eyes of some female readers.[1]

Granted, Davis's fiction is not flawless realism, and granted, it is not uncompromised feminism. The impediment to productive reading, however, is not as much Davis's work as the perspectives we have brought to it. Contemporary critical reception of Davis's work indicates that, in her own day, her efforts toward realism and toward a liberal vision of womanhood were considered advanced. Today, however, she seems very much a woman of her time. For this reason, her texts really open to us only when we understand them in the context of the culture that shaped both the author and her fiction.[2] For productive reading of Davis's work, the most important cultural influence to be aware of is the ideology of domesticity—actually a composite of four belief systems: the doctrine of gender spheres, idealism, sentimentalism, and evangelicalism.

## The Ideology of Domesticity

Understanding of nineteenth-century domesticity begins with the doctrine of gender spheres: the codification of the head-and-heart dichotomy as gender-linked attributes. Historically, the industrial revolution further entrenched the separation of spheres. Women, remaining in homes that were no longer productive in order to care for children, abandoned their economic roles. But as the relativity and materialism of the marketplace became the world of men, the perpetuation of morality fell to women.

Associated with the doctrine of gender spheres were idealism, sentimentalism, and evangelicalism. Idealism, which led fiction writers to use fact as an inductive approach to spiritual mystery, caused women to perceive of their role and their sphere typologically. Like Christ, their self-sacrifice was redemptive; like heaven, their home was a haven of loving peace. Related to idealism was sentimentalism, with its vision of a benevolent God. The supremacy of love as the definition of the Godhead was a primary force behind the elevation of woman in the nineteenth century; hers was the affective domain of loving. Sentimentalism, with its stress on the demonstration of love through self-sacrifice and on the social benefits of altruistic cooperation, was the antithesis of romanticism's defiant egoism. A sentimentalized vision of domesticity also provided a way to view female self-abnegation as messianic.

Idealism and sentimentalism, which confirmed the affinity between Christian and feminine values, also led to an optimistic faith in the eventual success of both. This millennial vision of social reform through spiritual transformation was evident in evangelicalism. Like other aspects of domestic ideology, evangelicalism, while it pervaded the culture, was experienced primarily by women. The only way that women writing within the web of these values could combine their multiple vocations as authors, women, and reformers was by writing moral fiction. As realism developed an aesthetic of objectivity, the genre became problematic for female writers who, with identities shaped by domestic ideology, saw themselves as preachers through fiction. Nineteenth-century domesticity, while it limited female self-definition, also infused women with a sense of power. It provided the impetus behind both the temperance movement and the suffrage movement. Ironically, while requiring that women accept their preordained place in society, domesticity also provided them with a mandate to reform it.

When we read within the context of this value system, we find in "Iron-Mills" a new, rewarding dimension. The "flaws" in Davis's realism and the "compromises" to her feminism reveal a complex imaginative response to the ideas and mores that shaped her world. Furthermore, approaching "Iron-Mills" as a text informed by nineteenth-century domestic ideology actually enriches our study of it as realism and feminism, revealing the tension between each of those sensibilities and her received domestic values. This perspective provides greater access to Davis's other works as well, since they, too, are strongly influenced by domestic ideology.[3]

## Responses to Domestic Ideology

For what it reveals about a writing woman's various responses to domestic ideology, "Iron-Mills" remains a valuable literary artifact. Like a great deal of Davis's fiction, her story of a coal miner's suicide illuminates a woman's perspective on nineteenth-century experience. "Iron-Mills" reveals four different ways that Davis as a female writer responded to domestic ideology: mediation, confrontation, ameliora- tion, and rationalization. She mediates gender limitations through her narrative strategies. She confronts the mores of domestic ideology in her female characters, who are either victimized by domesticity's false material values or empowered by its true spiritual ones. She ameliorates the crimes of society with plots that allegorize social reform through spiritual transformation. And, finally, she rationalizes her own thwarted and guilty ambitions in stories of compromised artists. Domestic ideology, the most influential force in Davis's life, affected both how she wrote and what she wrote.

Davis demonstrates many ways of mediating the limiting effect that the doctrine of gender spheres had on her natural literary expression. Domesticity and realism, the two sensibilities shaping Davis's texts, were distinctly gender-associated and traditionally incompatible. Women upheld the sentimentality that shaped domesticity, and men championed the objectivity that shaped realism. Born into a worldview premised on the total separation of gender spheres, Davis continually argues for a sensibility that contains both female and male attributes. The con- temporary writer Elizabeth Stuart Phelps describes Davis's style in "Iron-Mills" in androgynous terms: "Her intensity was essentially feminine, but her grip was like that of a masculine hand" (p. 120).[4]

In both the form and content of her fiction, Davis attempts to resolve this schism. For instance, Davis often creates a sexually ambiguous protagonist, as she does with Hugh Wolfe in "Iron-Mills." Wolfe has "a meek, woman's face. . . . In the mill he was known as one of the girl-men." They call him "Molly Wolfe" (p. 24). Davis's male and female protagonists are always sexual anomalies in societies codified by gender distinction.

Davis mediates gender coding in her narrative technique, which attempts to transcend female restrictions by acquiring male license. To this end, she often assumes a masculine narrative voice, as she does in "Iron-Mills." Her narrator's sex is not designated in this tale; and therefore, particularly in 1861, it would be assumed to be masculine. Independence and freedom of movement, male prerogatives, enable the narrator to relate his "story of this old house into which I happen to come today" (p. 13). Clearly not one of the "masses of men, with dull, besotted faces bent to the ground," the narrator, nevertheless, is able to walk about freely in the "air saturated with fog and grease and soot" (p. 12). A female narrator would have to explain her presence in this demimonde. The narrator ends his story with another statement that reflects the subtle kind of freedom that a man would assume but a woman could not. He offers no explanation for his behavior when he states, "The deep of the night is passing while I write" (p. 64). A female narrator would have to defend her sleepless night of writing and contemplation. She could not have told a story of sordid life in the iron mills without pulling the focus away from the story to explain her knowledge of it.

In addition to the many ways that Davis mediates the limitations of gender codification by denying them, she occasionally mediates by emphasizing them. In her treatment of Hugh and Deborah Wolfe, the complementary protagonists of "Iron-Mills," she employs gender-specific attributes to her own advantage. Bifurcating the role of the protagonist, she splits focus and significance between Hugh and Deb, assigning to each motives appropriate to his or her sex. While Hugh enacts the human need for freedom, Deb demonstrates the driving motive of love. Hugh enacts Davis's dark deterministic vision and egoistic desire, while Deb asserts Davis's optimistic faith and self-sacrifice. The pessimism that shaped Davis's social criticism was considered unacceptable in a woman. Her fiction did not elevate or ameliorate as much as readers thought a woman's should. Davis's strategy, therefore, was to split the central figure so that the part enacted by Hugh Wolfe could confront brutal reality while the part enacted by his cousin Deb could recognize hopeful spirituality. Just as Davis creates a male voice to tell her horrific story of life in the iron mills, she also creates Hugh, a male who has the ironic freedom to reject the world through suicide after voicing his despair that "all the world had gone wrong" (p. 51).

But also shaping Davis's reformist vision is a traditionally feminine spiritual optimism. As in "Iron-Mills," carriers of millennial hope in her work are usually women. Although Hugh is ostensibly the protagonist of this story, the plot does not conclude with his suicide. Rather, the narrator, trying to comprehend Deb's story, returns the focus to where it began, with Deb: "a soul filled with groping passionate love, heroic unselfishness, fierce jealousy" (p. 21). After Hugh's death for a crime which she had instigated, Deb is redeemed through the love of an old Quaker woman. The story ends not with the despair associated with the mills or the prison, which could be voiced acceptably only by a male, but with the optimistic vision of a Friends' meetinghouse, where Deb enjoys the fellowship of a loving community.

This story's development of a male tragic hero also illuminates Davis's mediation of gender-based sensibilities. Hugh Wolfe's character suggests much about female literary imagination, although it is camouflaged by several personas. The narrator's account of Hugh Wolfe is an attempt to understand the mystery embodied in his female image of the korl woman with "not one line of grace in it . . . the powerful limbs instinct with some one poignant longing" (p. 32). Davis projects her animus through a male narrator and a male protagonist and, further, through them into their shared anima-projection, the korl woman. It is this female object that communicates "something pure and beautiful, which might have been and was not: a hope, a talent, a love, over which the soul mourns" (p. 64).

In addition to her narrative mediation of polarized gender sensibilities, Davis also confronts the influence of domestic values in various ways through her characters. When we examine her female characters, who are affected by social definition just like their real-world counterparts, we see still more clearly Davis's reaction to the mores of her society. While she endorses the power of sentimental domestic reform, she criticizes the intellectual and physical prohibitions within the woman's sphere. Her female characters either offer a critique of domestic mores as oppressive—like Deb, who is victimized by her femininity, or they provide a model of domestic ideals as empowering—like the old Quaker, whose quiet strength lies as much in her feminine wisdom as it does in her Christian faith. Often, like the writers of sentimental "woman's fiction," Davis makes symbolic emblems of her characters, as she does the redemptive Quaker and the redeemed Deb, giving her plots the force of allegory. Yet, as in the case of Deb, she also manages to develop many of them as individual characters reacting to realistic situations.

In the brutal world of immigrant laborers, Deborah Wolfe is clearly a victim. Davis uses her as an emblem of powerlessness:

> [Deb is] not an unfitting figure to crown the scene of hopeless discomfort and veiled crime: more fitting, if one looked deeper into the heart of things,—at her thwarted woman's form, her colorless life. . . . (p. 21)

Compared to Hugh's pretty friend Janey, who has that death-frail beauty so admired in the nineteenth century, Deb, who is "deformed, almost a hunchback" (p. 15), has a frailty that is only repulsive. Hugh loves and protects Janey; no one loves and protects Deb. The contrast of the two women confronts the reality that in the subtle and complex hierarchy of our ostensibly classless society, the bottom rung belongs to an ugly woman. Davis's depiction of deformed Deb's anguish to be loved underscores the objectification of all women. Looking at Deb's unloved face, the narrator broadens his contemplation to include all unloved women in a world that objectifies their value:

> One sees that dead, vacant look steal sometimes over the rarest, finest of women's faces,—in the very midst, it may be, of their warmest summer's day; and then one can guess at the secret of intolerable solitude that lies hid beneath the delicate laces and brilliant smile. (p. 22)

The first appearance of Davis's most frequent emblem of female wisdom, the Quaker woman, is also instructive. Putting "her strong arm around Deborah" (p. 62), this unnamed "homely body, coarsely dressed in gray and white" (p. 61), involves herself in Deb's sordid world of poverty, crime, and death in order to bring comfort and solace to a stranger. But like Deb, this character also has the power of the real. Quaker women in Davis's fiction primarily assert strength of integrity and purpose. Their defiance of social norms challenges the false value of domesticity. These women refute the popular belief that purity requires innocence, the assumption that most forcefully kept women within the protected limits of the home.

Davis's subsequent fiction contains many other images of the nineteenth-century woman confronting her social condition. Many of her later female protagonists register some degree of discontent with the restrictions of domesticity (see "The Wife's Story," "Anne," *Margret Howth,* and *Waiting for the Verdict*). Capable, intelligent, energetic women in Davis's fiction are frustrated by their limitations, humiliated by their dependency, and angry at their decorative uselessness. However, her women often champion the sentimental ideals of domesticity. Thus, we see in Davis's characters' confrontation with society the same split attitude toward their domestic context that we see illustrated in other aspects of her writing.

"Iron-Mills" further typifies Davis's fiction in that it articulates many goals of nineteenth-century social reform. Asserting feminine attributes like loving self-abnegation and spiritual purity as Christian ideals, domestic ideology encouraged women to perceive their role as messianic. Like the Quaker in "Iron-Mills," who intrudes herself into the jail, the defense of feminized Christianity often placed women at odds with social and institutional values. Real personalities who were acquaintances of Davis, like Lucretia Mott, Frances Willard, and Catharine Beecher, were all impelled by this force in a variety of directions.[5] Domestic reformers maintained a typological perception of the domestic sphere which affirmed faith in their power to ameliorate social ills. Home and family were believed to be the earthly manifestation of heaven and loving connectedness. For Davis and many of her contemporaries sharing this vision, allegorical narratives were not inherently at odds with the principles of realism, particularly critical realism. She asserts her resolutions in "Iron-Mills" and elsewhere to be as realistic as her problems; it is just that her problems are actual, and her solutions are potential.

As with the other aspects of domesticity in Davis's fiction, "Iron-Mills" illustrates her use of the ideology as a reformative plan. Like most of her other stories, it promotes affective femininity, sentimental theology, spiritual integrity, maternalism, and agrarian familial communities. The story is based on scenes of home and family, the *topoi* of domestic valuation. "Iron-Mills," which dwells on the power of both physical place and ideological institutions to affect the human spirit, begins in a home. It is "low, damp,—the earthen floor covered with green slimy moss,—a fetid air smothering the breath" (p. 16). Here human beings are forced to "breathe from infancy" only "vileness for soul and body" (p. 12). However, the Quaker community envisioned at the end affirms society's ability to create for itself a positive environment in which the individual spirit can thrive. The fact that the external force of the Quaker's love, rather than any action of her own, saves Deb defines *affection* as the ultimate power of God's design. This transformation of domestic environments from the beginning of the tale to its conclusion outlines a scheme for social reform.

After Hugh's suicide, Deb's concern with his burial place further reinforces the idea that a healthful atmosphere is necessary for the human spirit as well as for the body. Deb, with her rather primitive sense of the grave as a final home, agonizes that the mill's slums, where Hugh has spent his life, will also be his eternal resting place. Her Quaker friend responds with assurances that humanity can build pastoral communities that replicate heaven and that answer the soul's needs. She promises to take Hugh's body to rest there: "Thee sees the hills, friend, over the river? Thee sees how the light lies warm there, and the winds of God blow all the day? I live there" (p. 62). As she tells Deb, "Thee shall begin thy life again,—there in the hills," the Quaker also offers hope for rejuvenation within a healthful environment.

Davis's narrator concludes "Iron-Mills" with a note of optimism by depicting an ideal home that is the antithesis of the "kennel-like rooms" that open the story. But like the opening, this setting is also a house:

> There is a homely pine house, on one of these hills, whose windows overlook broad, wooded slopes and clover-crimsoned meadows,—niched into the very place where the light is warmest, the air freest. It is the Friends' meeting-house. (p. 63)

"Iron-Mills" urges not the external reform of labor unions, but an internal, spiritual transformation, which asks society to structure itself on Christian, feminine ideals. Here, Davis bases her ameliorative vision on the woman's domestic sphere, asserting the home and family as emblems of ideal, sentimental human relationship. This domestic vision of social reform is her project in "Iron-Mills," and it continued to be her project throughout most of her career.

A much more personal response to domestic ideology in Davis's fiction is her rationalization of egoistic artistic desire. For women, acceptance of the egoism implicit in artistic self-assertion was antithetical to the passive, self-abnegating service that defined femininity. If a writer like Davis denied her creativity, she willingly crippled her sensed potential; but if she denied her womanhood, she annihilated her sense of self. Davis quite typically alleviated the guilt and frustration inherent in this double-bind by becoming her own worst enemy—creating fictional projections of herself as artist and then negating their power, punishing them, or having them recant their unacceptable artistic impulses. Her treatment of artists, or rather artists manqué, offers a paradigm of ambivalence toward the female situation experienced by many intelligent, creative women in the nineteenth century.

Davis's ambivalence toward her frustrated creative desire and her guilt about being a woman with this desire are nowhere more evident than in this story. Though male—a rationalization in itself—Davis's first artist, Hugh Wolfe, articulates the frustration commonly experi-

enced by female artists. Oppressive external forces thwart his development, silence his expression, and inhibit his self-comprehension. He
sculpts in korl, an industrial waste product, and creates the massive
figure of a woman. The image of the korl woman is proof that
compromised artists produce compromised art:

> Nothing remains to tell that the poor Welsh puddler once lived,
> but this figure of the mill-woman cut in korl. I have it here in a
> corner of my library. I keep it hid behind a curtain,—it is such
> a rough, ungainly thing. Yet there are about it touches, grand
> sweeps of outline, that show a master's hand. Sometimes,—to-
> night, for instance,—the curtain is accidentally drawn back, and
> I see a bare arm stretched out imploringly in the darkness, and
> an eager, wolfish face watching mine: a wan, woeful face, through
> which the spirit of the dead korl-cutter looks out, with its thwarted
> life, its mighty hunger, its unfinished work. (p. 64)

This scene powerfully illuminates Davis's guilty anxiety about the
artist's role. The fictive narrator—a writer, an artist, and a musician—
sits in the library amid such value-laden objects as "a broken figure of
an angel pointing upward," a "dirty canary chirp[ing] desolately in a
cage" (p. 12), and "a half-moulded child's head" (p. 65). Pondering
the mystery of the sculpture, the narrator understands the "spirit of
the dead korl-cutter." The statue of the korl woman, to which the
narrator has fallen heir, is kept "in a corner of [the] library" in order
to "keep it hid behind a curtain." But like any repressed desire,
sometimes, at night, "the curtain is accidentally drawn back," and "its
mighty hunger, its unfinished work" are painfully visible.

While providing a rationale for Davis's own life, her artists also
reveal the insidious power of ideology to limit potential. In "Iron-
Mills," Hugh Wolfe is frustrated by the inhumane economic forces that
determine his inability to fulfill his creative desire. As a result, he fails
in that his death causes his creation to remain incomplete and hidden.
Creativity offers him no solace. Most of all, his statue fails him as
communication. His korl woman is a puzzle to the mill officials who
discover it—"some terrible problem lay in this woman's face, and
troubled these men," but they could not solve that puzzle (p. 34).
Furthermore, as expression stimulates greater comprehension, the statue's full meaning remains outside her creator's ken also; all Wolfe can
say is "she be hungry" (p. 33). Like the statue, Hugh Wolfe fails to
satisfy his hunger, to use his power, to find his voice. He kills himself.
Davis's protagonist, like artists in all her stories and like those in the
fiction of most other female writers of this period, is a frustrated,
unfulfilled failure.

An artist like her character, Rebecca Harding Davis, a woman in the nineteenth century, was forced to make choices that made inevitable some degree of frustration or failure. Like the statue of the korl woman, which seems to contain "the spirit of the dead korl-cutter," Davis's fiction remains as a valuable literary artifact to remind us, in her own words, of "thwarted life," "mighty hunger," and "unfinished work." Like the narrator, for whom the story of Hugh and Deb Wolfe brings an enriched context of meaning to the statue of the korl woman, we also gain a richer appreciation of "Life in the Iron-Mills" and all of Davis's writing by contextual reading. Like a great deal of Davis's fiction, this story of an inarticulate iron worker and a hunchbacked mill girl illuminates a woman's perspective on nineteenth-century experience.

Domesticity, the ideology that shaped Davis's life, determined women's proper sphere of influence in fiction just as it did in every other endeavor. Female writers like Davis, who aspired to the objectivity of realism or the creative autonomy of authorship, were impelled by deep-seated values to mediate these possibilities with more socially acceptable domestic perspectives. Davis personally attempted to free herself from the restrictions that the domestic sphere placed on the matter of her fiction by frequently appearing to focus on male subjects in male situations. Having accomplished an acceptable public voice, female authors, through their fictive alter egos, could confront the social mores of domesticity that oppressed women by offering alternative liberating visions. Women could also use their creative imaginations to ameliorate the crimes of a misdirected society by showing the possibilities of spiritual transformation. However, even when writing within their proper mode, many women were forced to develop narrative strategies by which to rationalize their unfeminine perspective. Davis's stories of failed or frustrated artists reflect her need to integrate the values of domestic ideology with her own values as a woman and a writer. Contextual reading reveals that Rebecca Harding Davis was indeed a pioneer critical realist but that she was also in many ways a typical nineteenth-century woman, thoroughly enmeshed in the web of beliefs that comprised domestic ideology.

## Notes

1. Gilbert and Gubar (1979) define *males manqués* as female authors "who disguised their identities and, denying themselves, produced most frequently a literature of bad faith and inauthenticity" (p. 72). One further reason for this lack of attention is the frequent misattribution

to Davis of an anti-feminist diatribe. For proof of this error, see Eppard 1975.

2. For sympathetic and insightful inquiry into the values operating in middle-class nineteenth-century America and shaping its fiction, see Tompkins 1985.

3. These imaginative responses to domesticity's influence, first appearing in "Iron-Mills," resonate as motifs through the more than five hundred essays, stories, and novels that Davis wrote during her fifty-year career (for bibliography, see Rose 1990).

4. In an essay published shortly after Davis's death in 1910, Phelps, an admirer of Davis, assesses the distinct quality that marks the best of Davis's fiction (p. 120).

5. The Quaker Mott was a force in the abolition and suffrage movements. Willard was founder of the Women's Christian Temperance Union and coauthor of the feminist biographical resource *A Woman of the Century* (1893). With the assistance of her sister, Harriet Beecher Stowe, Catharine Beecher was the architect of home economics as an educational discipline and coauthor of an influential nineteenth-century treatise, *The American Woman's Home* (1869).

# References

Beecher, Catharine E., and Harriet Beecher Stowe. 1971 [1869]. *The American Woman's Home: or Principles of Domestic Science; Being a Guide to the Formation and Maintenance of Economic, Healthful, Beautiful, and Christian Homes.* New York: Arno-New York Times.

Davis, Rebecca Harding. 1985 [1889]. "Anne." In *"Life in the Iron-Mills" and Other Stories,* edited by Tillie Olsen. Old Westbury, N.Y.: Feminist Press.

———. 1985 [1861]. "Life in the Iron-Mills." In *"Life in the Iron-Mills" and Other Stories,* edited by Tillie Olsen. Old Westbury, N.Y.: Feminist Press.

———. 1970 [1862]. *Margret Howth: A Story of To-day.* Upper Saddle River, N.J.: Gregg.

———. 1968 [1867]. *Waiting for the Verdict.* Upper Saddle River, N.J.: Gregg.

———. 1985 [1864]. "The Wife's Story." In *"Life in the Iron-Mills" and Other Stories,* edited by Tillie Olsen. Old Westbury, N.Y.: Feminist Press.

Eppard, Philip. 1975. "Rebecca Harding Davis: A Misattribution." *PBSA* 69: 265–67.

Gilbert, Sandra M., and Susan Gubar. 1979. *The Madwoman in the Attic.* New Haven: Yale University Press.

Olsen, Tillie. 1972. Biographical Interpretation. In *"Life in the Iron-Mills" and Other Stories,* edited by Tillie Olsen. Old Westbury, N.Y.: Feminist Press.

———, ed. 1985. *"Life in the Iron-Mills" and Other Stories.* Rev. ed. Old Westbury, N.Y.: Feminist Press.

Phelps [Ward], Elizabeth Stuart. 1910. "Stories that Stay." *Century* 81: 118–24.

Rose, Jane. 1990. "The Writing of Rebecca Harding Davis: A Primary Bibliography." *American Literary Realism* 22, no. 3 (Spring).

Spiller, Robert E., et al., eds. 1946. *Literary History of the United States.* 2 vols. 3rd. ed., rev. New York: Macmillan.

Tompkins, Jane. 1985. *Sensational Designs.* New York: Oxford University Press.

Willard, Frances E., and Mary A. Livermore. 1967 [1893]. *A Woman of the Century.* Rev. ed. Detroit: Gale. (Also reprinted as *American Women,* Gale, 1973.)

# 15 Local Canons: Professing Literature at the Small Liberal Arts College

Bobby Fong

In the fall of 1989 Bobby Fong moved from Berea College, in Berea, Kentucky, to become dean of arts and humanities at Hope College, in Holland, Michigan. His essay draws on his long tenure at Berea College, where he began teaching in 1978. Berea College is a small private four-year liberal arts institution that is distinctive in that it has no tuition, its students must fulfill a universal labor requirement (ten hours a week helping to maintain the institution), and its curriculum is specially focused on the southern Appalachian mountain region.

During the 1988–89 academic year, Professor Fong chaired the Department of English at Berea, which has a full-time faculty of fourteen and graduates fifteen to twenty majors each year. Typically each semester he taught a writing course, a literature course, and a course in the college's general education sequence. During the January short term, he had the opportunity to offer a course that mirrored his training or current interests—in recent years, courses in American literary realism and naturalism, the American small town, Dickens, and utopian literature. About his department, he notes, "We were a service department, but we offered a goodly variety of literature courses, and in recent years enrollment in those courses exploded."

Professor Fong's essay developed from his response to the second Summer Institute as expressed in a letter exploring his concern over the differences between the responsibilities and demands of teaching in a research institution and those in a small college. One letter led to another, and then to the essay that follows.

Questions of canon formation have enlarged our conception of what materials constitute the literary heritage of England and America. The work of feminist and ethnic scholars, the new-historicist emphasis on the social context of nonprivileged classes, and the renewed interest in the mimetic and political dimensions of texts have brought forward an immense body of works for serious consideration by teachers and students. But the very wealth of materials vying for places in the curriculum has also created a crisis of evaluation. What deserves classroom time, and who decides?

One attempt to answer these questions was the 1988 Summer Institute for college teachers sponsored by the National Council of Teachers of English. The presentations by Sandra Gilbert, Susan Gubar, and Henry Gates sparked animated discussions among participants as to how our teaching might incorporate the new scholarship on women and blacks. The occasion, however, led me back to basic pedagogical reality: the way in which individual teachers deal with questions of canon is heavily dependent on the institutional contexts in which they work. As a professor in a small private liberal arts college, my strategy for incorporating the new scholarship must be different from that of Gilbert, Gubar, and Gates. They helped me think through some of the theoretical issues involved in canon formation, but given their affiliations with prestigious research universities, they could not know of the curricular constraints and opportunities that teaching at a small college entails and that necessarily bear upon the implementation of the new scholarship.

College professors, given their graduate training, have been exposed to the ethos of the research university. The reverse, however, is not true. Many of our most eminent scholars and critics have no professional acquaintance with the operations of a small college. And yet, even though the research universities, by virtue of their scholarly production, may set much of the agenda and tone for American higher education, they are relatively atypical of the majority of institutions that engage in undergraduate education. In the "Report on the 1983–84 Survey of the English Sample" (1986), a study of the profession commissioned by the Association of Departments of English, Bettina Hube and Art Young make the following observations:

1. Ph.D.-granting institutions account for only 6 percent of all English departments (p. 40).
2. English programs in very small institutions, that is, with enrollments of fewer than 3,000 students, account for 58 percent of the college and university departments of English. Programs in small institutions, with enrollments between 3,000 and 10,999, account for another 20 percent (p. 41).
3. The "typical" department of English offers no graduate program and has a regular (i.e., tenure and tenure-track) full-time faculty of five to eighteen members (p. 46).
4. A large part of the "typical" department's instruction load involves lower-division writing and literature courses (p. 46).

While research scholars have led the way in thinking about issues of canon formation, the curricular implications of the debate are being worked out in arenas—the small colleges—in which university faculty may have little experience. It is here that a small-college teacher might contribute to the dialogue. Drawing from a decade's work at Berea College, with its enrollment of 1,500 students and fourteen full-time English, speech, and theatre faculty engaged solely in baccalaureate education, I would like to discuss how particular strategies of canon formation reflect institutional structures and how the small colleges need to think about canon formation in ways distinctive to their own size and missions.

## Approaches to Canon Formation

Jay B. Hubbell's *Who Are the Major American Writers?* (1972) exemplifies one way of thinking about canon formation. Hubbell charts the opinions of influential writers and critics from the early American republic to the 1960s as to which authors they considered significant and likely to endure. In his very approach, Hubbell assumes the existence of a largely unified literary establishment within which individuals might disagree, but whose collective pronouncements regarding the "greats" has prescriptive force. Although the book demonstrates that the collective wisdom of one generation may be considered collective wrongheadedness by the next, and that reputations rise and fall according to the changing critical values brought to the works, Hubbell is basically sympathetic to this procedure: a species of voting for a literary Hall of Fame, certain members of which can be tossed out by the next cycle of electors. Indeed, Hubbell expresses dismay that modern anthologies of major American writers are apt to include too many authors (pp. 277–78), since this presumably debases the standard for greatness and evades the responsibility for making distinctions. In sum, canon formation for Hubbell is a sort of "top-down" process, where the most influential writers and critics of a generation effectively decide what is "major" and what is not. The desired result is a largely uniform—and short—list of authors and works that can be taught as the major tradition. The list can be revised by the next generation, but the procedure will be the same.

A contrasting approach to canon formation is found in the organization of Paul Lauter's *Reconstructing American Literature* (1983). The book is a collection of American literature course syllabi from teachers determined to incorporate recent scholarship on minorities and women.

Lauter and his contributors welcome the proliferation of materials with a claim to classroom time. The challenge is to accommodate a multiplicity of literary traditions rather than to reduce all works to a single standard of greatness. Considerations should include the historical, social, and political significance of works as well as their aesthetic value. At the very least, this approach expands the dimensions of a single canon far beyond what Hubbell might imagine or approve. More ambitiously, it creates a number of alternative canons that can be organized by race or gender or region or class. At the extreme, it can eradicate the very notion of "canon" in favor of combinations of readings that differ from classroom to classroom depending on the interests of the instructor and the needs of the students. Lauter's collection is a "bottom-up" approach, where individual classroom experiments form a network of alternatives from which instructors can fashion their own courses of reading.

Although these two procedures to canon formation could be characterized as polar opposites of one another, they are really but two faces of literary study in the modern research university. In *Professing Literature* (1987), an institutional history of literary studies in the American research university, Gerald Graff notes that from the outset, "the transmission of humanism and cultural tradition in the Matthew Arnold sense was indeed the official goal of the literature department" (p. 3). This humanistic tradition, I think, includes Jay Hubbell and the approach to canon formation which he represents. Moreover, note the academic and institutional credentials of the editors of the Norton, Macmillan, and Harper anthologies of literature. It is mainly research-oriented academics in the twentieth century who arbitrate the canonicity of works through that most powerful of vehicles: the textbook anthology. Nonetheless, according to Graff, the humanistic goal of literary studies has always been undermined by the way that the modern university organizes these studies according to the *field-coverage principle*. Writes Graff,

> For reasons having to do equally with ensuring humanistic breadth and facilitating specialized research, the literature department adopted the assumption that it would consider itself respectably staffed once it had amassed instructors competent to "cover" a more or less balanced spread of literary periods and genres, with a scattering of themes and special topics. . . . Its great advantage was to make the department and the curriculum virtually self-regulating. By assigning each instructor a commonly understood role—to cover a predefined period or field—the principle created a system in which the job of instruction could proceed as if on

automatic pilot, without the need for instructors to debate aims
and methods. (pp. 6–7)

This structure has compartmentalized learning and produced research
that challenges the unitary tradition of knowledge. That Hubbell's
notion of canon seems so dated testifies to the degree to which the
very notion of a universal canon clashes with the specialized orientations
of literary scholars. The vehemence with which the lack of a common
cultural tradition has been bemoaned by critics such as Allan Bloom
arises from a sense that the academy is organized about courses of
study that make a common tradition impossible. At the same time,
Graff writes,

> The second advantage of the field-coverage principle was to give
> the institution enormous flexibility in assimilating new ideas,
> subjects, and methods. . . . [I]nnovation even of a threatening kind
> could be welcomed by simply *adding* another unit to the aggregate
> of fields to be covered. It is only the field-coverage principle that
> explains how the literature department has managed to avoid
> incurring paralyzing clashes of ideology during a period when it
> has preserved much of its earlier traditional orientation while
> incorporating disruptive novelties such as contemporary literature,
> black studies, feminism, Marxism, and deconstruction. (p. 7)

It is this aspect of the field-coverage principle that has troubled feminists
and ethnic studies advocates. The university makes room for a new
approach by adding courses, and not by integrating that approach into
ongoing curricula. The effect is to marginalize the approach, minimize
its potential impact, and, when budget tightening comes, make courses
embodying the approach among the first dropped from the catalog.

Graff's institutional analysis of literary studies suggests how the
procedures represented by both Hubbell and Lauter have been compromised, in different ways, by the structure of the modern research
university. Whether one advocates a "top-down" or a "bottom-up"
approach to canon formation, the field-coverage principle will frustrate
attempts at coherence and discourage integration of new knowledge
across the literary curriculum. The organization of an educational
institution can subsume and subvert the best intentions of scholars and
critical movements. Attention, then, must be paid to how knowledge
is organized in a curriculum, not just what knowledge is valuable to
know and teach.

## Canon Formation at the Small College

To the extent that colleges employ the field-coverage principle, they
face problems similar to those in the research university. However, the

question of canon formation for college teachers is different from that for university faculty precisely because the scale of operations in a small college has usually made a pure field-coverage approach to curriculum impracticable. Graff himself acknowledges that his institutional history of literary studies, based on the research university model, "does not do justice to the small-college experience" (p. 2). In the remainder of this essay, I want to discuss three intertwined questions:

1. How does the size of the institution affect the way English departments at small colleges think about questions of curriculum and canon?

2. What kinds of scholarship from English departments at research universities would most help small-college teachers deal with the pedagogical implications of canon formation?

3. What resources and alternatives available to English departments at small colleges can be brought to bear in incorporating new scholarship on women and minorities into the curriculum?

## The Consequences of Institutional Size

In a small college, incorporating new scholarship is not ordinarily accomplished by simply adding a new course or even by an individual instructor introducing new works into existing courses. Characteristically, if a new course is to be taught, an instructor needs to be released from an old one. If an existing course is to significantly change its emphasis, then the rest of the curriculum needs to be reconsidered by the entire department to ensure that what gets dropped is either covered elsewhere or is now deemed unimportant. In short, small-college instructors are less independent than are their university counterparts. These realities are dictated by the structures of the small college. First, hiring is enrollment-driven, and unless both departmental and institutional enrollment are increasing, the odds are that a new position cannot be easily found. (Given that the number of English majors has dropped nationally, and that most small colleges maintain a policy of steady-state enrollment in order to stay small, English faculties at such institutions do not normally expect to staff new courses by hiring.) Second, small-college English departments do not have the redundancy of offerings found at universities. This means that available courses are more closely articulated in order to assure the widest range of experiences for students.

At large institutions, students gain a preliminary knowledge of, say, the Victorians through the sophomore English survey. Those interested in the period might proceed to a class in the Victorian novel or poetry, or in Dickens or George Eliot. In their senior year, they might take seminars in "Women in Victorian England" or the Pre-Raphaelites. At each point, there is comparative freedom for an individual instructor to fashion a classroom canon according to topic, critical orientation, personal taste, and current research interests. The need for inclusiveness is not a particularly important criterion for syllabus design because students have other opportunities, if they desire, to make up gaps in knowledge.

This is not the case at most small colleges. At my own institution, whose literature program was praised by external university examiners as having an unusually rich offering of courses for a college its size, "Romantics and Victorians" is a one-semester course taught every other year. A student interested in further study of the Victorians can take "Early English Novel" (a survey from Defoe to Hardy), or arrange an independent study. That's it. Furthermore, because my working-class students frequently have never heard of Matthew Arnold or William Thackeray before entering the courses, instructors must start with at least some of the chestnuts. Small-college teachers are thus constrained, by the limitations of curriculum and frequently the inexperience of their students, to continually confront the question of relative literary value. For example, if I had to construct a "local canon" of novels for a fourteen-week course on the eighteenth- and nineteenth-century novel, what novels should be considered, and by what criteria should I do the gleaning? If I had to choose between an Alice Walker novel and one by Toni Morrison for a course in twentieth-century American literature, what criteria should I use?

## How University Scholarship Can Help the Small-College Teacher

These questions of criteria, the aesthetic-historical-social-moral standards of judgment, underlie any discussion of canon or syllabus. And it is here that college teachers most need the aid of their university counterparts. Mere lists of which works merit teaching are insufficient, for appeals to self-evident quality are not enough: teachers need to read and hear discussions as to the criteria by which other scholars and teachers make selections. On the one hand, Hubbell's book is valuable for its lists of what has been esteemed over time. On the other, it frustrates because it cannot, as a compilation of authoritative choices, detail the reasons and standards by which individual critics make one choice as opposed to another. In reading criticism and attending summer seminars, I have been struck by how university scholars reflexively think about how a literary work relates to their writing, but college teachers necessarily think about how a literary work fits into their teaching. To be useful for us, theory needs to be grounded in pedagogical implications. My own desire is that research and writing in literature become more cognizant of the need to bridge the gap between cutting-edge scholarship and classroom pedagogy.

The new scholarship on literature by women and minorities makes itself felt on the small-college level through discussions of suggested readings and through anthologies. *Reconstructing American Literature* has been important to teachers because it suggests specific texts by minorities and women which can be found in print and which have been successfully incorporated into courses. Just as important, the works are embedded in discussions of syllabi that suggest some of the ways that the texts can be used to highlight one another. Moreover, an anthology like Gilbert and Gubar's *Norton Anthology of Literature by Women* not only makes available otherwise inaccessible texts but also provides a series of intertextual connections in its survey of women's literature in English. Teachers and students obtain from it a sense of continuity of concerns, themes, and forms from writer to writer.

## The Resources and Promise of the Small-College Experience

No one can teach the whole of a reading list or anthology. Each teacher necessarily picks and chooses from the wealth of selections, in effect creating a "local canon" for a particular class. Nonetheless, small colleges which recognize the need to rethink the limits of older literary traditions must do so in a more comprehensive way than universities have done because of the aforementioned need for teachers to coordinate their efforts. Lauter's "bottom-up" approach, while useful, is ultimately an inappropriate model for small-college curricular change because the unit of innovation in the small college is not the individual instructor but the department. On the one hand, the rethinking of an entire departmental curriculum is necessarily a slower process than simply introducing some new courses. On the other hand, there is less danger of new studies being marginalized the way they are in the university because the need for an articulated curriculum encourages an integration of materials across courses. Such coherence of learning is an objective more easily met at the small college than at the university because small-college teaching staffs are so much smaller. Faculty have to talk across specialties because at a small college you are likely to be the only person working in your specialty. In addition, staffing needs at the small college typically require most faculty to rotate through the gamut of courses offered. This generalist orientation, combined with small staff size and the need to maintain an articulated, coherent set of curricular offerings, means that canon formation becomes a corporate affair of the department, and the collective "local canon" that is developed reflects a departmental vision of literary studies, not only that of individual instructors.

At the same time, the small college can avoid another pitfall, the sense that whatever succeeds the traditional canon should itself be a unitary model for literary study across the nation. Recent anthologies of American literature have gone beyond the traditional readings to make room for Hispanic, Native American, Black, and Asian-American works. But despite the aim of such anthologies to expand the literary canon, they still share with Hubbell the sense that a single canon can serve all American readers. Moreover, the space accorded these new selections frequently allows for little more than snippets of these authors and works. By adding new materials to the old, they again run the danger of marginalizing the new. The small college, freed from the need to define a canon for the nation, often establishes what I have called a "local canon." A California college may well need a strong emphasis on Hispanic and Asian-American contributions to literature. A Mississippi institution needs to represent Black, women's, and Southern regional writing in its offerings. At my own institution, Berea College, where by charter 80 percent of the students are drawn from the Appalachian region and Kentucky, the English department offers a course in Appalachian literature as part of an institution-wide commitment to Appalachian studies. The institutional mission, the regional context, and student interest make such offerings a natural and even essential part of the curriculum. Even at small colleges which may lack an explicit institutional identity or regional commitment, the makeup of the student body may necessitate that a canon be customized for its needs. It is a commonplace that older notions of a unified literary tradition were based upon a student audience of upper-class white males, now only a small portion of the heterogeneous population pursuing higher education. At the same time, most small colleges draw from local areas, and the student bodies are generally homogeneous in background and preparation. It is generally more practicable in fashioning a local canon to address the particular student profile in terms of race, gender, and class than to encompass the heterogeneity of the entire nation.

The majority of my students are the first in their families to attend college. My responsibility is to introduce them to mainstream ways of knowing and learning without suggesting that the worlds from which they come have no place in their future lives. Education means affirming the Appalachian past while preparing to live in New York. Literary canon making must encompass both the students' roots and their aspirations. This is why I have come to believe in local canons, customized for the particular college population that one serves. Such canons can only be designed by faculty on the scene. There can be no top-down prescription for local conditions, whether those unitary lists be conservative or progressive.

At this point, I hope, the distinctive situation and promise of the small college is becoming clear. Because it does not wholly share the field-coverage principle of research universities, because its structure compels community among its scholars, who necessarily must serve as generalists to particular homogeneous student populations, the small college can be more coherent in its educational vision in the local area of its influence. With regard to canon formation, it may draw from but cannot limit itself to either top-down formulations of a uniform canonicity nor bottom-up strategies that depend on the autonomy of individual instructors. I see a middle ground between the two approaches to canon formation that may avoid both of their dangers. Literary humanism, which seeks to transcend particulars of the human situation to penetrate to universal norms, is too sweeping because it ignores the reality that we recognize our humanity only through particular lives mediated through particular cultures at particular times. In turn, literary egalitarianism, which emphasizes the individuality of works, instructors, and students, is too atomistic because it ignores the reality that we differentiate ourselves only by common reference to some community standard of values. In devising local canons, the small college is able to create a community of readers without insisting that that community be a microcosm of the world.

To read a canon, however, involves matters of theory and methodology, not only content. Here too, I think, the small college has its own distinctive bent. Because we are necessarily generalists, I have found that colleagues at my own and similar institutions are more interested in the tools for interpretation provided by literary theories than in their ideology. For example, of late the New Criticism has been derided for its treatment of texts apart from context, as if the play of words had no reference to historical or biographical reality. But for college teachers, New Criticism is the method of reading that continues to be valuable, not, as some have suggested, because it allows them to deal with students devoid of a historical or social sense, but because the New Critical approach insists that one can begin to engage literature before one is an expert in the period or the author. Most students in introductory literature courses do not go on to further work in literature, and very few proceed to graduate study. They need to feel empowered to avail themselves of literary texts without the intercession of authorities. Their appreciation of a work is no doubt enriched by the historical and biographical contexts, but they should not expect to wait until they have those contexts before they begin to read. College teachers quickly become eclectic, mixing New Critical formalism, the affective fallacy (which we now privilege under reader-response theory), Marxist historicism, and psychoanalytic approaches to authorial intent. The result may be a nightmare to a theorist, but this flexible and eclectic approach permits the teacher to value the student's own knowledge while opening the doors to new knowledge.

These, then, are the contexts within which I see small-college teachers doing their work. As I have sought to demonstrate, these conditions influence how we approach literary study in general, and, in particular, how the question of who decides the canon might be resolved. Further, an understanding of these contexts, I hope, will help university scholars to more effectively address the needs of college teachers. The opportunity, from the perspective of one who has been university-trained but who has professed literature in a small college for a decade, is that the small college represents a fertile field for the rethinking of canon and the teaching of literature precisely because it is so different from the university.

## References

Gilbert, Sandra, and Susan Gubar, eds. 1985. *Norton Anthology of Literature by Women.* New York: Norton.

Graff, Gerald. 1987. *Professing Literature: An Institutional History.* Chicago: University of Chicago Press.

Hubbell, Jay B. 1972. *Who Are the Major American Writers?* Durham, N.C.: Duke University Press.

Huber, Bettina J., and Art Young. 1986. "Report on the 1983–84 Survey of the English Sample." *ADE Bulletin,* no. 84 (Fall): 40–61.

Lauter, Paul, ed. 1983. *Reconstructing American Literature: Courses, Syllabi, Issues.* Old Westbury, N.Y.: The Feminist Press.

# 16 The Structuralist Community College Student in a Post-Structuralist Age

Judy Arnold and Benjamin S. Howard

Judy Arnold and Benjamin S. Howard both teach in the Roane State Community College system in Tennessee but at campuses fifty miles apart. At the Oak Ridge campus, Judy Arnold is an assistant professor of English, and at the Harriman campus, Benjamin Howard is a professor of English and German. Both teach within departments of humanities that house music, art, foreign languages, philosophy, and, of course, English. The campuses are similar in size (1,800–1,850 students). The two English departments together employ ten to twelve full-time faculty members, many of whom teach on both campuses.

Professor Arnold teaches five courses each semester, including American literature surveys and composition sections. Before coming to Roane State in 1985, she taught for fourteen years at the high school level. Professor Howard began his career teaching German, but when foreign language study became optional he went back to graduate school in comparative literature, a field that allowed him to "tie together a number of interests." He has been at Roane State since 1972, teaching honors sections in English (composition and a two-semester survey of world literature) and courses in German language and literature.

Judy Arnold attended the 1987 Summer Institute and as a result was asked by her department chair to present an "inhouse workshop for English faculty in order to explain 'what went on.'" When the call for papers for this book went out, she showed it to Ben Howard, who had attended her workshop, and the result is the collaboratively written essay that follows.

Teaching literature at a two-year college is a special challenge. Many students at these colleges do not enjoy reading and are therefore skeptical about the value of literature. Their reading and writing skills are, on the average, lower than those of their counterparts at four-year institutions,[1] and their weakness in communications skills is accompanied by a strong vocational orientation: according to one ACT Profile, their "most typical planned educational major and first vocational

211

choice" is business and commerce; the second is health professions (ACT 1988–89). Yet there comes a time in the two-year college curriculum when all students, however poorly prepared or uninterested, have to read literature and have to write about what they have read. Literary analysis often perplexes these students, who, in turn, perplex their teachers. In this situation, does literary theory offer any help?

Even though the heyday of structuralism is long past, our classroom experiences at Roane State Community College have encouraged us to recognize the potential appeal structuralist analysis may have for the "resistant" student of literature. In Ben Howard's composition class, one that emphasizes writing about literature, the students read and wrote about Frank O'Connor's "My Oedipus Complex." One of them, without ever having heard of structuralism, discovered a structural pattern that proved helpful in overcoming the class's initial resistance to studying this particular story. In Judy Arnold's American literature course, students read and discussed *The Scarlet Letter* and, approaching this work from a structuralist perspective, did not experience the usual initial aversion to the writings of Hawthorne. Based on these classroom experiences, we find that a structuralist approach has an inherent appeal to some resistant readers and can therefore be a useful pedagogical stratagem in the classroom, one that opens new possibilities to both students and teacher.

## "My Oedipus Complex"

When Ben Howard taught the O'Connor piece, he was impressed by a student who wrote an essay containing the germ of a structuralist interpretation of the work—even though she had never heard of structuralism. "My Oedipus Complex," a frequently anthologized story, lends itself to a psychological reading, but the title is, of course, ironic. Although the stages through which Larry, the main character, progresses appear to be textbook Freud, the reader senses that the mechanism at work is far too overt, too out-in-the-open, and that O'Connor must be poking fun at the Oedipal interpretation. In fact, it seems that Freud is not really the point at all; the point is the double perspective: the narrator does not understand as a child but does understand as an adult. The narrative is retrospective and reflective, a story told by a narrator looking back to his relationship to his mother, understanding now at least some of the humor implicit in the crises of those childhood days.

One of Howard's student readers, however, continued to read from the child's perspective and saw that for the child the world had two foci: the mother's bed and the child's bed. The story moved, as it were, from bed to bed. Here is the student's analysis:

> O'Connor has based the whole story around a bed scene. First, a little boy wants to get in bed with Mummy. As long as he is able to do this, everything is good. Once the little boy is rejected from the bed, the little boy behaves like a little boy. Larry's actions are exactly the way you would expect a little boy to react.
>
> Finally, O'Connor presents another scene. This is a scene of an adult man being ejected from Mummy's bed. O'Connor tells us that Daddy and son behave the same way when sent away from Mummy's bed because of someone else. They both act like little boys and get mad as hell. However, they have the traditional model train (that fathers have bought for years) to console themselves.

Working from what the student wrote toward a deeper understanding, the instructor divided the story into three parts: (1) the boy's close relationship with his mother while his father is off at the war; (2) the boy's defeat and loneliness when his father returns from the war and resumes his place in the family and, of course, in the bed; and (3) the boy's new close relationship with the father after the baby is born and both father and son are displaced from the mother's affections.

This outline, and the student's reading, is the beginning of a structuralist reading that emphasizes the polarities and parallels illustrated in Figure 1.

Larry's access to his mother's bed, and his subsequent loss of that access, represents a move from "Paradise" to "Paradise Lost." Larry sees his early-morning visits to his mother's bed as a daily ritual: waking early each morning, he puts a chair under the window, climbs up, and looks out at the dawn; he then goes to his mother's room and climbs into her bed; he tells her his plans, or "schemes," for the day; he falls asleep, waking only when he hears his mother downstairs making breakfast. In later years he humorously notes that this ritual, performed daily while his father was away at the war, made the war "the most peaceful period of my life" (p. 283). Then the father returns and Larry can no longer come to his mother's bed. He has been ejected from paradise, and declares open warfare on his father.

Then, in a transformation of the earlier pattern, Larry's father finds himself ejected from paradise, replaced by the new baby, Sonny. Larry and his father become allies instead of enemies. In fact, one night

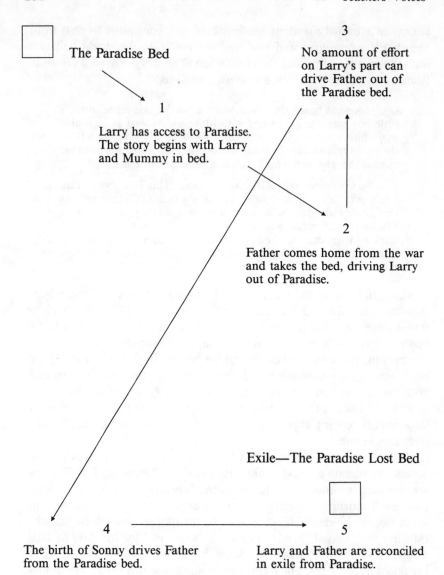

The Paradise Bed

3

No amount of effort
on Larry's part can
drive Father out of
the Paradise bed.

1

Larry has access to Paradise.
The story begins with Larry
and Mummy in bed.

2

Father comes home from the war
and takes the bed, driving Larry
out of Paradise.

Exile—The Paradise Lost Bed

4

The birth of Sonny drives Father
from the Paradise bed.

5

Larry and Father are reconciled
in exile from Paradise.

Figure 1. A structuralist diagram of the movements around the "Paradise Bed" and the "Paradise Lost Bed" in "My Oedipus Complex."

Larry wakes to find someone beside him in bed. For one "wild moment" he imagines that it is Mother who has "come to her senses." But he hears the new baby "in convulsions" in the next room, and hears Mother saying, "There! There! There!" and realizes that it is his father lying awake beside him, breathing hard and "apparently mad as hell" (p. 295). The story ends with the formation of a new alliance:

> After awhile it came to me what he was mad about. It was his turn now. After turning me out of the big bed, he had been turned out himself. Mother had no consideration for anyone but that poisonous pup, Sonny. I couldn't help feeling sorry for Father. I had been through it all myself, and even at that age I was magnanimous. I began to stroke him down and say: "There! There! There!" He wasn't exactly responsive.
>
> "Aren't you asleep either?" he snarled.
>
> "Ah, come on and put your arm around us, can't you?" I said, and he did, in a sort of way. Gingerly, I suppose, is how you'd describe it. He was very bony, but better than nothing.
>
> At Christmas he went out of his way to buy me a really nice model railway. (p. 295)

A structuralist would consider the ways in which the movements between the two scenes—the "Paradise" bed and the "Paradise Lost" bed—were foregrounded. And the inquiry might naturally proceed to the cause: what happened to cause the exile from paradise? The story's title forces us to think in Freudian terms: Larry is sexually attracted to his mother and experiences the father as rival. He is punished for his desire (by the superego?) and is denied paradise. The author plays with this pattern, undercutting it, as he follows his narrator's thought train as he wonders why his parents sleep together:

> It all seemed to hinge around that unhealthy habit of sleeping together, so I made a point of dropping into their bedroom and nosing around, talking to myself, so that they wouldn't know I was watching them, but they were never up to anything that I could see. In the end it beat me. It seemed to depend on being grown-up and giving people rings, and I realized I'd have to wait. (p. 311)

The narrator announces directly that when he grows up he will marry his mother and they will have "lots and lots of babies," and he believes his mother would be "relieved to know that one day Father's hold on her would be broken" (p. 311). Freud's view, that the son is attracted to the mother and is at war with the father, is played out literally, ironically, and humorously in the structure of the story. The student who discovered this structure had an interesting and valid approach which led to a vigorous class discussion of the story's materials as they contributed to structure.

## The Scarlet Letter

Knowing how a structuralist approach had enlivened Ben Howard's teaching of the O'Connor story, Judy Arnold decided to see what kind of discussion she could generate by deliberately introducing a structuralist interpretation of *The Scarlet Letter*. On the first day of class, she introduced standard topics—Hawthorne's use of irony, symbolism, and atmosphere. The students' response to this material was predictable: some had read the book, some had not; some were interested in the topics introduced, some were not. At the end of the session, Arnold noted that Hawthorne's novel had an interesting structure: twenty-four chapters divided neatly into three sections. As the class left the room, she noticed that several students were looking at the chapter and section divisions in the novel's table of contents. The mention of a structure— and, perhaps, particularly a *symmetrical* structure—seemed to give the students a way of approaching the novel. And what was particularly interesting to the teacher was that the students who were looking at the structure of the text as they left the room were not the same students who had participated in the class discussion. There seemed to be two groups: those who responded to conventional pedagogy and those who responded to structure.

The teacher opened the next class period with a question: "In each of the three sections of the novel, what is the important focal point for the characters that is carried throughout the entire story?" The result was an interesting discussion of the three scaffold scenes. Moving from scene to scene, more students were engaged in the discussion than had been engaged in earlier discussions. This lively discussion led to a diagram (Fig. 2).

As the discussion evolved, the teacher began to think like a structuralist while the students—now more comfortable in their understanding of Hawthorne's novel—began to identify with the characters and their feelings. It was at this point in the process that the instructor began to see parallel structures and polar oppositions that she had not seen so clearly before. In her earlier readings, she had found Hester strong during her ordeal on the scaffold, weak when she returned to the prison, and strong after her many years of suffering the effects of the scarlet letter. Further, Hester was stronger than Dimmesdale, and

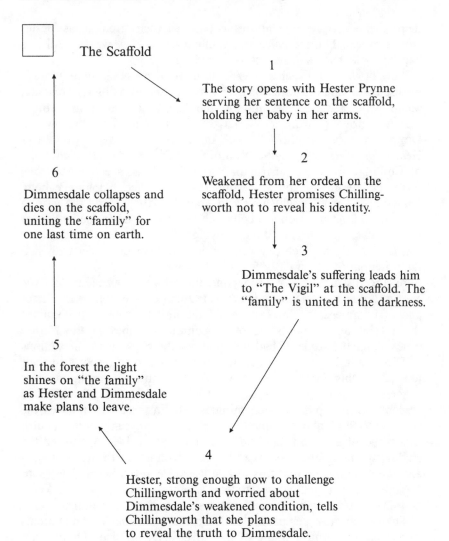

The Scaffold

1

The story opens with Hester Prynne serving her sentence on the scaffold, holding her baby in her arms.

2

Weakened from her ordeal on the scaffold, Hester promises Chilling-worth not to reveal his identity.

3

Dimmesdale's suffering leads him to "The Vigil" at the scaffold. The "family" is united in the darkness.

6

Dimmesdale collapses and dies on the scaffold, uniting the "family" for one last time on earth.

5

In the forest the light shines on "the family" as Hester and Dimmesdale make plans to leave.

4

Hester, strong enough now to challenge Chillingworth and worried about Dimmesdale's weakened condition, tells Chillingworth that she plans to reveal the truth to Dimmesdale.

Figure 2. A structuralist diagram resulting from a discussion of the scaffold scenes in *The Scarlet Letter.*

there was a reciprocal relationship between their strength: as Hester grew stronger, Dimmesdale, and Chillingworth, grew weaker. All this had been clear to the instructor in earlier readings.

Now, however, through a consideration of the novel's structure forced by discussion and diagram, the instructor discovered a different reading, one in which Hester, Pearl, and Dimmesdale came together as a family that was growing stronger—a fact that is announced to the town as Dimmesdale dies on the scaffold. Considering the novel's structure— Hester's growing strength, the "dimming" of Dimmesdale, the "chilling" of Chillingworth—the instructor was led to a perspective that one might call feminist, and she wondered what effect Sophia Peabody (Hawthorne's wife) might have had upon Hawthorne and the writing of the novel. At this point, a colleague recommended to the instructor David Leverenz's article "Mrs. Hawthorne's Headache: Reading *The Scarlet Letter,*" in which Leverenz argues that Hawthorne certainly had the potential to be an early feminist writer.[2]

As the instructor was discovering this new-to-her reading of *The Scarlet Letter,* the students continued to focus on the feelings of Hester and of Dimmesdale. The last day of the unit brought with it one of those "shining moments" Eliot Wigginton describes in the *Foxfire* series. After the students had talked about the physical manifestations of Dimmesdale's mental anguish, they were asked to respond in their journals to this question: "Have you (or has someone you know) ever suffered so much mental anguish that you became physically ill?" The students wrote rapidly for ten minutes. The instructor then asked the students to think about a time they had felt the greatest mental anguish as a result of an event that had occurred in their lives. She asked the students to remember how they felt, and to hold on to that feeling— and then to imagine that this feeling lasted for seven years. The room was absolutely quiet. Some students silently wept. "Now you know how Dimmesdale felt," the instructor said, and the class ended.

The structuralist perspective had, almost paradoxically, led students to a deep, empathic reading of the novel being studied. Though not itself the point, the structuralist approach was the point of departure. For the instructor, the approach opened up a new reading of the novel. For the students, the approach seemed to offer comfort. They understood the novel's structure, and, when they found they understood this aspect of the novel, they decided they could think, talk, and write about other aspects of the novel, too. For these students, the structuralist approach was a useful first step, an apparently necessary precondition to the kind of reading we are hoping for: a deep, personal understanding of the universal elements in the fiction.

## The Appeal of Structure

How is it that a structuralist approach opens up literature to our normally resistant students? We believe that the answer lies both in the approach and in the special nature of our students. Students at two-year colleges have not often had rewarding experiences with literature, and they come to class expecting further distasteful encounters. Moreover, they have difficulty in distinguishing between the literal and the figurative, and in their attempts to analyze literature often err in the direction of the literal. These students enjoy their classes in the sciences and mathematics, because in these subjects they find structure. The structure in these subjects makes sense to them; they wonder why literature does not make sense in the same way. And, since most of the students are vocationally oriented, they see the reading of literature, this personally unrewarding struggle, as a waste of time because there is no apparent link between its subject and their highly specific educational goals. Perhaps for this reason, few students at Roane State major in English, and the brightest and best are most likely to choose areas of study other than English. Our experience suggests to us that these students, who find so much to admire in the apparent clarity of the sciences and mathematics, are natural structuralists looking to find the patterns of science in their literary studies.

Given our particular set of students, most of whom are looking for something "solid," a structuralist approach has a number of attractive features. First, it is much more comfortable, much more at-home-seeming than post-structuralist theories of literary criticism. For our students, who need to believe in text before they can accept its unreality, the idea that the text is not "there," central—a notion itself central in post-structuralist criticism—upsets their notions of study. A structuralist approach is the least radical, most logocentric of the approaches since the New Criticism—and it is therefore the least threatening to the students' intuitive sense that the text is indeed there, an object to be studied.

In addition, a structuralist approach calls for visual representation, and although we do not mean to link the visual and the structural too tightly, we have seen structural analysis produce meaningful diagrams that in turn engender meaning. For example, in discussing the characters in Arthur Miller's *The Crucible,* the instructor might diagram the characters by placing them in two columns: the accused and the accuser. Once this division has been made and made visual, the instructor could encourage the class to look for other patterns, perhaps those based on where the people live and/or their social status. Our students respond to practically any visual presentation—even moments when the instructor briefly uses the blackboard to illustrate a point. Most will, at these moments, take notes, feeling that something *important* is happening (as opposed to other times, when the instructor is lecturing or leading a discussion). An instructor informed by a structuralist approach provides a visual route to understanding—a chart, a pattern, the "science" that makes the language meaningful.

That structuralism appeals to a particular type of thinking, the type of thinking that just might be characteristic of the "nonliterary" student, is suggested by Terry Eagleton (1983) in *Literary Theory: An Introduction*. Eagleton traces the history of structuralism in America to the 1950s, when American culture valued the "scientific" and it was felt that literature itself needed to become more like science. Eagleton cites Northrop Frye, who argued in 1957 that "criticism seems to be badly in need of a coordinating principle, a central hypothesis which, like the theory of evolution in biology, will see the phenomena it deals with as parts of a whole" (Eagleton, p. 16). Eagleton sums up Frye's position thus: "Literature was in a sorry unscientific mess and needed to be smartly tidied up" (p. 91). The subjective nature of literary criticism could be tidied up because literature itself was objective and systematic. Structuralists found their systems in the structural linguistics of Ferdinand de Saussure, the formalism of Roman Jakobson, the semiotics of the Prague school, and the narratology of Gerard Genette—and thus moved literature into the realm of science (p. 96). Structuralism, as Eagleton puts it, "represents a remorseless *demystification* of literature" (p. 106). Further,

> Loosely subjective talk was chastised by a criticism which recognized that the literary work, like any other product of language, is a *construct*, whose mechanisms could be classified and analysed like the objects of any other science. The Romantic prejudice that the poem, like a person, harboured a vital essence, a soul which it was discourteous to tamper with, was rudely unmasked as a bit of disguised theology, a superstitious fear of reasoned enquiry which made a fetish of literature and reinforced the authority of a "naturally" sensitive elite. (pp. 106–7)

If our students were asked what they hated about literary study, they might respond in language that echoes Eagleton's. Many have known only the "subjective talk" of their teachers (" 'To Autumn' is a beautiful poem") and have resisted ("Why do I have to read this stuff?").

We do not mean to suggest that a structuralist approach is a miracle cure—that it will convert the resistant student or rejuvenate the exhausted teacher. We do know from experience, however, that certain classroom approaches are doomed from the outset. What does not work is to assign the conventional analysis of literature (theme, character, plot, atmosphere) to two-year college students who would, on the whole, rather be studying, reading, doing something else. These students, and their counterparts at four-year colleges, can be brought to a point where they are willing to participate in literary analysis and can be confident of the value of their thoughts and insights that grow from this activity. We find that a structuralist approach is one means of encouraging our students to be readers, and students, of literature.

In considering a seventeenth-century sermon, Stanley Fish (1980) concludes that our lives are sequential, just like the life of the reading experience, just like the progress of the sermon, "proceeding from point to point, but in a progression that is not generating meaning but merely creating new spaces into which the meaning that is already there expands" (p. 193). Our thoughts about the literature we had been teaching for years were not new thoughts, but, through our new approach to the literature, we were "creating new spaces"—for our students and for ourselves.

## Notes

1. At four-year colleges and universities, students enrolled in courses considered developmental make up approximately one-fourth of the population; at two-year colleges, they represent almost half. These figures are based on a memorandum from the chancellor of the State Board of Regents to members of the Committee on Academic Policies and Programs, and pertain therefore to the state of Tennessee. Because testing and placement vary among institutions, we do not want to use the actual percentages reported, but nonetheless believe that *approximately* is an accurate description here, and that what is true in Tennessee is generally true in other states.
2. Leverenz also discusses the Freudian aspects of the novel, mentioning the Oedipal theme suggested by the two men (Dimmesdale and Chillingworth) in flight from a strong woman (p. 213).

## References

American College Testing Program. 1988–89. *The ACT Class Profile Service Report: Tennessee Public Junior Colleges System Comp Report.* Iowa City: American College Testing Program.

Eagleton, Terry. 1983. *Literary Theory: An Introduction.* Minneapolis: University of Minnesota Press.

Fish, Stanley. 1980. *Is There a Text in This Class?* Cambridge: University of Harvard Press.

Leverenz, David. 1985. "Mrs. Hawthorne's Headache: Reading *The Scarlet Letter.*" Ithaca: University of Cornell Press.

O'Connor, Frank. 1981. *Collected Stories.* New York: Alfred P. Knopf.

# 17 Gender Differences: Both/And, Not Either/Or

Nancy Vogel

Nancy Vogel is professor of English at Fort Hays State University, which has an enrollment of 5,000 and is under the Kansas Board of Regents. One of fifteen full-time faculty members in English, Professor Vogel teaches two composition courses and two literature courses each term. Her range includes courses in technical/professional writing, the American dream, and pedagogy; her special interests are young adult literature, biography and auto-biography, and the poetry of Robert Frost. She is currently working on a book, tentatively titled *The American Eve,* which links the psychological developmental stages of women with characters in fiction.

Professor Vogel spent the spring of 1988 as a fellow at Menninger in Topeka, Kansas, studying the relationship between psychology and literature. She read about the 1988 Summer Institute in the *ADE Bulletin* and wrote us to find out about any bibliographies that might have come out of the program as well as to find out about any other meetings on a similar theme: issues of gender and the canon. Her paper that follows is an extension of her interest in these issues.

Given our growing awareness of gender differences in a democratic society that values equality, where do teachers of literature turn to construct a syllabus with readings of "comparable worth"? How can we create a syllabus that pairs male and female characters in similar situations in texts authored by writers of the same sex as their protagonists, all this ideally in works composed somewhat contemporaneously? Several conditions make this balanced reading list difficult to achieve.

First is the lack of easy access to writing by women. Even though women have always written, much of that writing has not survived. True, some of what has been saved is now beginning to appear in various volumes, but the loss of original texts and lack of published material present major difficulties.

A second problem is the nature of the professoriate—overwhelmingly male, even though classes in English tend to enroll more women than men. A predominantly male professoriate is not apt to be receptive to a gender-balanced syllabus.

A third difficulty, perhaps psychological but certainly cultural, is that women tend not to paint the grand murals of life—the *Iliad* and the *Odyssey*—but seem more attracted to inner journeys—diaries and autobiographies. These genres are not valued by the culture generally and are therefore seldom included in the canon.

Given the problems—the inaccessibility of texts, resistance by faculty, and the differing relationships among gender, subject, and genre—why even attempt to balance a syllabus in, say, an American literature course? As a recent occasional paper from the American Council of Learned Societies points out, "Developments in modern thought . . . have made us alert to what is left out when 'the best that has been thought and written' is selected or when discussion focuses on 'man' " (Levine et al. 1989, p. l6). The point that the directors of humanities centers make in the ACLS paper is also mine:

> We have learned to ask whether universalist claims do not in fact promote as a norm the concerns of a particular group and set aside as partial or limited those of other groups. Characteristically in literary studies, for instance, a boy's experience of growing up has been deemed universal and a girl's marginal. (p. l6)

In our teaching, in our reading lists, we cannot neglect valid cultural/ developmental differences between young men and young women. To expand the canon by including the work of women is to introduce a new perspective, to create diversity, and to make it easier to achieve one of the generally accepted aims of literary study: to expand, to liberate the imagination. Indeed, according to William Empson, "The central function of imaginative literature is to make you realize that other people act on moral convictions different from your own" (Levine et al. 1989, p. l6). The ACLS report continues,

> A particular virtue of literature, of history, of anthropology, is instruction in otherness: vivid, compelling evidence of differences in cultures, mores, assumptions, values. At their best, these subjects make otherness palpable and make it comprehensible without reducing it to an inferior version of the same, as a universalizing humanism threatens to do. The dramatization of social and cultural pluralism is one of the major roles of humanistic study. (p. l6)

Because English courses are at the core of humanistic study, and because otherness and pluralism exist and are to be valued, we should try to balance our syllabi. Anne Bradstreet, Emily Dickinson, Edna St. Vincent Millay, Adrienne Rich, and other poets have made such an impact that finding comparable poems or poets is not too difficult. Fiction and nonfiction, however, are another matter.

According to Peggy McIntosh at the Center for Research on Women at Wellesley College, there are five stages to transforming college curricula:

> In the first stage, women are nonexistent or totally excluded. The second stage examines only a famous few, while the experiences of most women remain invisible.
>
> Treating women as an "anomaly" or a "problem" is the third stage. At this point, the focus begins to shift from the exceptional to everyday women, and questions are raised about who "defines" history. In the next stage, women are the sole subject matter and only their experiences are examined.
>
> The final phase represents "history redefined" to include both men and women. . . . Here, women are considered an integral part of history, but they are discussed as a heterogeneous group of individuals with different racial, ethnic, class, and sexual identifications. (McMillen 1987, p. A16)

According to the Wellesley scale, many American literature classes are in stage two. Hardly a course exists in which either Anne Bradstreet, Emily Dickinson, or Willa Cather is not discussed—the "famous few." But before stage five can be reached—and reach it we must—we must read more women writers so that we can raise and discuss the question of who "defines" literature. At some schools, discussion has gone beyond this third stage and into the fourth stage, where women writers and their writings form the whole content of courses. *The Norton Anthology of Literature by Women* is one book tailored for just such a course. Yet this stage is not the ultimate one. Stage five, the transformation of courses, is the ideal.[1] In the pages that follow, I will suggest a strategy that may help us move closer to this ideal.

## Gender Differences in the American Novel

What two novels can elicit a discussion of gender differences? Initially, *The Adventures of Huckleberry Finn* (1885) and *Anne of Green Gables* (1908) may seem an unlikely pairing separated by many years,[2] but studied together, the books reveal the contrasting patterns of development for a young man and a young woman. Although Huck and Anne are orphans, their patterns of development highlight their differences in gender. Questions pointed to these gender differences can help faculty and students see clearly the characters' different cultural patterns:

1. What are the tasks of the youth?

2. What is the role of the mother?
3. What is the role of the father?
4. How is separation an issue?
5. How difficult is individuation?
6. Who values attachment?
7. Who values what Harvard professor Carol Gilligan identifies as "separation, autonomy, individuation, and natural rights" (1982, p. 23)?
8. What is the nature of commitment?
9. What additional movement is necessary before the protagonists reach adulthood?

If students write their answers to questions like these, they become aware of differences that previously many had ignored or accepted. And teachers reading these responses may find themselves viewing familiar texts from different perspectives.

The growing-up process that results in individuation has different results for Anne and Huck because gender and cultural differences lead to different quests. Kathryn Zerbe (1988), a psychiatrist at the C. F. Menninger Memorial Hospital, explains that from ancient times, men's heroic quest has been to find their father. Women, on the other hand, have had a heroic quest to find a lover or have a baby. At some deep level, then, Huck is seeking a father and Anne a mate. At the conclusion of *Anne of Green Gables,* Gilbert Blythe, who has tolerated the antics of Anne for years, forgiven her for impudence beyond sauciness, and, by today's standards, waited interminably long for her, gently but firmly admonishes Anne that the future will be theirs, together: "We were born to be good friends, Anne. You've thwarted destiny long enough. I know we can help each other in many ways." The book ends with Anne whispering, " 'God's in his heaven, all's right with the world' " (p. 240). That, as Joseph Campbell (1988) would say, is "bliss" (p. 148).

How is Huck's coming of age different? Having fled the home of Widow Douglas, Huck will flee Aunt Sally's, too. Huck's abusive and alcoholic father scares Huck so much that the young man fears for his life and runs away, stopping first at the island in the river, where he joins up with another runaway, Jim. When the book begins, Huck says, "I felt so lonesome I most wished I was dead" (p. 8). Soon warmed by the prospect of a relationship with Jim, Huck says, "Well, I warn't long making him understand I warn't dead. I was ever so glad to see Jim. I warn't lonesome, now" (pp. 37–38). In a mysterious way, Jim becomes a surrogate father, and life on the raft becomes life with Father: "We said there warn't no home like a raft, after all. Other places do seem so cramped up and smothery, but a raft don't. You feel mighty free and easy and comfortable on a raft" (p. 95). Life together terminates near the delta when Jim becomes a free man, but Huck, having grown to know love as well as remorse under Jim's tutelage, now is free to seek his own identity. This good bad boy can search for his bliss somewhere beyond the covers of the book. Twain leaves Huck's potential latent, much as America once assumed America's to be, somewhere out in the wild blue yonder of the uncharted future.

These differences in cultural patterns underlie other contrasts. At the end of *Huckleberry Finn,* Huck says, "I reckon I got to light out for the Territory ahead of the rest, because Aunt Sally she's going to adopt me and sivilize me and I can't stand it. I been there before" (p. 226). The American hero, before Huck and after Huck, has wanted to "light out," to take off, just as America took off from Europe (the manor, the state, the church, and especially royalty). It is a pattern deep in the American (male) psyche: the search for freedom. Juxtapose with this the ending of *Anne of Green Gables,* where quite the opposite happens: the orphan stays with her adoptive mother and, upon reaching maturity, "adopts" the ailing and lonely Marilla.

Another major difference lies in the notion of friendship. Anne has a talent for making friends, and she comes to have one close friend, Diana Barry. Before she meets Diana, Anne asks Marilla if she thinks she will ever have a bosom friend on Prince Edward Island:

> A bosom friend—an intimate friend, you know—a really kindred spirit to whom I can confide my inmost soul. I've dreamed of meeting her all my life. I never really supposed I would, but so many of my loveliest dreams have come true all at once that perhaps this one will, too. Do you think it's possible? (p. 46)

Except for Tom Sawyer and his tomfoolery, Huck is a loner. His character fits what Gilligan (1982) identifies as the male developmental pattern:

> For boys and men, separation and individuation are critically tied to gender identity since separation from the mother is essential for the development of masculinity. For girls and women, issues of femininity or feminine identity do not depend on the achievement of separation from the mother or on the progress of individuation. Since masculinity is defined through separation while femininity is defined through attachment, male gender identity is threatened by intimacy while female gender identity is threatened by separation. Thus males tend to have difficulty with

relationships, while females tend to have problems with individuation. (p. 8)

But boys have little difficulty with same-sex groups, as the activities of "Tom Sawyer's Gang" amply demonstrate.

The central images of the two novels are also gender-related. Twain sets his story on the mighty Mississippi. The raft is a portable home— disposable, portable, pitchable. It lets Huck stay on the move. In *Anne of Green Gables,* the image is one of settlement, a garden with trees, reminiscent of Eden: the island is "the bloomiest place" (p. 13). On her first night with Matthew and Marilla Cuthbert, Anne says she could even sleep in a cherry tree:

> I'm very glad to see you [Matthew Cuthbert]. I was beginning to be afraid you weren't coming for me and I was imagining all the things that might have happened to prevent you. I had made up my mind that if you didn't come for me tonight I'd go down the track to that big wild cherry-tree at the bend, and climb up into it to stay all night. (p. 11)

Forsaking life as a dryad, Anne comes to revere Green Gables; Huck has no such attachment to a place. Reflected in Anne and Huck is the tension in society: stability versus mobility, roots versus wings.

## Gender Differences in the Personal Essay

Gender differences can illuminate the American novel, as I hope I have shown. They can also illuminate and enrich our teaching of the personal essay. Comparing Joan Didion's "On Going Home" (1967) and E. B. White's "Once More to the Lake" (1941) reveals different gender-based perspectives. First, the similarities: Didion takes her daughter home; White takes his son to the camp of his boyhood. Both writers convey the pang of the realization of time's passing, the loss of childhood, and the chilling realization that death is closer at midlife than at adolescence. Next to Quintana's crib, Didion muses,

> She is an open and trusting child, unprepared for and unaccustomed to the ambushes of family life, and perhaps it is just as well that I can offer her little of that life. I would like to give her more. I would like to promise her that she will grow up with a sense of her cousins and of rivers and of her great-grandmother's teacups, would like to pledge her a picnic on a river with fried chicken and her hair uncombed, would like to give her *home* for her birthday, but we live differently now and I can promise her nothing like that. I give her a xylophone and a sundress from Madeira, and promise to tell her a funny story. (p. 169)

Similarly, at the Maine camp where his father took the family every August, White realizes his son's vulnerability as his son decides to join other campers and swim in the rain:

> He pulled his dripping trunks from the line where they had hung all through the shower and wrung them out. Languidly, and with no thought of going in, I watched him, his hard little body, skinny and bare, saw him wince slightly as he pulled up around his vitals the small, soggy, icy garment. As he buckled the swollen belt, suddenly my groin felt the chill of death. (p. 202)

Both Didion and White are observers of offspring. Given that much in common, they then develop their essays in separate ways, predictably along gender lines.

Like Anne of Green Gables, Didion expresses a love for home; she seems to wish she could wrap it up like a present: "I . . . would like to give her *home* for her birthday." The images are domestic: teacups and fried chicken. Let Old Man River roll on by: she does not want to raft on it, just picnic beside it. The action is sedentary, not peripatetic. Like Huck, White and his son have been civilized long enough to escape; they seek not the frontier but the past, the idyllic rural past, the forest "primeval" (p. 198). White's images are action-oriented, undomestic:

> We went fishing the first morning. I felt the same damp moss covering the worms in the bait can, and saw the dragonfly alight on the tip of my rod as it hovered a few inches from the surface of the water. . . . We caught two bass, hauling them in briskly as though they were mackerel, pulling them over the side of the boat in a businesslike manner without any landing net, and stunning them with a blow on the back of the head. (pp. 198–99)

White initiates his son into what Jean McClure Kelty (1980) calls "the cult of the kill" (p. 238). It is a gender-based rite, one that Ike learns in Faulkner's "The Bear," that Jody learns in *The Yearling,* that Huck draws upon when, fearing Pap's violence, he kills a pig and uses its blood to feign his murder and cover his escape from the cabin. Yet for women within our culture, the mystique of the kill and the acceptance of it tend to be just that, a mystique—foreign to the world of Green Gables and of Didion and Quintana.[3]

Both Didion and White share a love of the land, a love of nature, even a nostalgia for simpler times. Didion's writing, though, reveals the dominant pattern for women's lives, a "web of relationships" (Gilligan 1982, p. 32); these many connections are what Robert Frost calls "countless silken ties of love and thought" ("The Silken Tent"). They constitute a natural hope most mothers have for their daughters. White, on the other hand, expresses no such dream for his son. In fact, both White and his son seem very much alone, separate, even when they are together at camp, a camp reached, as Gilligan would note, by separation from the mother. These two essays, then, exemplify important gender-based cultural patterns: separation and attachment. To use Gilligan's (1982) terms, White's son finds (or "defines") a self via separation (p. 35), Didion's daughter via attachment (although Didion senses somewhat regretfully that Quintana's connections will be more limited than hers have been).

As my doctoral adviser, Oscar M. Haugh, used to say about many things, "It's both/and, not either/or." So it is with gender differences: it is not either books about men or books about women; it is both books about men and books about women. The social sciences, notably the work of Natalie Shainess, Carol Gilligan, and Harriet Goldhor Lerner, offer us insights into gender differences, but even there, further work is needed. As Gilligan puts it,

> The myth of Persephone . . . [reminds] us that narcissism leads to death, that the fertility of the earth is in some mysterious way tied to the continuation of the mother-daughter relationship, and that the life cycle itself arises from an alternation between the world of women and that of men. Only when life-cycle theorists divide their attention and begin to live with women as they have lived with men will their vision encompass the experience of both sexes and their theories become correspondingly more fertile. (1982, p. 23)

Humanists face a similar challenge in the exploration of not only gender differences but differences of the "other." Research in the social sciences continues to provide greater understanding about gender differences; as research about the same topic advances in the humanities, teachers and students of literature can also expect valuable insights. The American Council of Learned Societies provides a cogent rationale for such study:

> We urge that humanities programs continue to teach the great works of the traditional canon in relation to historical scholarship and critical theory. In addition, experiments with the canon should be the norm, not the exception, and texts representing traditionally marginal voices or other national contexts should always be taught, and for these reasons: first, because our students are not themselves drawn from a single homogeneous culture; second, because the nation is increasingly involved in cultural and business exchanges with other nations; third, because one of the humanities' most fundamental responsibilities is to expose and question the aesthetic, moral, cultural, and epistemological assumptions which govern our behavior and our society. (Levine et al. 1989, p. 33)

As we change and enlarge the canon, we will not only change our students' assumptions but our own. Balancing our syllabi by gender is a start, but let it begin—with you, with me.

## Notes

1. For an example of how to overcome faculty resistance to stage five, see the model at Towson State University, recipient of a grant of $250,000 from the Fund for the Improvement of Postsecondary Education. There, professors from many disciplines volunteered to meet once a week for a workshop. The codirector of the Towson State project, Elaine Hedges, explains the initial resistance of the faculty: "Most faculty members have a lot invested, in their education, their degrees, their classes, their authority. They can have an extraordinarily defensive position. You can't force it down people's throats." Yet, as one professor of English stated, "If we can change people's heads, you institutionalize it all across the campus. . . . You can't lower a raised consciousness" (McMillen 1987, p. A17).

2. In my research, I have noticed that women's thematic counterparts to men's writings tend to be delayed by a generation or so, a point worth exploring.

3. The blood rite for young women is menstruation—internal, silent, and mysterious—celebrated in print privately, as in Anne Frank's diary, if at all. Young adult fiction, however, is the exception. There, one does find this feminine counterpart to the masculine "cult of the kill."

## References

Campbell, Joseph, with Bill Moyers. 1988. *The Power of Myth.* New York: Doubleday.

Clemens, Samuel Langhorne. 1962 [1885]. *Adventures of Huckleberry Finn.* Norton Critical Edition, edited by Sculley Bradley, Richmond Croom Beatty, and E. Hudson Long. New York: Norton.

Didion, Joan. 1981. "On Going Home." In *Slouching Towards Bethlehem,* 166–69. New York: Washington Square.

Gilligan, Carol. 1982. *In a Different Voice: Psychological Theory and Women's Development.* Cambridge: Harvard University Press.

Kelty, Jean McClure. 1980. "The Cult of Kill in Adolescent Fiction." In *Young Adult Literature: Background and Criticism,* compiled by Millicent Lenz and Ramona M. Mahood, 237–44. Chicago: American Library Association. (Reprinted from *English Journal* [Feb. 1975]: 56–61.)

Lerner, Harriet Goldhor. 1985. *The Dance of Anger.* New York: Harper and Row.

———. 1988. *The Dance of Intimacy.* New York: Harper and Row.

Levine, George, et al. 1989. *Speaking for the Humanities.* ACLS Occasional Paper, No. 7. New York: American Council of Learned Societies.

McMillen, Liz. 1987. "More Colleges and More Disciplines Incorporating Scholarship on Women into the Classroom." *Chronicle of Higher Education,* 9 September 1987, pp. A15–A17.

Montgomery, Lucy Maud. 1985 [1908]. *Anne of Green Gables: Three Volumes in One.* New York: Avenel Books.

Shainess, Natalie. 1969. "Images of Woman: Past and Present, Overt and Obscured." *American Journal of Psychotherapy* 23, no. 1: 77–97.

White, E. B. 1977. "Once More to the Lake." In *Essays of E. B. White,* 197–202. New York: Harper and Row.

Zerbe, Kathryn. 1988. "Women Artists and the Men around Them." Psychocultural Series. Topeka, Kans.: Menninger, 19 December 1988.

# Editors

**Charles Moran** is professor of English at the University of Massachusetts at Amherst, where he has directed the university writing program since 1982. He has written on the teaching of literature, the teaching of writing, computers and writing, and the training of new and inservice teachers. He has received his university's Distinguished Teaching Award and has been given the F. Andre Favat Award by the Massachusetts Council of Teachers of English. A member of the group that planned the first Summer Institute, he remembers well the intensely hot July meetings in Urbana, where, with Lynn Troyka, Jim Raymond, Joe Skerrett, Jane Christensen, and Jack Maxwell, the structure and intent of the Summer Institutes was hammered out. He credits Elizabeth Penfield with the idea that, two years later, has become this book.

PHOTO: J. SHERRILL

**Elizabeth Penfield** is professor of English at the University of New Orleans. Having spent a number of years running the freshman English program, directing the Greater New Orleans Writing Project, chairing the Department of English, and working as associate dean of liberal arts, she rejoices at being back in the classroom, where she teaches courses in both writing and literature. She has written on the teaching of writing and the administration of writing programs and departments of English.

# Contributors

**Judy Arnold** is an assistant professor of English at the Oak Ridge campus of Roane State Community College, in Tennessee. She teaches five courses each semester, including American literature surveys and composition sections. Before coming to Roane State in 1985, she taught for fourteen years at the high school level.

**Lloyd Dendinger** is professor of English at the University of South Alabama. His publications include articles on the works of Robert Frost in the *Southern Review* and *American Quarterly*, and on the work of Stephen Crane in *Studies in Short Fiction*. In addition to his teaching, Professor Dendinger is active in community outreach programs. He lectures and does dramatic readings in the schools and at community functions.

**Joseph Dupras** is an associate professor at the University of Alaska–Fairbanks, where he teaches a wide variety of courses, including graduate seminars in British literature of the Victorian and Romantic periods and undergraduate courses in literary criticism, nineteenth-century British literature, and writing. He has served as acting head of his department and director of undergraduate studies, and has been a judge in the NCTE Achievement Awards in Writing program. Professor Dupras has published frequently on the works of Robert Browning and the Brontës. Recently, he was cited in Lisa Birnbach's *College Book* as one of the three best teachers at his university.

**Janet Emig,** president of NCTE in 1989, is University Professor of English Education at Rutgers University. She is the author of *The Composing Processes of Twelfth Graders; The Web of Meaning: Essays on Writing, Teaching, Learning, and Thinking;* and articles and poems in a broad range of scholarly journals. She is cofounder of the New Jersey Writing Project, and a recipient of the MLA's Mina Shaughnessy Award.

**Bobby Fong** is dean of arts and humanities at Hope College, in Holland, Michigan. Previously he chaired the Department of English at Berea College, in Berea, Kentucky, and taught courses there in writing and literature, as well as special short-term courses in American literary realism and naturalism, the American small town, Dickens, and utopian literature.

**Henry Louis Gates, Jr.,** is W.E.B. DuBois Professor of Literature at Cornell University. Among his works are *The Signifying Monkey: Towards a*

*Theory of Afro-American Literary Criticism;* the *Schomberg Library of Nineteenth-Century Black Women Writers* (editor); and publications on Zora Neale Hurston, Wole Soyinka, Jean Toomer, Frederick Douglass, and Phillis Wheatley. For the past several years, Professor Gates has been working as general editor for the forthcoming *Norton Anthology of Afro-American Literature.* In 1983, he received the Yale Afro-American Cultural Center Faculty Prize.

**Walker Gibson** is Emeritus Professor of English at the University of Massachusetts–Amherst. He has published two volumes of poetry and two writing textbooks, and has edited a number of anthologies. His book *Tough, Sweet, and Stuffy: An Essay on Modern American Prose Styles* was selected for the Scholar's Library by the Modern Language Association. Professor Gibson helped initiate NCTE's Committee on Public Doublespeak and has served as a member of the College Section Committee, the Commission on the English Curriculum, and the Executive Committee of CCCC. He served as president of the Council in 1972–73, and in 1988 he was given the Council's Distinguished Service Award.

**Irene Goldman** is an assistant professor of English at Ball State University, in Muncie, Indiana, where she teaches an undergraduate survey of American literature, a graduate/undergraduate course titled "Women in Literature," and a graduate seminar in American literature, most recently in Twain, James, and Wharton. Professor Goldman is firmly committed to the university's Women's Studies program, and for this program organizes a lecture series and a "women's week" of activities for, by, and about women.

**Benjamin S. Howard** is professor of English at the Harriman campus of Roane State Community College, in Tennessee. He teaches honors sections in English (composition and a two-semester survey of world literature) and courses in German language and literature.

**Myra Jehlen** is professor of English at the University of Pennsylvania, where she normally teaches two courses each semester—one graduate and one undergraduate. In both her teaching and scholarship, she examines the relation of literature and culture. Author of *Class and Character in Faulkner's South,* Professor Jehlen has recently published *American Incarnation: The Individual, the Nation and the Continent,* a study of the ways that assumptions about the nature of America and Americans inspire the form as well as the content of eighteenth- and nineteenth-century writings. Her current research is on the period of discovery and exploration.

**Steven Lynn** is associate professor of English at the University of South Carolina–Columbia, where he teaches courses in writing, in the history of rhetoric, in eighteenth-century literature, and in critical theory. In addition to his teaching, Professor Lynn directs the university's Writing Center. His essays have been published in journals as various and distinguished as

*Eighteenth Century Studies, The Journal of Developmental Education,* and
*The Journal of Technical Writing and Communication.*

**Steven Mailloux** is professor of English at Syracuse University, where he has
just completed a three-year term as chair of the English Department.
During his tenure, the department established a new undergraduate major
in English and Textual Studies, one that reconceptualizes the literary
studies curriculum as a "culture studies" program. Professor Mailloux is
the author of *Interpretive Conventions: The Reader in the Study of American
Fiction; Rhetorical Power;* and *Interpreting Law and Literature: A Hermeneutic Reader.*

**James Raymond** is professor of English and director of freshman English at
the University of Alabama. He is also editor of *College English,* the official
journal of the College Section of NCTE. In addition to numerous articles
and reviews, he has published a composition textbook, *Writing (Is an
Unnatural Act),* coauthored a book on legal writing (*Clear Understandings,*
with Ronald L. Goldfarb), edited a collection of essays on literacy (*Literacy
as a Human Problem*), and coedited a collection of essays on linguistics
(*James B. McMillan: Essays in Linguistics by His Friends and Colleagues,*
with I. Willis Russell).

**Jane Atteridge Rose** is an assistant professor at Georgia College, in Milledgeville, Georgia, where she teaches composition, American literature, modern
fiction, and black literature.

**Warren Rosenberg** has taught English since 1970 at a variety of levels and
schools—both full- and part-time—in high schools, community colleges,
and four-year institutions. He is now an associate professor at Wabash
College, in Crawfordsville, Indiana, where he teaches American literature
to 1900, composition, ethnic literature, black literature, literature and film,
and women's studies.

**Jane Tompkins** is professor of English at Duke University. She is author of
*Sensational Designs: The Cultural Work of American Fiction, 1790–1860*
and editor of *Reader-Response Criticism: From Formalism to Post-Structuralism.* In addition, she has written articles on a wide range of subjects,
including canon formation, *Uncle Tom's Cabin,* the American Indian in
history and literature, and the use of the personal voice in academic
criticism. Professor Tompkins teaches courses in American literature,
popular culture, and women's studies, and is now completing a book on
the Western, seen from a feminist perspective. The book's title: *West of
Everything: The Construction of Male Identity in American Popular Culture.*

**Nancy Vogel** is professor of English at Fort Hays State University, where she
teaches two composition courses and two literature courses each term. Her
range includes courses in technical/professional writing, the American
dream, and pedagogy; her special interests are young adult literature,

biography and autobiography, and the poetry of Robert Frost. Professor Vogel is currently working on a book, tentatively titled *The American Eve,* which links the psychological developmental stages of women with characters in fiction.

**Joel Wingard** is an associate professor of English at Moravian College, in Bethlehem, Pennsylvania, where he teaches each semester a section of freshman writing and a section of introductory literature. In addition, he teaches courses in twentieth-century British literature and in newswriting. He advises the student newspaper, directs interns in journalism, and advises English/journalism majors.